Ages 5–10

The SUPER-SIZED Book of Bible GAMES

Features Over 250 Games

Lindsey Whitney

HENDRICKSON PUBLISHERS

ROSE KiDZ®

The Super-Sized Book of Bible Games

RoseKidz® is an imprint of
Rose Publishing, LLC
140 Summit Street
P.O. Box 3473
Peabody, Massachusetts 01961-3473
www.hendricksonrose.com

Cover and Interior Design: Keith DeDios

ISBN: 978-1-628625-46-2
RoseKidz® reorder number R50016
RELIGION / Christian Ministry / Children

Printed in the United States of America 01 3.2018.VP

Table of Contents

Introduction

Have you ever faced one of these situations?

- You've used up your entire lesson, but the pastor seems to still be going strong. You've got at least 10 minutes to fill and no idea what to do!
- You love the content of your curriculum, but it seems to be lacking the fun factor. You'd love to come up with a few games to go along with the concepts you're already teaching.
- You've got a group of preschoolers who all seem a bit shy and timid. You know a game would help them all to feel more comfortable, but it's hard to adapt the more traditional games to fit this age level.
- You're finishing up a lesson series and would love to have a review week that is both memorable and exciting for the kids. You're puzzled on how to use all those review questions in a way that will keep kids engaged.

If so, you've picked up the right book!

We know fun is an integral part of working with kids, and is there anything more fun than a game? Isn't it delightful to see the excitement and anticipation on the faces of those little ones around you when you announce it is time for a game? However, we know it's not always easy to come up with a game that fits your topic or your situation.

That's why we've created a resource packed full of fun and games! With over 250 games divided up into fourteen different sections, you're sure to find something to fit your needs. We've included games for every season, every age group, and for almost any size space or noise level. Browse through the Table of Contents and you'll see games specific to certain Biblical accounts, wet and wild games, no prep games, games specifically for little ones, and even games to play in the snow!

Games help unite kids and help them build memories that cause them to keep coming back again and again for more Bible teaching. We pray that this resource will help you create lessons that are a blast for you to teach and exciting for kids to participate in.

Keep on serving the Lord!

Lindsey Whitney

GrowingKidsMinistry.com

How To Use This Book

This Book is Divided Into The Following Sections				
Old Testament Games	New Testament Games	Ice Breaker Games	Indoor Active Games	Outdoor Games
Wet and Wild Water Games	Shivering Ice and Snot Games	Small Group Games	Large Group Games	Games for Little Ones
Quiet Games	Quick/No-Prep Games	Lesson Review Games	Memory Verse Review Games	

Most of the games in this book work with children ages four to twelve–and beyond! Games that are more suited for older elementary children (ages six to twelve) are **bolded** in the Table of Contents. For your younger ones (ages two to five), we have a section designed specifically for them, Games for Little Ones. There is something for everyone!

Each Game Includes:

- Time Needed
- Age Range
- Overview
- Supply List
- Preparation
- Scripture Connection
- Step-By-Step Instructions
- Teachable Moments Script
- Needed Reproducible Pages (located in the back)
- Discussion Questions

(Note: The last two sections are designed for review of lessons already taught and doesn't include Teachable Moments or Discussion Questions).

Who Can Use This Book?

This book is an excellent resource for:

- Church Volunteers
- School Teachers
- Daycare Workers
- Homeschooling Families
- VBS
- Parents looking for home-devotion ideas

Added Bonus Material:

Find tips throughout the book on:

- Behavior
- Development
- Special Needs
- Discipline
- Saving money

Indexing

Indexing is provided in the back for at-your-fingertips searching! Look for a game by Scripture reference. OR Find just the right game for any situation by the following types:

• Individual Games or Races • Team Games or Races • Partner Games • Tag Games • Seek and Find Games • Circle Games • Guessing Games • Relay Races • Card Games

OLD TESTAMENT GAMES

DAYS OF CREATION

Individual Game

OVERVIEW

This game is played much like the classic Red Light, Green Light, but kids are only allowed to move when their specific assigned part of creation is called.

SCRIPTURE CONNECTION:
Genesis 1:1-2

SUPPLIES:
- Large area
- Optional: Washable markers

PREPARATION:
Optional: Write creation assignments on kids' hands if they tend to forget.

SOME IDEAS FOR ASSIGNMENTS:
Sun, moon, stars, fish, land animal, tree, bird, flower, plants, etc.

PRESCHOOL TIP:
Draw a simple picture of the part instead of the word. Have the adult call out the parts of creation to keep things moving.

HOW TO PLAY:

1. Have players line up in a single file line across one side of the play area.
2. Assign each player a part of creation. For example, you could assign one player to be the sun, several players to be birds, a few to be flowers or trees, etc. (See sidebar for ideas.)
3. Pick one child to be "It." Place "It" about 50 feet away from the line of players.
4. "It" faces away from the group and calls out something from creation. It can be something specific like "the sun" or something more general like "all the lights in the sky."
5. The players who have been assigned those things begin to move towards "It." After a few seconds, "It" calls out, "STOP!" and spins around to face the group. "It" calls the name of any player seen moving. Named players return to the start line.
6. This play continues until someone reaches and tags "It." That child then becomes "It," and a new round of play begins.

TEACHABLE MOMENT:

Say: Isn't it amazing to think about all the things that God created? We can read all about God's creation in Genesis 1. We read that he made the sun, moon, stars, plants, and all the animals—whether in the sky, sea, or land.

DISCUSSION QUESTIONS:

- How hard do you think is was for God to create everything?
- What is your favorite part of creation?
- Take a minute to thank God for all he has created.

GOOD FRUIT OR BAD FRUIT

Seek and Find

OVERVIEW

In this game, children gather up fruit to score points, but a hidden twist makes the game more interesting!

SCRIPTURE CONNECTION:
Genesis 2:15-16

SUPPLIES:

- Fake fruit,at least one or two per child; available at most dollar stores
- Index cards
- Timer

PREPARATION:
Hide fruit around the area. Decide on a point system for each fruit. (Prepare to change the point system on the fruits after the first round). Make up a score card that gives each fruit a different point value. Pick one fruit to have a negative point value.

$ TIP:
If you cannot get fake fruit, try using small colored balls, small fruit-looking erasers, or multi-colored pom-poms.

HOW TO PLAY:

1. Set the timer to three minutes. On your signal, children search for and collect the fruits. Inform them that different fruits are worth different points.
2. Allow kids to search for the fruit. When they are done, reveal the score card and tally up each of the scores. One child may receive a negative score if they get the "bad fruit."
3. Use the teachable moment points below and then play again if time allows. Be sure to change up the scores so the "bad fruit" will again be a mystery.

TEACHABLE MOMENT:

Say: When Adam and Eve were in the garden of Eden, God told them they could eat of any fruit except for the tree of knowledge of good and evil. That tree was in the middle of the garden. God was very clear about the rules and what fruit was off limits. (*Read Genesis 2:16–17.*) In this game though, it was a complete mystery which fruits were good and which were bad. Thankfully, God is still very clear about his rules and what is allowed and not allowed. You can find his commands in the Bibles. God is not trying to trick us or get us in trouble just for fun—the rules he makes are designed to keep us safe.

DISCUSSION QUESTIONS:

- What do you think it would have been like for Adam and Eve if they didn't know what was allowed and what was not allowed to eat?
- What did you think about the tricky "bad fruit" in this game? What a surprise it was to find out what had negative points!

NOAH'S ARK: FIND YOUR MATCH

Partner Game

OVERVIEW
Kids are assigned a specific animal and find their match (pair) by making the animal noise.

SCRIPTURE CONNECTION:
Genesis 6

SUPPLIES:
- Optional: Use Animal Cards, page 278.

PREPARATION:
Optional: Photocopy and cut apart the animal cards.

TIP:
Be on the lookout for children who are introverts and don't feel comfortable being silly and connecting with other children. You can help by going with them on their hunt, encouraging them or allowing them the option to help you or sit out. Try staying tuned in to how far you can try and stretch them or if you are just losing connection with them by pushing them too far out of their comfort zone.

HOW TO PLAY:

1. Whisper the name of an animal in the ear of each child. Optional: pass out the Animal Cards. Make sure you assign two kids to the same animals so that everyone can find a match.
2. Make sure kids keep their assigned animal a secret for now.
3. On your signal, kids will mill around the room making their animal noise. The goal is to find their match by listening to the sounds. When they think they have found their match, they will link arms and continue to make their animal noise until everyone has found their match.
4. When everyone is matched, children say their animal out loud or reveal their cards to check that everyone is matched correctly.

TEACHABLE MOMENT:

Say: When God flooded the earth, he provided safety for some of the animals along with Noah and his family. (*Read Genesis 6.*) Even though the ark was huge, it was probably crowded, smelly, and noisy. Our game was noisy too! In our game, you had to find your match by listening. Do you think this is how Noah had to gather up the animals for his ark?

DISCUSSION QUESTIONS:

- How did it feel to hear all those animal sounds at once?
- What do you think it would have been like to be on the ark for such a long time?
- If you were on the ark, what would be your favorite animal to hang out with?

BUILDING BABEL

Team Game

OVERVIEW
Kids compete in teams to build the tallest tower. In round two, things get complicated when kids can no longer speak to each other.

SCRIPTURE CONNECTION:
Genesis 11:1-9

SUPPLIES:
- Wooden blocks (preferably square)
- Flat area to build
- Timer or clock

PREPARATION:
Determine the number of teams you need for your group to build with blocks. Divide blocks into piles according to the number of groups.

TIP:
Young elementary children want to see how things work and learn best from hands-on, concrete discovery.

HOW TO PLAY:

1. Kids divide into teams. Divide the blocks into piles and give one pile to each team.
2. Set the timer for one minute. Kids build the tallest tower possible before time runs out.
3. When the timer beeps, measure the towers and declare a winner.
4. Kids take the towers down. Tell them that in this round, they cannot talk to each other. They can hum, squeak, say "La la la," or make other nonsense noises–but no intelligent language.
5. Set the timer for one minute. Kids build the tallest tower possible before time runs out.
6. When the timer beeps, measure the towers and declare a winner.

TEACHABLE MOMENT:

Say: In this game, you guys worked together to build a tower. The same thing happened a long time ago. People worked together to build a giant tower. They were hoping to reach all the way to the sky and become very famous. (*Read Genesis 11:1–9.*)

DISCUSSION QUESTIONS:

- Was it easier to build in the first round or the second round? Why do you think that is?
- How does this game remind you of the tower of Babel?
- Why do you think God confused the languages?
- Why do you think the people gave up when they couldn't understand each other?

OLD LADY SARAH

Circle Game

OVERVIEW
Kids will play a funny game, trying to say words without showing their teeth.

SCRIPTURE CONNECTION:
Genesis 17:1-4

SUPPLIES:
- None

PREPARATION:
None

TIP:
This is also a no-prep game.

HOW TO PLAY:

1. Kids sit in a circle, facing each other. **Say:** Abraham and Sarah were very old when they had their baby, Isaac. Sometimes old people have trouble with their teeth falling out! In this game, we're going to pretend we're very old with no teeth.
2. Have everyone pick a favorite fruit or vegetable and say it out loud.
3. Begin with one player and have them say their favorite fruit or veggie with their lips over their teeth—no teeth can be showing! Go on to the next player who has to say the previous fruit/veggie two times and then their favorite fruit/veggie.
4. For example, the first player will say "Banana."
   The second player will say "Banana, Banana, Grape."
   The third player will say "Grape, Grape, Potatoes."
5. Continue until everyone has had a turn.

TEACHABLE MOMENT:

Say: Have you ever heard of Abraham and Sarah before? They were very old when Sarah became pregnant with her son Isaac. It must have been pretty unbelievable at first—to have such old people expecting a baby—but we know, with God, all things are possible.

DISCUSSION QUESTIONS:

- This was a pretty funny game. Was it hard to keep from laughing?
- There was a time in the Bible when Sarah found it hard to keep from laughing too! (*Read Genesis 18:12.*)
- Why do you think Sarah laughed?
- Can you name something that is too difficult for God to do?

JOSEPH'S COAT OF MANY COLORS

Seek and Find Game

OVERVIEW
Kids will gather up strips of cloth to symbolize Joseph's coat of many colors.

SCRIPTURE CONNECTION:
Genesis 37:3

SUPPLIES:
- Strips of colored cloth (red, orange, yellow, green, blue, purple)
- Large field to play in, or a room with plenty of good hiding places
- Optional: Checklist of Colors, page 279.

PREPARATION:
Before kids arrive, hide the strips of cloth throughout the playing space. Hide at least three to four strips of each color.

TIP:
Developmental
Children move from playing alongside each other in preschool to interacting and playing with each other. Peers are becoming more and more important to school-age children.

HOW TO PLAY:

1. When kids arrive, divide them up into teams (three to five kids per team work best). Make sure you have hidden enough strips for each team to find one of every color.
2. Explain to the kids that they find one strip of fabric for every color in the rainbow.
3. The first team to find all six colors and brings them to you, the leader, wins.

TEACHABLE MOMENT:

Say: In Genesis 37:3, we read about a special gift that a young man named Joseph received from his father. It was a coat of many colors. It might have had a special pattern or been made from many fabrics like we have today. Does gathering up these colors remind you of anything from the story of Joseph? This special coat was the beginning of a bad relationship between Joseph and his brothers. They were jealous of Joseph.

DISCUSSION QUESTIONS:

- How do you think you would feel if one of your siblings got special coat and you got nothing?
- How does it feel to receive something really special?
- Have you ever felt jealous of something someone in your family has? What made you jealous?

MOSES CROSSING THE RED SEA

Circle Game

OVERVIEW
Children try to make it through the "sea" without being tagged by pool noodles.

SCRIPTURE CONNECTION:
Exodus 14:14

SUPPLIES:
- Blue pool noodles, one for each child.
- Long narrow playing space.

PREPARATION:
None

TIP:
If you can't find enough blue noodles, any color will do. You may also use palm branches or squirt bottles to create obstacles for children to get through.

HOW TO PLAY:

1. Kids divide into two groups. Place each group on opposite sides of the play area. They should be about 10 feet apart.
2. Give each child a pool noodle and pick the first "Red Sea Crosser." **Say:** Do you remember in the Bible, when the Israelites crossed the Red Sea? I wonder if the water still sprayed at them or if they crossed with smooth walls of water on either side? In this game, our walls of water are going to be a little crazy.
3. Instruct the two groups to shake and wave their pool noodles. The volunteer must "cross through the sea" without getting tagged with a pool noodle.
4. If the game is too difficult, have the two groups take a few steps back to allow more room for passing through.
5. Once the first volunteer has made it through, have them take a pool noodle and join a group to allow another child to take a turn.

TEACHABLE MOMENT:

Say: How did it feel to cross our "Red Sea?" How do you think the Israelites felt to cross the real Red Sea? The Israelites also had Pharaoh's army after them. That must have been frightening! (*Read Exodus 14:14.*) The Lord told the Israelites that he would fight for them. Splitting the sea in half was an amazing battle plan.

DISCUSSION QUESTIONS:

- What unexpected things has God done in your life?
- Describe a difficult situation you have been in where you couldn't see a solution. What did you do?
- God is amazing, and nothing is impossible for him! Let's spend a few minutes praying difficulties we might be facing.

JERICHO TAG

Tag

OVERVIEW
Children run along a circle trying to tag everyone in their path.

SCRIPTURE CONNECTION:
Joshua 6:1-5

SUPPLIES:
- Very long rope
- Large play area

PREPARATION:
Set up the play area by laying the rope on the ground, the shape of a circle. The circle should be approximately 20 feet in diameter.

$ TIP:
Don't have a rope? Use masking tape or chalk to mark off the circle.

HOW TO PLAY:

1. Kids stand along the rope. Select one child to be "It."
2. Kids run along the rope (and only along the rope) as they try to escape the clutches of "It." "It" also runs along the rope and try to tag as many kids as possible. Anyone can change directions at any time, but be careful to stay on the rope!
3. At first, there will be a lot of kids getting out, but as the numbers dwindle, the game becomes much more difficult for "It"

TEACHABLE MOMENT:

Say: In this game, we went around in a circle! Does this remind you of anything from the Bible where the people had to walk around in a circle many times? It reminds me of the battle at Jericho. (*Read Joshua 6:1–5.*) In this battle, the people walked around the city walls once a day for six days and then seven times on the seventh day. It may have been boring during those first six days, but on the seventh day, something amazing happened! As the people finished their marching, they began to shout and blow trumpets, and the walls of that great city collapsed. Can you imagine all the dust and noise? What a day to remember!

DISCUSSION QUESTIONS:

- Have you ever seen a construction project where they were demolishing a large building or structure?
- What do you remember about the event?
- What kind of things do you think the Israelites would have remembered from the battle at Jericho?

DAVID AND GOLIATH

Individual Game

OVERVIEW
Children try to hit a cardboard Goliath with Ping-Pong balls.

SCRIPTURE CONNECTION:
I Samuel 17:48-49

SUPPLIES:
- Simple slingshot, available online or at outdoor supplies
- Ping-Pong balls
- Tall cardboard box
- Masking tape or cones
- Optional: Bucket

PREPARATION:
Draw a basic man shape the full length of the cardboard box. Use masking tape or set up cones to make a start line on one side of the play area. Optional: Place Ping-Pong balls in bucket.

TIP:
Have start lines at different distances, based on the ages of the kids.

HOW TO PLAY:

1. Try shooting from the start line a few times yourself to determine a good distance for the cardboard box. A good place to start is about 5 feet from the box. Move the box closer or farther from the line, depending on the distance that works best.
2. Players line up behind the cones and use a slingshot to try to hit the cardboard Goliath with the Ping-Pong balls. Give each kid five tries. If you have two slingshots, you can make the game a race to see who can hit Goliath first.

TEACHABLE MOMENT:

Say: David probably didn't have a slingshot like this one—his was more of a piece of fabric folded into a pouch. It was probably even harder for David to use than this, and the Bible tells us that he slung the stone while running! (*Read 1 Samuel 17:48–49.*) God was with David in the battle and helped him defeat Goliath. God is with us during hard times as well.

DISCUSSION QUESTIONS:

- What did you think of this game?
- Was it easy or hard to hit Goliath? Why?
- Raise your hand if you were able to hit him right in the head.
- Do you think it was easy or hard for David to hit Goliath?
- Tell us about a time when God helped you do something that was tough or scary.

CAN YOU HIDE YOUR SIN?

Seek and Find

OVERVIEW
Children run along a circle trying to tag everyone in their path.

SCRIPTURE CONNECTION:
Psalm 32:5 and
2 Samuel 12:13

IDEAL GROUP SIZE:
5+ kids

SUPPLIES:
- Small note card
- Optional: Table

PREPARATION:
Write the word "sin" on note card.

HOW TO PLAY:

1. Pick a child to go first. Give them the note card with "sin" written on it and have the rest of the kids cover their eyes. Optional: Kids put heads down on the table.
2. Have the volunteer child hide the sin card somewhere in the room and then return to the table to sit.
3. When the sin card is hidden, allow the rest of the kids to uncover their eyes and search for the sin card.
4. Whoever finds the sin card hides it next. Continue to play until everyone has had a turn to hide the sin card.

TEACHABLE MOMENT:

Say: David was a king of Israel. He loved God and tried to do the right thing, but one day he made a big mistake. Not only did he sin, but he also tried to hide his sin. God wasn't pleased, and God does not want us to hide our sin. Just like David tried to hide his sin, we tried to hide a sin card in this room. No matter how clever the hiding place, the sin card was found. The same is true in life. No matter how we try to hide our sin (maybe we even lie about it!), God knows the truth and, other people will find out about our sin, too. We can't hide sin. It is better to confess and repent so that we can continue following God's way.

DISCUSSION QUESTIONS:

- In this game, was it easy to hide the sin? Why or why not?
- Was it easy or hard to find the sin?
- When is a time a kid your age might try to hide sin? Why might a kid want to hide sin?
- How does it end up making a bigger mess?

WHICH WAY IS RIGHT?

Partner Game

OVERVIEW
Kids will help their blindfolded friend through a series of obstacles.

SCRIPTURE CONNECTION:
Proverbs 14:12

IDEAL GROUP SIZE:
5+ kids

SUPPLIES:
- Large space to play in
- Obstacles such as chairs to go around, ropes to jump over, safety cones to avoid, etc.
- Blindfold

PREPARATION:
Place obstacles around the play area.

HOW TO PLAY:

1. To begin, blindfold a volunteer and have them stand at one end of the playing field.
2. Pick another child to be a guide. Tell the blindfolded child that they should ONLY listen to their guide. Meanwhile, tell the other children that they should try and confuse or trick the blindfolded child as they make their way through the playing field.
3. On your signal, the blindfolded child will walk through the obstacle course, trying their best not to touch anything along the way. If they do touch an obstacle, you can either deduct points or end their turn. Continue to play, rotating the roles of \blindfolded child, guide, and tricksters.

TEACHABLE MOMENT:

Say: After everyone has had a chance to play in some capacity, kids sit in a semi-circle around you. Ask the kids if it was hard to listen to just the guide. (*Read Proverbs 14:12.*) Sometimes our friends or people in our lives try to get us to do things that we aren't quite sure are right. At first, it might seem okay, but in the end–it leads to destruction (or trouble). In our game, the guide was trying to help get you to safety, but there were a lot of other voices too! The closer we are to God, the easier it is to listen to only his voice. He will show us the right way to go.

DISCUSSION QUESTIONS:

- Have you ever faced a situation where it was difficult to make a decision? Tell us about it.
- How do you spend time with God?
- Tell us about people in your life that can help you make decisions based on the Bible.

PASS THE MANTLE

Seek and Find

OVERVIEW

One child will place a cloak on a friend, much like Elijah did for Elisha. However, in our version, there is a little more mystery in the passing of the cloak.

SCRIPTURE CONNECTION:
I Kings 19:19

IDEAL GROUP SIZE:
5+ kids

SUPPLIES:
- Bathroom, towel, shawl, or large piece of material
- Table

PREPARATION:
None

HOW TO PLAY:

1. Kids sit around the table, putting their heads down and covering their face with their arms. Be sure to watch for little peeking eyes!
2. Choose one child and give them the cloak (quietly!).
3. Have that child place the cloak on a friend's shoulders and then quietly return to their seat.
4. When the giver of the cloak is safely seated again, instruct all the kids to look up.
5. Whoever has been given the cloak guesses who the giver of the cloak was. Give them three tries to guess and then reveal the answer.
6. Play again as time permits, choosing a new giver of the cloak for each round.

TEACHABLE MOMENT:

Say: In this game, we placed a cloak (or shawl) on each other's shoulders. Something like this happened in the Bible as well. Does anyone know the story? (*Read 1 Kings 19:19.*) Elijah wanted to choose a helper to do God's work with him. He found a man named Elisha and placed his cloak (or mantel) on Elisha's shoulders. This meant that Elijah chose Elisha to be his helper.

DISCUSSION QUESTIONS:

- How did it feel to be chosen to receive the cloak when we were playing our game? How do you think Elisha felt when he was chosen?
- Have you ever been a helper to someone in your life?
- What are some ways kids your age can help others now?

DANIEL AND THE LIONS' DEN

Tag

OVERVIEW
In this version of tag, the lions try to get Daniel while the angels try to tag the lions.

SCRIPTURE CONNECTION:
Daniel 6:21

SUPPLIES:
- Large play area
- Optional: Colored bracelets, bandanas or vests

PREPARATION:
None

HOW TO PLAY:

1. Divide the kids into two groups. Half the kids will be "angels," and half the kids will be "lions." Optional: Kids wear colored bracelets, bandanas, or vests to indicate teams because things could get confusing very quickly!
2. Pick one child to be "Daniel."
3. In this game, there are a few goals. First, Daniel does not want to get tagged by any lions. If he does, the game is over.
4. Second, the lions do not want to get tagged by any angels. If they do get tagged, they lay or sit down and pretend they are asleep.
5. The ultimate goal is to have all lions put to sleep by the angels before Daniel is tagged by any of the lions.

TEACHABLE MOMENT:

Say: Wow, that was an intense game, wasn't it? Do you think it was like that for the Daniel when he was in the lions' den? We are told in Scripture that angels shut the mouths of the lions. (*Read Daniel 6:21.*) It is amazing how God protects his people.

DISCUSSION QUESTIONS:

- Can you think of a time when you were worried or afraid, and God protected you?
- What is the scariest animal you have ever seen?
- What would it be like to be trapped in a cave with that animal?
- Daniel was a man of prayer. When are some times each day that kids your age might pray?
- Do you pray alone or with others?

RUN AWAY JONAH

Individual Race

OVERVIEW
Kids will run to a corner of the room based on a city that is called out.

SCRIPTURE CONNECTION:
Jonah 1:1-4

SUPPLIES:
- Pre-made signs hung in the four corners of the room.
- Fairly large playing area for kids to run.

PREPARATION:
On the signs, print "Nineveh," "Tarshish," "'Under his bed," "In the sea." Put them in corners around the room.

DEVELOPMENTAL ALERT:
Look for ways to alter the game to accommodate those children with physical challenges or delays. Perhaps send them off in stages by calling out color of clothes. This way you can control who goes first and level the playing field.

HOW TO PLAY:

Say: Jonah was told by God to go to Nineveh, but he didn't obey right away. In this game, I'm going to call out a location, and you all need to run to that space. The last child to reach the space is out.

1. Kids start in the center of the playing space. Call out one of the places you wrote on the signs. Kids dash there as quickly as they can. The last child to arrive is out.
2. The child who just got out calls the next location. Repeat game until there are only one or two kids left. These kids answer one of the Discussion Questions below.

TEACHABLE MOMENT:

Say: In this game, you ran to where you were told, but in real life, Jonah did the exact opposite! (*Read Jonah 1:1–4.*) When God told Jonah to go to Nineveh, he hopped on a boat and headed somewhere else entirely! God cannot bless us when we are acting in disobedience–we saw the consequences for Jonah–a giant storm! God wants us to be part of his kingdom work, but that can only happen when we listen to and obey God.

DISCUSSION QUESTIONS:
- Why do you think Jonah disobeyed God?
- Do you ever feel like Jonah? Have you ever felt God's leading to do something, but you did the exact opposite? What was it?
- What are some consequences kids your age might face when they disobey God or their parents?

LEFT-HANDED EHUD

Individual Game

OVERVIEW

Play this quick game with the left hand to honor our left-handed hero, Ehud.

SCRIPTURE CONNECTION:
Judges 3:15

SUPPLIES:
- Pennies
- Stopwatch

PREPARATION:
Count out twenty-five pennies and place them in piles.

TIP:
Lessen the number of pennies for especially young kids.

OPPORTUNITY:
Have children raise their hand if they are left-handed. Have them raise their hand if they are right-handed. Have them jump up if they love to play sports. Have them get on their knees if they like video games. Continue this way pointing out how God made each of us the same yet different in many ways.

HOW TO PLAY:

1. Select four volunteers from the group and give them twenty-five pennies each.
2. Players stack the pennies in a tower, moving only one penny at a time, using only their left hand.
3. Begin the stopwatch and have the players begin to stack. Whoever can accomplish the task in under a minute, wins.
4. Allow more volunteers to play as time allows.

TEACHABLE MOMENT:

Say: For some of you, it might have been really hard to stack pennies with your left hand. However, if you were left-handed already, I bet that game was a piece of cake! There was a great warrior in the Bible named Ehud who fought with his left hand. It was very uncommon for a person to do battle with their left hand and Ehud used that to his advantage. He was able to trick the guards by hiding his sword in an unlikely place and then was able to kill the evil king. (*Read Judges 3:15–16.*)

DISCUSSION QUESTIONS:

- Have you ever heard the account of Ehud and the evil king Eglon before? What is your favorite part of the story?
- Do you know anyone who is left-handed? Do you think there are advantages to being left-handed?
- Isn't it interested that God used something as simple as being left-handed to bring down an evil king?
- Can you think of any other accounts in the Bible that have an interesting twist like that?

EZEKIEL AND BONE DIG

Team Race

OVERVIEW
Kids dig for bones in a dry and sandy valley.

SCRIPTURE CONNECTION:
Ezekiel 37:10

SUPPLIES:
- Small plastic bones (found online) or padded ear-cleaning swabs
- Large flat bin (think under bed storage) filled with sand
- Timer
- Paper and pen for recording score.

PREPARATION:
Fill bin with sand and bury twenty to thirty bones in the sand.

TIP:
If you have a large group (more than twenty kids), set up two bins so one player from each team can play at the same time.

HOW TO PLAY:
1. Kids divide into two teams.
2. Choose one player from the first team and have them sit next to the bin. Set timer for thirty seconds and have the child dig through the sand trying to find as many bones as possible. After the time is up, count the bones and record the score for the team.
3. Repeat the process for a player on the other team.
4. Continue this way until everyone has had a chance to play.
5. When everyone has had a turn, add up the bones and announce totals.

TEACHABLE MOMENT:

Say: That was a lot of bones you dug up there. Do you know that the Bible talks about a valley that was filled with dry bones? There was once a prophet named Ezekiel and God took him to a valley filled with bones. The bones were dry and old, but God made them come back to life! (*Read Ezekiel 37:1–10.*)

DISCUSSION QUESTIONS:
- What would you think if you saw the dry bones come to life?
- What do you think Ezekiel was thinking when he heard the rattling sound and saw the bones moving?
- Why do you think God brought these bones back to life?

AGES: 4–12 TIME NEEDED: 10 MIN

GATHER UP THE GRAIN (RUTH)

Team Race

OVERVIEW
Kids scramble to gather the most grain.

SCRIPTURE CONNECTION:
Ruth 2:2

SUPPLIES:
- Scraps of fabric or strips of paper from a shredder
- Differently colored bucket, one for each team of four to six players
- Scale
- Timer
- Large space to spread out the pretend grain.

PREPARATION:
Scatter the "grain" all over the room. Set the team buckets at one end of the room.

HOW TO PLAY:

1. Kids divide into teams of four to six players. Make sure each team knows which is their bucket.
2. Set the timer for one minute.
3. On your signal, kids will run out and gather grain and then return to their bucket and place it inside. Kids can make as many trips as they want during the time limit.
4. When the timer goes off, teams gather as you weigh the buckets. Team with the most grain answers one of the Discussion Questions below.

TEACHABLE MOMENT:

Say: Wow, there sure was a lot of activity on the pretend field out there! Gathering grain in the Bible time would have been similar, but a little less crazy. People would go up and down the rows gathering grain, but the Bible specifically told landowners to leave the corners untouched, so poor people could come and gather grain. When Ruth and Naomi moved back to Bethlehem, they had no food or relatives to help them. Ruth relied on this provision to gather food for her family. (*Read Ruth 2:15–16.*)

DISCUSSION QUESTIONS:

- What do you think Ruth and Naomi were thinking and feeling when they returned to Bethlehem? Do you think God specifically led Ruth to Boaz' field or was it something that just happened?
- What did Boaz do to help Ruth?
  How do you think this made her feel?
- When is a time when God provided for you?

NEW TESTAMENT GAMES

MARY VISITS ELIZABETH

Team Race

OVERVIEW
Kids pretend to pack a bag for a journey.

SCRIPTURE CONNECTION:
Luke 1:35-39

SUPPLIES:
- One small bag or suitcase for each team of four or five players
- Variety of things someone might pack for a trip (See optional checklist or Tip below.)
- Optional: Checklist of Things to Pack, page 280
- Optional: Cones or rope

PREPARATION:
Gather the same number of items for each team. Spread out all the items on one end of the room or play area. Optional: Set up cones or rope to make start line.

TIP:
Things to pack: shirt, pants, socks, comb, empty shampoo bottle, toothbrush, washcloth, towel, swimsuit, etc.

HOW TO PLAY:
1. Kids divide into teams of four or five players. If you are using the checklist, hand each team a checklist.
2. Give each team a suitcase or bag (should all be approximately the same size).
3. At the start of the game, the first person on each team will take the bag, run to the other end of the play area, grab an item, put it in the bag, and return to their team with the bag.
4. The next player will repeat the process, taking the bag to the items, placing something inside, and returning to their team. Each item placed inside the bag must be unique (the bag cannot contain two toothbrushes or two pairs of shorts, etc.).
5. The first team to have all players pack their bag answers one of the Discussion Questions below.

TEACHABLE MOMENT:
Say: In our passage today, Mary went on a trip to visit her cousin Elizabeth. (*Read Luke 1:35–39.*) She might have packed some of the same things in her bag. Why was Mary going to visit her cousin? Mary received some great news—she was going to be mother of the Savior! She wanted to share the good news with her cousin, Elizabeth, who was expecting a baby too!

DISCUSSION QUESTIONS:
- Have you ever gone on a trip? What kind of things did you pack? How do you think Mary felt as she packed for her trip?
- How do you think she felt when she arrived at Elizabeth's house?
- Do you think she felt nervous about it?

JESUS IS BORN

Team Game

OVERVIEW
Christmas trivia game where kids compete to answer questions.

SCRIPTURE CONNECTION:
Luke 2

SUPPLIES:
- Jesus Is Born Questions, page 281
- Notecards
- Pen or marker
- Sheet of paper

PREPARATION:
On note cards, print the clues/questions. Print the category and point value for each clue on the back of the card. Place cards clue-side-down on a table.

TIP:
If you have a large group of kids, set up the clues on pieces of construction paper instead. You could also write the clues in a PowerPoint program and project them onto a wall.

HOW TO PLAY:
1. Kids divide into teams of five to eight players, and chooses a team name.
2. Allow the first team to pick a category and point value. If they get the question/clue correct, they earn the point value on the back of the card. If they get the question incorrect, the other teams have a chance to steal the points.
3. Keep score on the sheet of paper.
4. Rotate between all the teams so everyone has a chance to pick a clue. Clues can be answered individually, or a child can ask their teammates for help (you may wish to set a thirty-second answer timer, so the game doesn't drag on too long).
5. The game ends when all the clues are gone. Team with the highest score wins.

TEACHABLE MOMENT:
Say: That was certainly a lot of information about Christmas! Wasn't it great to have teammates to help us out when we didn't know an answer? God loves it when we help each other out–whether it is in a game like this or real life.

DISCUSSION QUESTIONS:
- What are some ways we can help others during the Christmas season?
- What is your favorite part of Christmas?

JESUS IS BORN QUESTIONS

SONGS (Fill in the blank):
- 100: O Little Town of __________ (Bethlehem)
- 200: O Come, O Come __________ (Emmanuel)
- 300: O Come, All Ye __________ (Faithful)
- 400: Hark, the Herald __________ (Angels Sign)
- 500: God Rest Ye Merry __________ (Gentlemen)

TRADITIONS
- 100: Name a Christmas decoration
- 200: Why do we give gifts? (Because the wise men did)
- 300: What is the time/month leading up to Christmas called? (Advent)
- 400: What were the first Christmas tree lights? (Candles)
- 500: Name the eight original reindeer (Dasher, Dancer, Prancer, Vixen, Comet, Cupid, Donner, Blitzen)

EVENTS
- 100: We were in the field tending the sheep when something exciting happened. What was it?
- 200: After being warned in a dream about King Herod's evil plan, what did Joseph do? (Egypt)
- 300: T or F: Prophets were telling about the birth of Jesus more than 400 years before it happened. (True)
- 400: After the angel Gabriel visited Mary, she sang a song. Where can we find her song? (Luke 1) Bonus: Find it in the Bible.
- 500: Why did Mary and Joseph have to travel to Bethlehem (to be counted for the census). Bonus: Bethlehem was called the city of __________ (David).

CHARACTERS (4-5 Year olds only)
- 100: I am Jesus' mother
- 200: We traveled from afar, following a star
- 300: I didn't have any room for Jesus (inn keeper)
- 400: I am Mary's cousin–the one she visited after she was pregnant (Elizabeth)
- 500: I tried to kill all the baby boys when I found out about King Jesus. (King Herod)

PLACES
- 100: Where was Jesus born? (Bethlehem)
- 200: Where was Mary when the angel came to visit? (Her house)
- Bonus: What was his name? (Gabriel)
- 300: Where was Joseph when the angel came to visit? (In his bed, sleeping)
- 400: Where did the first Christmas tree show up? (Germany)
- 500: Where did the wise men stop in order to ask about the new baby king? (Jerusalem)

281

AGES: 4–12 | TIME NEEDED: 5 MIN

THAT SPICE IS NICE (WISE MEN)

Circle Game

OVERVIEW
Kids will sniff spices and try to name what they are smelling.

SCRIPTURE CONNECTION:
Matthew 2:1-11

SUPPLIES:
- Various spices (cinnamon, cloves, coriander seeds, cumin, oregano, basil, black pepper, garlic, sage, thyme, mint, nutmeg, etc.)
- Small containers with lids (available at dollar stores)
- Pen
- Two sheets of paper

PREPARATION:
Before kids arrive, pour each spice into a separate container. Place lid on top. Number container. Record which spice is in which container on sheet of paper. Keep answer sheet hidden from the kids. On another sheet of paper, print the name of each spice.

TIP:
You can use resealable plastic bags.

HOW TO PLAY:

Warning: When smelling something new, it's best to do so by waving your hand over the item to draw the scent to you (wafting).

1. Have all the kids sit in a circle and bring out the first spice. Let them pass it around, waft the smell towards them, and guess what spice it is.
2. After everyone has had a chance to smell and guess, you can reveal the answer.
3. Play again with the remainder of spices.

TEACHABLE MOMENT:

Say: Those were some interesting spices. Did you know that the wise men brought spices as gifts to Jesus when he was born? The spices that Jesus received were frankincense and myrrh. They were very expensive spices. (*Read Matthew 2:1–11.*)

DISCUSSION QUESTIONS:
- How would you like to get a spice as a gift?
- What was your favorite spice that we sniffed today?
- What was your least favorite spice?
- Do you think that Jesus and his family were happy to get spices for gifts?

SOWER AND THE SEEDS

Individual Game

OVERVIEW
Kids toss seeds, hoping to get them to land in the "fertile" soil.

SCRIPTURE CONNECTION:
Matthew 13:18-23

SUPPLIES:
- Large seeds (pumpkin seeds or sunflower seeds)
- Four poster boards, each a different color
- Permanent marker
- Masking tape or cones

PREPARATION:
Place the four poster boards on the floor. Label each one based on the parable of the sower: On the path (eaten by birds), Rocky Soil, Thorny Soil, Good soil. The "good" soil poster board should be the farthest from the start line. Use masking tape or cones to create a start (or throwing) line about 5 feet away from the poster boards.

HOW TO PLAY:
1. Kids stand at the start line and throw their seeds at the poster board. The object is to get your seeds to land on the good soil poster board. Each child has five seeds to throw.
2. When everyone has had a chance to toss, you can have the kids sit in a circle.

TEACHABLE MOMENT:
Say: In our passage today, Jesus tells a story about four types of soils. Do you remember what each of the soils stands for? (*Read Matthew 13:18–23.*) Just like in our game, sometimes the seeds land on good soil, and sometimes they do not.

DISCUSSION QUESTIONS:
- The thorny soil stands for worries of life–what kind of worries or troubles do you think might keep someone from trusting Jesus or obeying God?
- How can help people continue to grow in their faith?

AGES: 6–10 TIME NEEDED: 5–10 MIN

WALKING ON WATER

Relay Race

OVERVIEW

Kids walk on "water" as Peter did. But they have to be careful where they step!

SCRIPTURE CONNECTION:
Matthew 14:29-30

SUPPLIES:
- Footprints drawn on cardstock or poster board.
- Clear packing tape or painters tape.
- Large open space for running.

PREPARATION:
Draw and cut out footprints on cardstock or poster board. Tape the foot prints to the floor in a walking pattern. Prepare one set of footprints for each team of five or six players.

HOW TO PLAY:

1. Kids divide into teams and line up behind the start line. At the start of the race, the first person in line runs along the feet, being careful to step ONLY on the feet.
2. They race to the end of the line, touch the ground and then return to tag the next person on their team, relay style.
3. Once a child has completed the "walking on water" run, they should sit down, so it is clear who still needs to run. The first team to have everyone sitting answers one of the Discussion Questions below.

TEACHABLE MOMENT:

Say: In this game, we pretended to run on water. We read about Jesus and Peter walking on the water in Matthew 14:29–30. At first, Peter was doing pretty good, but then he got nervous about the wind and the waves. Do you think this game would have been harder if there was a lot of wind? What happened when Peter began to doubt? Jesus reached out and saved Peter. God will also hear us when we cry out to him.

DISCUSSION QUESTIONS:

- What are some things that might make a kid your age feel nervous or worried?
- How do you spend time praying, asking God to help you with your concerns?
- What did you like about this game? What did you not like?
- What do you think it would feel like to walk on water?

BLIND MAN CAN SEE

Partner Game

OVERVIEW
Kids guide a blindfolded friend towards a goal.

SCRIPTURE CONNECTION:
John 9:1-12

SUPPLIES:
- Blindfolds, one for each team of three players
- Small objects, one for each team
- Large play area
- Optional: Timer

PREPARATION:
Space small objects around the middle of the play area.

TIP:
Optional: If the game is too confusing with all the callers, you could play with just one or two teams and time teams to see who can complete the task the fastest.

HOW TO PLAY:

1. Group divides into teams of three partners.
2. One partner in the team is the blind man and puts on blindfold, another person is the caller, and the last person is the navigator.
3. The blind man tries to follow his teammate's directions to walk to and pick up one of the objects.
4. The navigator watches the blind man and gives blind man directions by pointing up, down, left or right. The navigator does not speak.
5. The caller faces the navigator but face from the blind man. The caller watches the navigator's hand signals and shouts them to the blind man.

TEACHABLE MOMENT:

Say: In our Bible story today, Jesus healed a man who was blind from birth. It must have been very hard for this blind man to find his way around. He would have needed someone to help him just like you guys did. Jesus healed the man in a very strange way. He put mud on the man's eyes and told him to go wash the mud off. The man obeyed, and he was healed! *(Read John 9:3.)*

DISCUSSION QUESTIONS:

- What is the hardest part of being blind?
- Why did Jesus chose to heal this man?
- What would it have been like for the blind man to see for the first time?

WIDOW GIVES HER COINS

Individual Game

OVERVIEW
Kids toss their coins just like the widow in the story.

SCRIPTURE CONNECTION:
Mark 12:41-44

SUPPLIES:
- Cones, rope, or masking tape
- Toy or real coins
- Bucket

PREPARATION:
Use cones, rope, or masking tape to make a start line. Set the bucket a few feet away from the start line. Adjust the bucket's position based on the age and ability of the child throwing.

HOW TO PLAY:

1. Kids stand in single file behind the start line.
2. Give each child two coins.
3. Players take turns tossing the coins into the bucket.

TEACHABLE MOMENT:

Say: In our Bible account today, a very poor woman gives all she has to the temple. She only had two coins left. It doesn't seem like much, but it was the last of her money, so it was a very big sacrifice for her. Even though other people gave more money, Jesus said that she put in more than the others because she gave the money she needed to live. (*Read Mark 12:41–44.*)

DISCUSSION QUESTIONS:

- Why might it have been hard for the woman to give away her last two coins?
- Was it harder for you to toss away your last coin? Usually, you have more than just two chances in a tossing game, so it might have seemed like more was at stake with each toss.
- Why do kids your age give money to the church? Why might kids not give money to the church?

PASS THE FISH (FEEDING 5,000)

Team Game

OVERVIEW
Kids pass "bread and fish" down a relay line to remind them of the time Jesus fed a large crowd with only a few loaves of bread and some fish.

SCRIPTURE CONNECTION:
Matthew 14:13-21

SUPPLIES:
- Small crackers (like oyster crackers)
- Small fish snacks (gold fish, gummy fish, etc.)
- Buckets or bowls, two for each team

PREPARATION:
Place one bowl of small crackers and small fish snacks at the start of each team and one empty bowl at the end of each team line. The starting bowls should have roughly the same amount of "bread and fish" for every team.

TIP:
If you don't want to count out crackers and fish snacks, use a small kitchen or postal scale to weigh them instead.

HOW TO PLAY:
1. Kids divide into teams of seven to ten players.
2. Kids stand in a single file line (each team is one line).
3. On your signal, the first player in line picks up one small cracker or fish snack and pass it to the next player in line. As soon as the first player has passed on the first cracker, they pick up and pass another food item.
4. That second player in line passes each food item to the next player and in line and so on. Until it reaches the last player who places each food item into the bucket.
5. The goal of the game is to pass all the bread and fish down the line, one piece at a time, until the starting bucket is empty and the ending bucket is full.
6. You could make kids pass the food items over their heads, under their legs, without bending their elbows, etc.

TEACHABLE MOMENT:
Say: A long time ago, Jesus fed many people with only a few loaves of bread and two small fish. Maybe the disciples passed the food out like we passed the food down the line. We know that Jesus performed a miracle because the food never ran out. Jesus and his friends were able to feed everyone in the crowd with only a small bit of food. Afterwards, they even collected leftovers! (*Read Matthew 14:13–21.*)

DISCUSSION QUESTIONS:
- How long would it have taken for the disciples to get food to everyone in the crowd?
- What would you do if you had to feed that many people?
- What do you think the people thought as Jesus multiplied the small lunch?
- How could there be leftovers?

GO TO JAIL (PAUL AND SILAS IN PRISON)

Tag

OVERVIEW
Kids play a crazy game of tag involving jail, praise songs, and earthquakes.

SCRIPTURE CONNECTION:
Acts 16:22-26

SUPPLIES:
- Large play area
- Optional: Chairs
- Optional: Children's worship CD and player

PREPARATION:
Designate a small area/corner off to the side to be the pretend jail. Optional: Place chairs in the jail.

HOW TO PLAY:

1. Pick one or two people to be "It" and the rest to be Christians.
2. This game is played like Tag. The group runs around in the playing space, trying not to get tagged by "It." If they do get tagged, they are taken to jail where they sit in chairs and sing praise songs. Optional: Play children's worship songs.
3. After kids sing praise songs for about a minute, yell "Earthquake." All the people in jail go free.
4. After every earthquake, choose a new "It." Play continues as time and interest allow.

TEACHABLE MOMENT:

Say: This game reminds me a lot about a time that Paul and Silas were in prison. (*Read Acts 16:22–26.*) Paul and Silas spent the night singing praise songs to God and something amazing happened—an earthquake broke their chains and left the prison doors open. Paul and Silas decided not to leave though, and because of that, the guard and all his family accepted Jesus as their Lord and Savior.

DISCUSSION QUESTIONS:

- Do you think you would have acted like Paul and Silas and stayed in the jail? Or would you have bolted right away?
- Why do you think Paul and Silas chose to stay?
- What do you think caused the earthquake that freed the men?
- Why do you think the jailer chose to become a Christian?

LOVE SCRAMBLE

Seek and Find

OVERVIEW
Kids find all the foam hearts before the time is up.

SCRIPTURE CONNECTION:
I Corinthians 13:4-8

SUPPLIES:
- Permanent marker
- Craft-foam hearts, available online or in craft stores)
- Large area with plenty of hiding places
- Poster board
- Timer

PREPARATION:
On separate hearts, print key words from the "Love is . . ." Bible passage (I Corinthians 3:4-8). Use one word or small phrase such as "kind," "patience," "does not envy," etc. Print the complete passage on poster board. Hide the hearts in the play area.

HOW TO PLAY:
1. Set the timer for one minute and have the kids search to find all the hearts.
2. Encourage them to match up the hearts to the poster to make sure they find all the hearts.
3. If all the hearts are found in under one minute, the group wins!

TEACHABLE MOMENT:
Say: This game was all about love. The Bible tells exactly what love is in 1 Corinthians 13. Let's read the passage together. (*Read 1 Corinthians 13:4–8.*) It's not always easy to do everything that is listed in this passage. That's why we often need God's help when showing love to others. God pours love into us so that we can love others.

DISCUSSION QUESTIONS:
- What is the hardest part of showing love to others?
- Which one of these words or phrases do you struggle with the most?
- Who is someone who shows this kind of love in your life?
- Who is someone you can show love to this week?

WHEN IS JESUS COMING BACK?

Seek and Find

OVERVIEW
When the music stops, kids must make it to a hoop before it is too late.

SCRIPTURE CONNECTION:
Matthew 25:13, Luke 12:40

SUPPLIES:
- Hula hoops, one fewer than the number of players
- Children's worship CD and player

PREPARATION:
Scattered toy hoops on the floor or ground.

TIP:
Don't have enough hula hoops? Use masking tape to make circles or squares for them to stand in.

HOW TO PLAY:
1. Kids begin the game by walking around the room as the music is being played.
2. When the music stops, they immediately run to a toy hoop and stand inside it. Only one child per hoop.
3. If a child does not make it to a hoop, they are out.
4. Remove one hoop after each round so that there is always one less hoop than the number of players.
5. The game continues until there are only one or two kids left.

TEACHABLE MOMENT:
Say: In this game, the music could stop at any moment. We didn't know when to expect it. When it did stop, you had to hurry to a hoop, but not everyone made it in time. Some people treat Jesus' return the same way. They think they can wait until the last minute to repent and start living for God, but when Jesus comes back, it will be too late to "run for a hoop." We have to be ready for Jesus' return now. Just like we didn't know when the music would stop, we don't know when Jesus will return. The Bible tells us that no one knows the day or hour. If we want to go to heaven with Jesus when he comes back, we have to accept him as our Lord and Savior now. (*Read Luke 12:40.*)

DISCUSSION QUESTIONS:
- Why do you think people sometimes wait to start following God?
- What did it feel like when you couldn't make it to a hoop in time?
- What do you think it would feel like to be shut out of heaven?

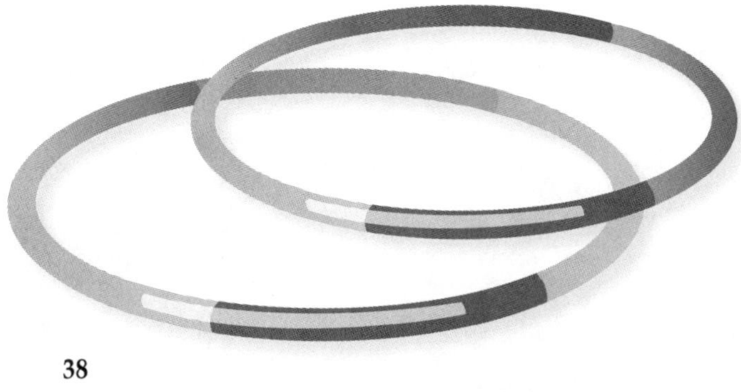

ARMOR OF GOD RELAY

Team Race

OVERVIEW
Kids race as teams to put on the full armor of God from a pile of discarded clothing.

SCRIPTURE CONNECTION:
Ephesians 6:10-18

SUPPLIES:
- One Bible for each team
- Armor of God cards, page 282
- Articles of clothing to coordinate with the armor of God
- Small bowl

PREPARATION:
Make one copy of the Armor of God cards for each team. Cut the cards apart and put them in a small bowl. Gather up discarded clothing and Bibles and put everything on one side of the room. You will need multiples of the clothing so that everyone can get a piece of armor on.

IDEAS OF COORDINATING CLOTHING:
- Belt of Truth = Belt
- Breastplate of Righteousness = shirt or jacket
- Feet fitted = shoes or slippers
- Shield of Faith = Umbrella or briefcase
- Helmet of Salvation = Hat
- Sword of the Spirit = Bible

HOW TO PLAY:
1. Kids divide into teams of six players.
2. Kids line up on one side of the room and place a bowl with the cards beside each beginning player.
3. On your signal, first player on each team will pick a card and then run to the opposite side of the room to find a coordinating piece of clothing. If player picked up the sword of the Spirit, player picks up the Bible.
4. When the first player returns, the next player takes a turn, picking up a card and finding a matching item.
5. The first team to grab a complete set of armor answers one of the Discussion Questions below.

TEACHABLE MOMENT:
Say: You might have heard of the full armor of God before. This is not real armor that we put on, but a type of spiritual armor. Clothing is important to keep us warm and protected, just like spiritual armor keeps us protected from our enemy–Satan. (*Read Ephesians 6:10–18.*)

DISCUSSION QUESTIONS:
- Why did we use a Bible for the sword of the Spirit? How does the Bible help us fight against Satan?
- How would putting on the armor of God help us fight against sin?
- How can we remember to put our armor on each day?

HIDDEN COINS (ZACCHAEUS)

Seek and Find

OVERVIEW
Kids will look high and low to gather up coins in this fast-paced game.

SCRIPTURE CONNECTION:
Luke 19:2

SUPPLIES:
- Pennies or toy coins
- Large space

PREPARATION:
Hide coins throughout the space. Make sure there are five or more coins per child. Base the number on how many children are expected, plus enough for one or two visitors.

HOW TO PLAY:

1. When kids arrive, tell them that you have hidden coins throughout the room and their job is to find the coins.
2. Give the youngest bunch of kids a ten-second head start.
3. On your signal, kids search for coins. After two or three minutes, when it seems like most of the coins have been found, gather the kids back together and have them count all their coins.
4. Whoever has the most coins answers one of the Discussion Questions below or chooses a volunteer to answer.

TEACHABLE MOMENT:

Say: There was a man who had a lot of coins. (*Read Luke 19:2.*) The Bible tells us that he was very wealthy. Unfortunately, he didn't gain his wealth through hard and honest work. He was a tax collector and often tricked people into giving him more money than what was required. His name was Zacchaeus and his life drastically changed when he met Jesus. One day, Zacchaeus heard that Jesus was in town. He went to see him and repented of his sin. He gave back the money he had stolen from people (by tricking them) and decided to live his life according to God's rules.

DISCUSSION QUESTIONS:

- Why do you think Zacchaeus made such a change in his life?
- What are some reasons people might decide to live God's way?
- Were there things you had to change or do differently?
- Do you think following Jesus is worth giving up all that money? Why or why not?

THAT'S A WRAP (LAZARUS)

Partner Game

OVERVIEW
Around and around the toilet paper goes. We've got to get Lazarus wrapped up tight!

SCRIPTURE CONNECTION:
John 11:43

SUPPLIES:
- Toilet paper roll, one for each pair of kids
- Timer

PREPARATION:
None

DEVELOPMENTAL ALERT:
Be sensitive to any children who have lost a loved one. Often children in Christian families know that family and friends prayed for healing. When God chooses not to grant healing, children can become confused. If needed, be prepared for that conversation with an answer your church shares in those difficult moments.

HOW TO PLAY:
1. Kids divide into pairs. Give each pair one roll of toilet paper.
2. Set the timer for two minutes.
3. Explain to kids that their goal is to completely cover their partner in toilet paper (one person will be wrapped, and the other will do the wrapping).
4. Begin the timer and let the kids get wrapping!
5. At the end of two minutes, have the kids stop wrapping. Whoever is the most covered wins.

TEACHABLE MOMENT:
Say: In our Bible story today, there was a man who was special to Jesus. His name was Lazarus. One day, Lazarus got sick and died. His sisters, Mary and Martha, were sad. They knew that Jesus could have healed him if only he had come sooner! They wrapped Lazarus in grave clothes and put him in the tomb. They thought that was the end of the story. Jesus surprised them three days later when he arrived at their house and raised Lazarus from the dead. (*Read John 11:43.*)

DISCUSSION QUESTIONS:
- Why do you think Jesus did not rush to Lazarus when he was sick?
- How did Mary and Martha feelings change when their brother was raised to life? What do you think were the first words Mary and Martha said to their brother? To Jesus?

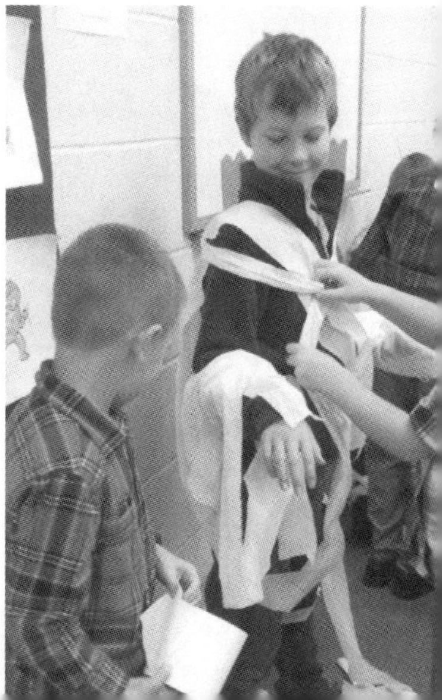

SERVING OTHERS

Drawing Guessing Game

OVERVIEW
Kids draw pictures of ways that they can serve others and then try to guess the artist.

SCRIPTURE CONNECTION:
Acts 9:36

SUPPLIES:
- Construction paper (white)
- Crayons
- Space for kids to spread out

TIP:
Brainstorm way your class can serve others with their families. Let parents know what their children want to do. Encourage them to create an action plan to carry out the serving opportunity as a family.

HOW TO PLAY:

1. Give each child a sheet of paper and some crayons. Children find a quiet place a bit separated from everyone else and draw a picture of a way they can serve others. Children keep their drawing a secret from the other kids.
2. After a few minutes, see if everyone is done drawing. Ask kids about their drawings and write a caption if needed. If they are finished, collect their drawings.
3. Gather in a circle. Show the group one of the pictures. Tell them what is happening in the picture. Have the other kids guess who the artist is. If they guess correctly, give the picture to the owner. After three guesses, set it aside to guess again later.
4. Continue in this way until all the drawings have been guessed and returned to their original owner.

TEACHABLE MOMENT:

Say: There was a girl who lived during Bible times who loved to help and serve others. (*Read Acts 9:36–40.*) Her name was Tabitha, and it seemed that her favorite thing to do was to sew clothes for others. You guys came up with a lot of good ways to serve others.

DISCUSSION QUESTIONS:

- What were some of your favorite ideas for helping others?
- What is something you can commit to doing this week to help others?
- What keeps us from helping others?
- How do you think others feel when we help them or serve them?

FOUR FRIENDS RACE (Jesus Heals Paralytic)

Team Game

OVERVIEW
Kids will carry a friend on a blanket as they race around the room.

SCRIPTURE CONNECTION:
Matthew 9:2

SUPPLIES:
- Blanket or beach towel
- Large room to run around or outside space
- Cones (to mark start and finish)
- Stopwatch

PREPARATION:
Set up the start and finish cones.

TIP:
Pick the smallest kids to be carried. They often struggle with physical tasks and their size will actually be a plus.

HOW TO PLAY:

1. Select five volunteers. Place blanket or towel on the ground. Four of the volunteers each hold a corner of the blanket or towel, and one child sits on it.
2. Start the stopwatch and signal kids to pick up their friend by lifting their four corners. Kids race around the perimeter of the room or between the start and finish cones. Keep track of their time.
3. After they complete the race, select five more volunteers and repeat the process. Play until everyone has a chance to race.
4. After everyone has raced, announce the fastest score and declare the winners!

TEACHABLE MOMENT:

Say: It wouldn't always be easy carrying around a friend like that, would it? There was a man who lived at the same time as Jesus who was paralyzed. (*Read Matthew 9:2.*) Back then, they did not have wheelchairs to help people. If this man wanted to go anywhere, he needed friends to carry him on a blanket like you did in this race. It would not have been easy, but the four friends in our passage today helped their friend. They brought him to Jesus. Jesus healed the man and forgave his sins.

DISCUSSION QUESTIONS:

- Why do you think these four friends chose to help?
- What must the paralyzed man have been thinking and feeling as his friends brought him to Jesus?
- What was the first thing the man did once he could walk again?
- Is there someone in your life that you can help?
- Is there someone in your life you could tell about Jesus?

BANDAGE BONANZA

Partner Game

OVERVIEW
Fingers will be flying as kids try to bandage up their friends as quickly as possible!

SCRIPTURE CONNECTION:
Luke 10:33-34

SUPPLIES:
- Box of bandages, one per pair of kids
- Timer

PREPARATION:
None

TIP:
Don't have money for all these bandages? Use painters tape instead.

HOW TO PLAY:

1. Put kids into pairs and give each pair a box of bandages.
2. Set the timer for two minutes and tell kids to stick as many bandages as they can on their partner within the timer limit.
3. After the time is up, count the number of bandages on their body and clothes and declare a winner.
4. Kids switch partners and play the game again.

TEACHABLE MOMENT:

Say: You were really in a rush to get those bandages on, but the man in our story (parable) today was not in a rush at all. He took the time to stop and help someone. (*Read Luke 10:30–37.*) The Samaritan cared for someone who was not like him and who may have treated him badly. Jesus says we should act the same way towards others we meet in our life.

DISCUSSION QUESTIONS:

- Why do you think the Samaritan man stopped to help?
- Why do you think some people pass by others who need their help?
- What are ways you can help others in a normal day?

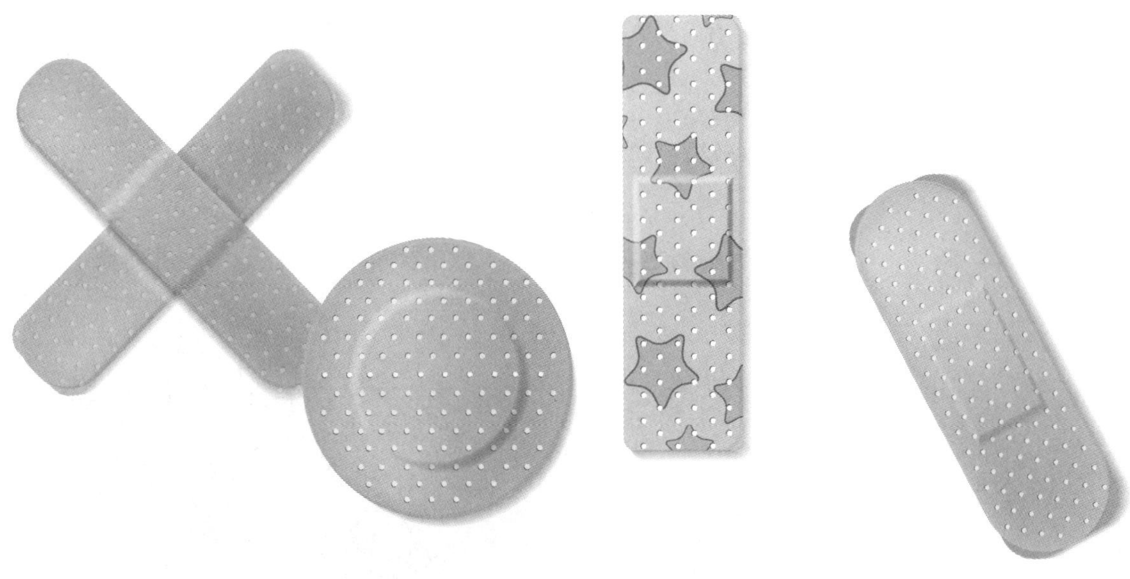

ICE BREAKER GAMES

TELEPHONE

Circle Game

OVERVIEW
In this classic game, kids pass a message from person to person by whispering in their ear.

SCRIPTURE CONNECTION:
Exodus 23:1

EXTRA PAGES:
- Shake the Box Guessing Game (Pre-Reader/regular)
- Who Am I?

SUPPLIES:
None

PREPARATION:
None

FUNNY PHRASES TO USE:
- A guppy in a shark tank goes blub, blub.
- Crunchy candy is my cat's favorite snack.
- Jack climbed a bean stock with a snake.
- Sister Suzy is sitting on a volcano with a glass of lemonade.
- Pass the razzleberry muffins as we go to the parade.

TIP:
This is also a good no-prep, no-prop game.

HOW TO PLAY:

1. Kids sit in a circle on the floor.
2. Begin by whispering a funny phrase to the child sitting next to you.
3. They turn and whisper it to the person sitting next to them.
4. This continues until everyone in the circle has heard the phrase. The last person in the circle says the phrase out loud. Often the phrase gets changed along the way, leading to a lot of laughter!

TEACHABLE MOMENT:

Say: The Bible talks a lot about spreading gossip and slander. Gossip is something negative we've heard about someone that we pass onto someone else. It might be true, and it might not be true, but usually, it's pretty hurtful to the person that it's about. The phrases that we used today were all silly, but imagine what might happen if we started talking about someone we knew. The message might get very twisted! (*Read Exodus 23:1.*) This verse tells us not to spread false reports. If you hear something about someone, ask the person if it's true. Don't just spread the news onto someone else.

DISCUSSION QUESTIONS:

- \Why do you think the Bible warns us again gossip and slander?
- Why did people spread false reports about other people?

PASS THE CARDS

Card Game

OVERVIEW
Pass the cards around the circle and then add the points.

SCRIPTURE CONNECTION:
1 Corinthians 12:4-11

SUPPLIES:
- Deck of cards (Uno cards can also be used)
- Rubber band
- Children's worship CD and player
- Optional: Calculator or pencil and paper

PREPARATION:
Put a rubber band around a deck of cards.

TIP:
SCORING: Each card is worth its face value. Jacks = 10, Queens = 15, Kings = 20, Aces = 25, and Jokers = 5

HOW TO PLAY:

1. Kids sit in a circle. Optional: Play music.
2. Each child takes two cards out of the deck and puts them in their lap. After they have taken their cards, they pass the deck to the child next to them.
3. The next child takes two cards and passes it on. This continues until all the cards are gone.
4. Add up the cards for each player. The team with the most points tells a sentence about the Bible story or says the memory verse. Optional: Use calculator or pencil and paper to add up scores.

TEACHABLE MOMENT:

Say: We all took cards from the same decks, but some of us ended up with some different scores! In 1 Corinthians 12, we learn that God the Spirit gives each person a gift. (*Read 1 Corinthians 12:4–11.*) Sometimes the gifts that God gives us look very different from the gifts he gives someone else, but they are all from God. All of our abilities and talents come from God and should be used to help others and build God's kingdom.

DISCUSSION QUESTIONS:

- What kind of talents and abilities do you have?
- How might you use your gifts to help others?
- What are some gifts that are listed in 1 Corinthians?
- Have you seen any of these gifts at work in your life or the lives of those around you?

HAVE YOU EVER...?

Circle Game

OVERVIEW
In this fast-paced game, the kids race to find a chair to sit in based on things they have done.

SCRIPTURE CONNECTION:
Psalm 139:1-4

SUPPLIES:
· Chairs

PREPARATION:
Set up chairs in a circle, seats facing in towards the center of the circle. There should be one less chair than the number of players.

HOW TO PLAY:

1. Choose a volunteer to be "It." "It" stands in the middle of the circle of chairs.
2. The rest of the players sit in the chairs. "It" says a phrase that begins with "Have you ever . . . ?" Some examples include:
   - Have you ever owned a pet?
   - Have you ever attended school?
   - Have you ever licked a lollipop?
   - Have you ever kissed a frog?
   - Have you ever gone swimming in the ocean?
3. If that phrase is true for any of the players who are currently sitting, they stand up and move quickly to a new, empty chair. In the meantime, "It" tries to sit in an empty chair.
4. Whoever is left without a chair to sit in is the new "It," and a new round begins.
5. Game continues for six to eight rounds or as interest allows.

TEACHABLE MOMENT:

Say: Did you know that God already knows everything about you? He made you, of course, but he also knows what you've been up to for your entire life. (*Read Psalm 139:14.*) God knows when we stand, sleep, the words we say and even our thoughts. That's amazing!

DISCUSSION QUESTIONS:

- When we were playing this game, did anything surprise you about your friends?
- How do you feel about God knows our every move?
- How does it feel to knowing God designed you as you are?

SHAKE THE BOX

Guessing Game

OVERVIEW
Kids rely on their sense of hearing to guess what is inside a closed box.

SCRIPTURE CONNECTION:
Exodus 15:26

SUPPLIES:
- 8 small boxes and lids
- 8 items to place in boxes
- Optional: Shake the Box Answer Key, page 283

PREPARATION:
Put the tiny things inside each box, one type of item per box. Close tightly and number each box. Optional: If you are using the answer key, choose items and place in boxes according to those listed in the answer key.

IDEAS TO PUT IN BOXES:
Safety pins, sea shells, dried beans, feathers, rice, coins, paperclips, Lego blocks, marbles, buttons, paper scraps, etc.

HOW TO PLAY:

1. Set the boxes out on a table and give kids a piece of paper to write down answers. Optional: For each child, make a photocopy of the Shake the Box Answer Key.
2. Allow children to rotate around and shake the boxes, trying to guess what might be inside. Have them write down their answers on their paper.
3. When everyone has a chance to listen to all the boxes, you can reveal the answers to the kids!

TEACHABLE MOMENT:
Say: Wow! That game took some pretty serious listening. You had to listen very carefully to get clues about what might be inside the boxes. Did you know the Bible talks about listening carefully too? (*Read Exodus 15:26.*) In this verse, Moses is advising the people to listen carefully to and obey the Lord's commands. Thankfully, reading God's commands is a lot easier than trying to guess what is in these boxes. We can read the Bible and learn how God wants us to live.

DISCUSSION QUESTIONS:
- Which one of these boxes was the easiest to guess? Which one was the hardest?
- Were you surprised by the contents of any of the boxes?
- How is listening to the boxes like listening to God's commands?
- How is it different?

PASS THE TISSUE PAPER

Team Game

OVERVIEW
Kids use straws to pass a piece of paper down the line.

SCRIPTURE CONNECTION:
Romans 12:12

SUPPLIES:
- Small squares of tissue paper
- Straws (at least one per child)

PREPARATION:
Cut tissue paper into small squares.

HOW TO PLAY:
1. Give each child a straw. Kids divide into teams of five or six players.
2. Arrange them in a straight line, about arms width apart.
3. Begin by placing a small square of tissue paper on a table. The first player on each team sucks up the tissue paper square with their straw. They hold the tissue paper on the end of the straw by sucking in.
4. With the tissue paper still on the straw (keep sucking in!), the first player will turn to the second player and attempt to transfer the tissue paper square to their straw. If a player drops a tissue, the player picks it up with their straw.
5. The tissue paper square continues down the line, being passed straw to straw until it reaches the last player who answers, or chooses a volunteer to answer, one of the Discussion Questions below.

TEACHABLE MOMENT:
Say: That was a pretty hard game since you had to keep sucking in air to keep the tissue paper on your straw. It took a lot of concentration and a lot of patience! The Bible talks quite a bit about patience and perseverance. There is one particular verse that I like in the book of Romans. (*Read Romans 12:12.*) Did you feel like you had to be patient in affliction in the game? It was hard to keep picking up the tissue paper when it dropped. God will help us with our hard tasks in life. He wants us to pray and ask him for help, and he will help us through anything.

DISCUSSION QUESTIONS:
- What was the hardest part of this game?
- Do you have tasks in life that seem exhausting too?
- Hard to do that require a lot of constant effort?

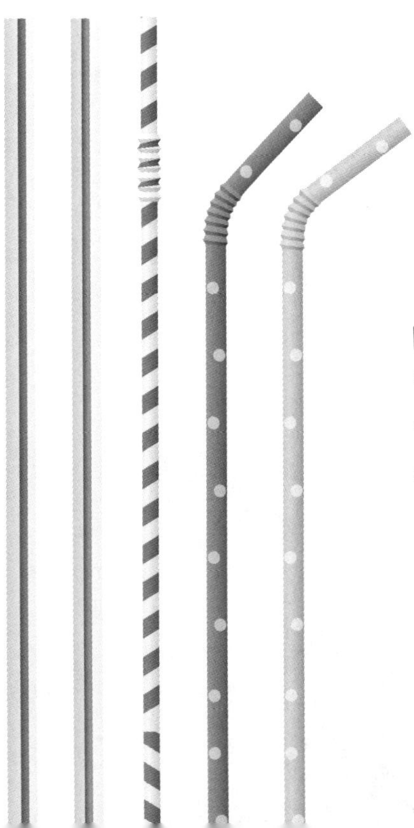

WHO AM I?

Guessing Game

OVERVIEW
Kids give each other clues to discover their "secret identity."

SCRIPTURE CONNECTION:
Hebrews 11

SUPPLIES:
- Who Am I? Cards, page 284
- Tape
- Optional: Children's worship CD and player

PREPARATION:
Make a copy of the reproducible page 260. You may wish to copy them onto cardstock to make them sturdier.

TIPS:
- Want to use the this game as a Bible-story review? Write the names of the people you've recently studied on index cards and use in game.
- If the game goes too quickly, mix the cards up and redistribute. This time, kids can only ask yes or no questions.

HOW TO PLAY:

1. When all the kids have arrived, tape a card to each child's forehead. Optional: Play music softly during game.
2. Encourage the children to walk around and ask each other facts about the person on their forehead. For example, they might ask:
   - Was my story in the Old Testament or New Testament?
   - Am I a man or woman?
   - Did I have any children?
   - Was I famous for anything?
   - Did I do something brave?
   - Did I travel far?
   - Did I have brothers and sisters?
3. When a child guesses their person correctly, they can remove the card from their head. They can continue to answer questions for other players until everyone guesses correctly.

TEACHABLE MOMENT:

Say: Many of the people from our game today came from a passage in the Bible called the "Hall of Faith." This passage tells about many great people who trusted God even when things didn't make sense. (*Read a few verses from Hebrews 11.*)

DISCUSSION QUESTIONS:
- Who is your favorite person from the Bible?
- What do you like about them?
- Was it easy or hard to figure out who the person was on your card? Why?
- How can we get to know the people in the Bible better?

ONE MINUTE WORDS

Team Game

OVERVIEW

Kids work together to come up with as many words as possible in one minute–all starting with the same letter.

SCRIPTURE CONNECTION:
Matthew 6:7-8

SUPPLIES:
- Timer
- Pen and paper

PREPARATION:
None

TIP:
Pray during the week for the lesson, the team and the children. Pray together as a team each week. Ask the children for prayer requests, pray for them, and then follow up with them the next week to see how it is going.

HOW TO PLAY:

1. Split the group up into teams of five to ten players.
2. Announce a letter and pick a team to go first.
3. Set the timer for one minute and allow the team to call out as many words as they can think of that start with the letter you chose. Keep a tally as they yell (try not to count repeats).
4. When the minute is up, pick a new letter and a new team and repeat the process.
5. Play again as time allows.

TEACHABLE MOMENT:

Say: Sometimes there were so many words flying at me at once that I couldn't understand you! In the New Testament, some people would stand up tall in church or the synagogue and go on and on with all kinds of words. (*Read Matthew 6:7–8.*) These people thought that God would hear them because of all their many words, but that just isn't the case. God hears us when we say just a few words, and he even knows what we're thinking! We don't have to try to impress him when we pray. God just loves to talk with us.

DISCUSSION QUESTIONS:

- Is it easy or hard to pray out loud? Why?
- Do you feel like you have to use just the right words?
- Where do you usually like to pray?
- How do you know God is listening to you when you pray?

CAN YOU REMEMBER?

Memory Game

OVERVIEW
Kids try to remember items on a tray before time it up.

SCRIPTURE CONNECTION:
Various

SUPPLIES:
- Small items (pencil, rubber duck, coffee mug, stapler, action figure, markers, crayon box, coins, pipe cleaner, deflated balloon, etc.)
- Tray
- Timer
- Pencils and paper

PREPARATION:
Place all items on tray.

TIP:
Elementary children want to see how things work and learn from hands-on discovery. Middle elementary children are becoming aware of their abilities or lack of them. It helps to expose them to new experiences so they can discover what they are capable of.

HOW TO PLAY:
1. When all the kids have arrived, tape a card to each child's forehead.
2. Give kids one minute to look at the tray (no touching).
3. After a minute, take the tray out of the room and give kids pencils and paper. Have them write down everything they can remember.
4. The person with the most items on their list wins.

TEACHABLE MOMENT:
Say: God can remember all things. He remembers every person he's ever created and what their life was like. Since we, as people, are so prone to forgetting things, God often set up remembrances so we could recall his good deeds. God gave us a rainbow to remember that he would never flood the earth again. God had the Israelites set up altars to remember his miracles. Every time we see a cross, we can remember Jesus' great big love for us.

DISCUSSION QUESTIONS:
- Was it hard to remember all of the items in our game? Who is someone who can remember everything?
- Can you think of a time that someone forgot something in the Bible (Ex. Joseph's inmates forgot to tell Pharaoh about Joseph)?
- Can God can remember everything we've ever said or done?
- Is it easy to remember the things God has done in our own lives?
- What is one way we can remember how God helps us?

WHERE IS MY SHOE?

Partner Game

OVERVIEW
Kids scramble to match shoes up to their partners.

SCRIPTURE CONNECTION:
Ruth 4:7-8, Luke 15:22

SUPPLIES:
- Chairs, one for every two kids
- Random shoes

PREPARATION:
Set chairs up in a circle, with seats facing out.

TIP:
Older Elementary children are very focused on developing friendships and sizing up where they are among their peers. Help them by setting up opportunities for them to connect to other children during games.

HOW TO PLAY:

1. Have everyone take off their shoes put them in the center of the chairs. While the kids are not looking, throw in a few random shoes.
2. Children pair up. One person sits in the chair, and the other stands behind the chair, facing from the middle.
3. On your signal, the standing children will go to the shoe pile, try to find their partner's shoes and get them back on their partner's feet. The sitting partner may give hints or descriptions, but they may not turn around and point to their particular pair.
4. Once all the seated partners are properly shoed, you can have the kids switch places and play the game again.

TEACHABLE MOMENT:

Say: What a rush to get those shoes on. Do you ever feel like that in real life? Have you ever had an emergency and had to run to get your shoes on and get out the door? Did you know that the Bible sometimes talked about shoes? Shoes were sometimes used to make deals or agreements with other people. (*Ruth 4:7–8.*) In another passage, a father puts sandals on his son to show him that he is welcomed back into the family (*Luke 15:22.*)

DISCUSSION QUESTIONS:

- Can you think of any other instances when the Bible talks about shoes or feet? (Moses takes off his sandals on holy ground, Jesus washes his disciples' feet).
- Do you think you would like to wash the feet of your friends? Why or why not?
- What was your favorite part of this game?
- What was the hardest part?

PASS THE PARCEL

Circle Game

OVERVIEW
Children pass the package (parcel) from person to person until the music stops.

SCRIPTURE CONNECTION:
Romans 6:23

SUPPLIES:
- Small box with a prize inside
- Tissue paper or wrapping paper
- Tape
- Scissors
- Children's worship CD and player

PREPARATION:
Wrap the box in several layers of wrapping. There should be at least one layer for every child who will be playing, plus a few extra.

TIP:
To introduce the Bible story, relate the prize to the lesson. For example, have seeds for the parable of the sower (Matthew 13), or a boat for Jesus walking on the water (Matthew 14), or some fruit shaped erasers for the Garden of Eden (Genesis 2-3).

HOW TO PLAY:

1. Kids sit in a circle.
2. Hand the parcel to one player and start the music.
3. Instruct kids to pass the parcel to their right as the music plays. After a few seconds, stop the music. Whoever is holding the parcel gets to take off one layer of wrapping.
4. The game continues in this way until the final paper is ripped away. Whoever is holding the box during the final unwrapping gets to keep the prize.

TEACHABLE MOMENT:

Say: This was a strange game, wasn't it? We didn't know who was going to end up with the gift. Every time another layer of paper was ripped off, I bet you wondered if the gift would finally be revealed. This reminds me of another type of gift–God's gift of salvation. Thankfully, God will give this gift to anyone who asks. We don't have to unwrap it or play a game to get it. God gives it freely. Romans 6:23 tells us that the gift of God is eternal life through Jesus. That's better than anything we can put in a box! .

DISCUSSION QUESTIONS:

- How did it feel to unwrap a layer of the gift?
- How did it feel not to know where the gift would stop?
- How do you feel knowing that we can have the gift of eternal life without having to do anything but ask for it?

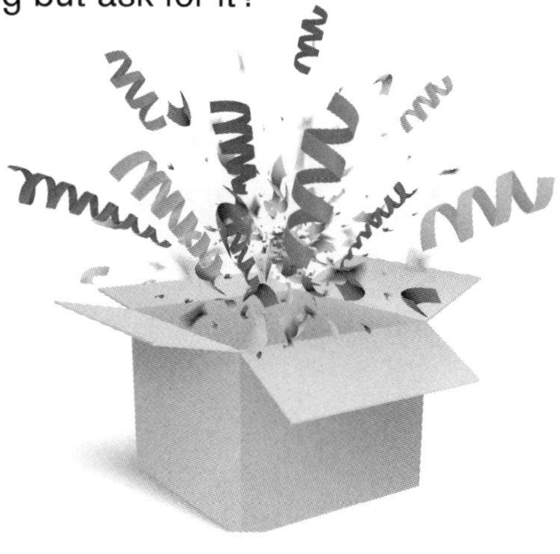

COMPLIMENTS

Guessing Game

OVERVIEW
Kids give each other compliments, but keep their identities a mystery. Can their friends guess who each compliment is about?

SCRIPTURE CONNECTION:
I Thessalonians 5:11

SUPPLIES:
• Paper and pencils

PREPARATION:
Write the name of each child on a card.

DEVELOPMENT:
At this age, peers are becoming a bigger influence on them. Encouraging good friendships is important. They're forming their self-image. Affirming them helps them sense their worth to you and God.

HOW TO PLAY:

1. Pass prepared cards out to each child randomly. Allow the children time to write something encouraging about the child on their card.
2. Collect the cards and read one aloud. Have the kids guess who the compliment is about. Reveal who it is by handing the card to that child.
3. Play again as time permits.

TEACHABLE MOMENT:

Say: The Bible instructs us to encourage each other and speak kindly to one another. You just practiced that right now! (*Read I Thessalonians 5:11.*)

DISCUSSION QUESTIONS:

- Is it easy to encourage each other and build each other up?
- Why do we sometimes forget to encourage each other?
- Do you remember a time when someone encouraged you? Tell us about it.

OPPOSITES

Circle Game

OVERVIEW
Kids think quickly in this game of opposites.

SCRIPTURE CONNECTION:
Jonah 1:1-3

SUPPLIES:
- Small ball

PREPARATION:
None

TIP:
Want some words to get you started? Start, clean, dirty, big, high, low, light, dark, soft, hard, easy, nice, flat, over, warm, loud, hungry, save, straight, open, on, many, after, up, above, empty, awake, alert, happy, wide.

HOW TO PLAY:

1. Begin by having kids sit in a circle.
2. Say a word and then toss the ball to someone. Whoever catches the ball says an opposite of the word. That player then takes a turn, saying a new word.
3. If a child gets stuck, that round is over (no one is out). The ball goes back to the last child who said a word and play begins again.

TEACHABLE MOMENT:

Say: Some of those were pretty easy to think of and some were a little tougher! There are times in life when we have a job or responsibility to do, but we feel like doing the exact opposite! That is what happened to a man named Jonah from the Bible. God told Jonah to go to a certain city, but Jonah hopped on a boat and went in the opposite direction! Maybe you know the story. Things didn't go too well for Jonah at first, but in the end, he obeyed God, and the people of Nineveh were saved!
(*Read Jonah 1:1–3.*)

DISCUSSION QUESTIONS:

- Why do we sometimes do the opposite of what we are told?
- Why do you think Jonah did the opposite of what God said?
- What do you think would have happened to the people of Nineveh if Jonah did not go?
- Are there people in your life you could tell about God?

WORD CHAIN

Circle Game

OVERVIEW
Quick thinking and a good grasp of the alphabet are needed to excel in this game!

SCRIPTURE CONNECTION:
Isaiah 5:21

SUPPLIES:
- Small ball

PREPARATION:
Write out words to use for easy reference.

INAPPROPRIATE BEHAVIORS:
Provide children with clear instructions and be as specific as possible. Use instructions such as hands down, come here, sit down, quiet hands, quiet voice, etc. State instructions clearly and concisely in an emotion-free voice. Be sure to tell children what you want them to do, not what you DON'T want them to do. For instance, instead of saying "Don't run," tell children to walk.

HOW TO PLAY:

1. Begin by having kids sit in a circle.
2. Say a word and then toss the ball to someone. Player who catches the ball says a word which begins with the LAST letter of the word that was just said. For example, if you say, "Tree," the player who catches the ball says a word that starts with *E*. That player then toss the ball and play continues.
3. If a player gets stuck, that round is over (no one is out). The ball goes to the last player to say a word and a new round begins.

Word Chain Example:
Tree ⇨ Elephant ⇨ Turtle ⇨ Egg ⇨ Gallop ⇨ Puzzle ⇨ Explain ⇨ Neck

TEACHABLE MOMENT:
Say: Sometimes I think I'm pretty clever and then I start playing a game like this and it's easy to get stuck! God warns against relying on our cleverness in life. (*Read Isaiah 5:21.*)

DISCUSSION QUESTIONS:

- Why do you think God warns against those who are "clever in their own eyes?"
- Do you think our attitude towards others changes when we begin to think we are smarter or cleverer than others? Why is that?
- Where does the ultimate source of wisdom come from?

RELATED WORDS

Circle Game

OVERVIEW
Let's see how easy it is to make connections.

SCRIPTURE CONNECTION:
Psalm 19:10

SUPPLIES:
- Small ball

PREPARATION:
Write out words to use for easy reference.

HOW TO PLAY:
1. Begin by having kids sit in a circle.
2. Say a word and then toss the ball to someone. Player who catches the ball says a word that is related to the first word. For example, if you say "Cat," the next player might say, "Mouse." That player then passes the ball to the child on the right.
3. If a player gets stuck, that round is over (no one is out). The ball goes to the last player to say a word and a new round begins.

Word Chain Example:

Cat ⇨ Mouse ⇨ Rat ⇨ Sewer ⇨ Drain ⇨ Water ⇨ Lake ⇨ Boat

TEACHABLE MOMENT:

Say: Those were some pretty crazy connections! It was interesting that we could start with one word (give an example) and get all the way to something completely different (give an example). I've got another set of words that might not seem related at first. They are "gold," "honey," and the "Bible." Can you guess the connection? In the book of Psalms, we learn that God's Word (or his commandments) are sweeter than honey and more precious than gold. (*Read Psalm 19:10.*)

DISCUSSION QUESTIONS:
- Why do you think God's word is more precious than gold?
- Why do you think God's word is sweeter than honey?
- Who wrote the book of Psalms (mostly)?
- Do you think David loved God's word?
- How can you tell when a person loves God's Word (the Bible)?

WHAT'S THAT NOISE?

Guessing Game

OVERVIEW
Children listen very carefully to try and discover the origin of mysterious noises.

SCRIPTURE CONNECTION:
I Samuel 3:4-5

SUPPLIES:
- Pre-recorded noises or a sound effects CD

PREPARATION:
Before meeting with the kids, use your phone or a tape recorder to make recordings of several household sounds (see tip box for ideas). Record each sound for at least 10 seconds.

TIP:
Need some ideas? Try recording these things: Running water, car starting, toilet flushing, doorbell ringing, garbage truck stopping, fridge door opening, dog parking, chair being pushed in, fan running, baby crying, etc.

HOW TO PLAY:

1. When kids arrive, play the sounds and have them guess out loud what they think the source might be. If they cannot guess after three to five attempts, reveal the answer.
2. Continue playing until you have made it through all of the sounds.

TEACHABLE MOMENT:

Say: Some of these things were pretty easy to guess—but some were a little tougher. You might have heard the sound before, but couldn't exactly name what it was. In our passage today, there was a young boy who heard someone calling his name. (*Read 1 Samuel 3:4–5*). Samuel thought it was his guardian, Eli, calling him—but it wasn't! Samuel, the young boy, ran to Eli several times before they finally figured out it was God calling Samuel. We don't usually hear God's voice like that anymore, but it must have been a cool experience for Samuel.

DISCUSSION QUESTIONS:

- Have you ever heard a strange noise and then followed it?
- Were you surprised by what was causing the noise?
- How do we usually hear from God now?
- How do you think Samuel felt when he was able to talk with God?

ICE BREAKER GAMES | AGES: 7–12 | TIME NEEDED: 10 MIN

NAME BINGO

Meet and Greet

OVERVIEW
Kids walk around and ask each other questions to fill in a Bingo sheet.

SCRIPTURE CONNECTION:
Exodus 9:16

SUPPLIES:
- Name Bingo Sheet, page 285
- Pens or pencils, one for each child
- Optional: Clipboards

PREPARATION:
Make copies of the Name Bingo Sheet for each child. Optional: Provide clipboards to make writing easier.

DISCIPLINE IN PRIVATE:
- Create simple and consistent rules.
- Keep in mind you are modeling God, forgiveness, and unconditional love.
- Remember your kids crave approval and connection.

HOW TO PLAY:
1. On your signal, kids should wander about the room, asking the questions found on their sheet. If someone answers "Yes," they sign in that square.
2. Kids don't simply hand the sheet to a friend and have them sign. They ask each person a specific question. If the answer is no, they move on to ask someone else.
3. For the first round, play until someone completes a row with names. Play a second round where players fill the card.

TEACHABLE MOMENT:
Say: What an interesting group of kids we have! We all have different talents, different experiences, and different interests. God made each one of use unique and for a specific purpose. In the book of Exodus, we read about something that God said to Pharaoh. (*Read Exodus 9:16.*) God wanted to show both the Egyptians and the Israelites his great power, and he used Pharaoh's stubbornness, and a hard heart to do it. God wants to use us, his people, in a different way. We can be more like Moses–using our gifts and talents to serve God.

DISCUSSION QUESTIONS:
- What are some gifts or talents you can use to serve God?
- What is something that makes you unique?
- What is something that makes you different, even from the people in your family?
- What keeps us from using our gifts and talents to serve God?

FIND THE SHOE

Team Race

OVERVIEW
In this quick and simple game, kids will find a partner based on a shoe and ask them a few quick questions.

SCRIPTURE CONNECTION:
Ruth 4:8

SUPPLIES:
- Whiteboard or projector with questions displayed.

PREPARATION:
None

TIP:
Looking for some ideas for questions? Here's a few to get you started:
- What is your favorite food?
- When do you normally eat your favorite food?
- What was your favorite family trip or vacation?
- What kind of sports do you like to watch or play?
- What kind of pets do you have?
- What kinds of pets do you wish you had?

HOW TO PLAY:
1. Kids divide into two teams. Have each team stand on opposite walls in the room.
2. Kids take off one shoe and put it against their team wall.
3. Members of Team #1 go to the opposite wall and each select a shoe. They then find the owner of that shoe and ask them one of the questions you provided.
4. Team #2 takes a turn.
5. Form new teams and play again as time and interest allow.

TEACHABLE MOMENT:
Say: Did you know that in Bible times, taking off your shoe was a sign that something important was about to happen? People used to make deals by taking off one of their shoes and handing it to the person who they were making a deal with. We see this in Ruth 4:8 and in a few other places in the Bible.

DISCUSSION QUESTIONS:
- How do we usually make deals or agreements today?
- How would you feel if you had to give away a shoe every time you agreed to something?
- What was your favorite question in this game?
- If you could ask your friends any questions, what would it be?

INDOOR ACTIVE GAMES

WATER, LAND & AIR

Listening Game

OVERVIEW
Children jump from place to place depending on a called-out word.

SCRIPTURE CONNECTION:
Genesis 1

SUPPLIES:
- Rope or masking tape
- Marker
- 2 sheets of paper

PREPARATION:
Use rope or masking tape to make a line on the ground that is long enough for all kids to stand next to.
Print "Land" on one sheet of paper and "Sea" on the other.
Place Land paper on one side of the rope, and Sea paper on the other side.

HOW TO PLAY:
1. Begin by having all players stand beside the prepared line.
2. Call out one of the three locations: land, air, or sea.
3. If you call out "Land," kids jump to the side of the rope with the Land paper.
4. If you call out "Sea," kids jump to the side of the rope with the Sea paper.
5. If you call out "Air," kids jump straight up in the air.
6. You can try to confuse the players by calling out the same location twice or calling out locations super fast. Whenever someone jumps the wrong way, they are out.
7. Play until one or two players are left. Remaining players answer one of the discussion questions below.

TEACHABLE MOMENT:
Say: There are a lot of places in the world, but they all end up being part of one of these locations–land, water, or air. God created everything that we see in the world–all the water, all the land, all the mountains, trees, and everything in the air. What an amazing God we have. You can read all about how God created the world in Genesis 1.

DISCUSSION QUESTIONS:
- What's a favorite place of yours in nature?
- What do you think is the most amazing thing God has created?
- If you could create something in nature, what would it be?

MUSICAL STATUES

Individual Game

OVERVIEW
Children dance to music until it stops. Then, they stand as still as statues.

SCRIPTURE CONNECTION:
Psalm 149:3

SUPPLIES:
- Children's worship CD and player

PREPARATION:
Pick out an upbeat song that is easy to dance to.

BEHAVIOR MANAGEMENT:
Consider what factors are playing out in the life of a challenging child that may be contributing to their behavior. Some of the conditions that could be factoring into their behavior: family issues, peer pressure, traumatic experiences, cultural confusion, awareness of weakness, special needs, world events, self-image.

HOW TO PLAY:

1. Play the music for the kids and encourage them to dance around like crazy.
2. After five to ten seconds, stop the music. When the music stops, the kids freeze exactly as they are and stand still as a statue.
3. If anyone moves after the music stops, they sit down in their spot. They are out.
4. Restart the music and play again until you have a winner.

TEACHABLE MOMENT:

Say: Did you know the Bible talks a lot about dancing? The book of Psalms has quite a few verses about music, singing, and dancing as a way to praise the Lord. (*Read Psalm 149:3.*) Isn't it wonderful that God made music for us to enjoy and to use as a way to worship him?

DISCUSSION QUESTIONS:

- What kind of music is your favorite?
- How can we dance as a way of worshiping the Lord?
- What is your favorite song about God?

DEADLY ARROWS

Team Race

OVERVIEW
Children toss bean bags in an attempt to knock over the opposing team's bottles.

SCRIPTURE CONNECTION:
Psalm 64:3

SUPPLIES:
- Large space to play
- Beanbags or balled-up socks
- Empty water bottles or two-liter bottles, five for each team
- Cones or rope

PREPARATION:
Divide room in half with cones or rope. Place five bottles at the back of each team's play area, setting them up bowling style. Place the bean bags or socks at the front of each team's play area.

TIP:
Fill bottles up with a few inches of water to make them stable and replace lids. If you have more than twenty kids playing, increase the number of bottles.

HOW TO PLAY:

1. Divide group into two teams. This is best played with ten or fewer kids on each team.
2. On your signal each team rushes to grab the bean bags and socks. The object of the game is to knock all five of the other team's bottles over (teams cannot cross the middle dividing line) before your own bottles are knocked over.
3. Kids can guard the bottles, but remind them they should also be trying to knock over the other team's bottles.
4. The first team to knock over all five of the opposing team's bottle answers one of the Discussion Questions.

TEACHABLE MOMENT:

Say: You guys were really moving out there! In order to knock those bottles over, you had to aim pretty carefully. This game reminds me of a verse from the Bible. (*Read Psalm 64:3.*) Sometimes people say cruel and hurtful words, and it knocks us right over–just like the bottles in this game.

DISCUSSION QUESTIONS:

- Has anyone ever hit you with some "deadly arrow" words? How did it feel?
- Have you ever thrown deadly arrow words?
- How did you feel after you said those things?

Say: Sometimes we say cruel and hurtful things when we are angry. We knock people right over with our words. We don't have to leave things like that though. We can apologize and start again. Sometimes other people don't apologize for the mean things they say. We can't do anything about that, but with God's help, we can forgive those people and move on with our lives.

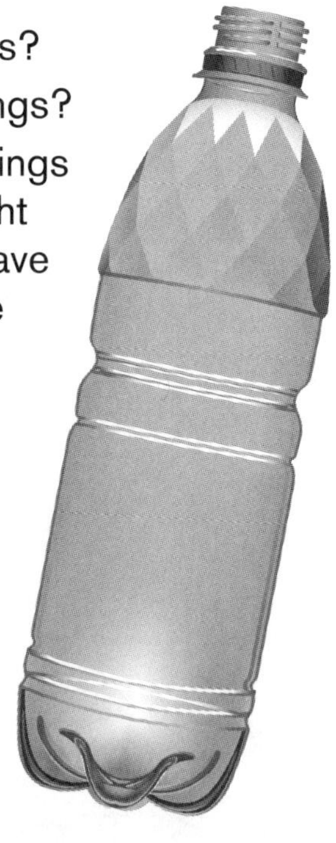

TAIL TAG

TAG

OVERVIEW
Kids race around trying to grab tails while making sure no one grabs their own!

SCRIPTURE CONNECTION:
I Timothy 6:11

SUPPLIES:
- Cones or rope
- Football flags or twelve-inch strip of cloth, one for each player
- Large play area
- Optional: Marker

PREPARATION:
Designate a safety zone with cones or rope. Optional: Use markers to write the words "righteousness," "godliness," "faith," "love," "endurance," and "gentleness" on separate strips of cloth before the game begins.

HOW TO PLAY:
1. Each child tucks a strip of cloth to into their waistband or belt loop.
2. Kids run around the gym trying to take other tails while keeping their own. If a player loses their tail, they are not out, but continue to try to capture other tails.
3. If a player gets another player's tail, player goes to safety zone to tuck newly acquired tails into their waistband or belt loop.

TEACHABLE MOMENT:
Say: In this game, we were running after the tails. The Bible tells us to run after things like righteousness, godliness, faith, love, endurance, and gentleness. Let's talk about what each of these things means.

- Righteousness–Doing the right thing
- Godliness–Being focused on God
- Faith–Trusting in God
- Love–Showing kindness to others
- Endurance–Working hard and not giving up
- Gentleness–Speaking kindly and touching carefully

DISCUSSION QUESTIONS:
- Was it easy to run after the tails? Why or why not?
- Do you think it is easy to run after the qualities we talked about?
- Which is hardest to put into practice in your life? (*Read 1 Timothy 6:11.*)

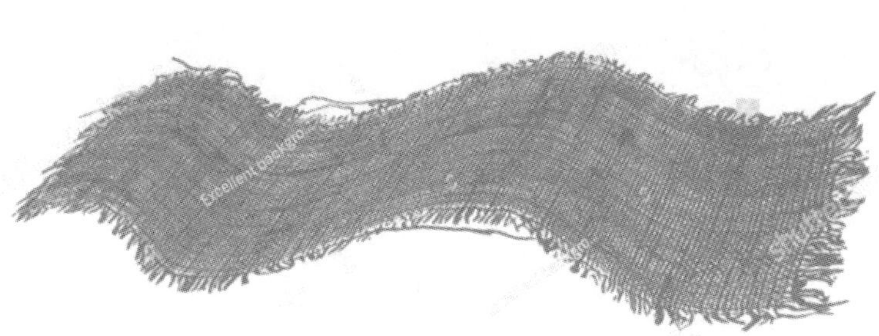

SPAGHETTI STRETCH RELAY

Team Relay Race

OVERVIEW
How far can you make a box of spaghetti stretch? Kids lay noodles end to end, racing to build a noodle line all the way to the finish line.

SCRIPTURE CONNECTION:
Proverbs 14:23

SUPPLIES:
- Box of long spaghetti, one per team.
- Cones or rope

PREPARATION:
Use cones or rope to make start and finish lines.

HOW TO PLAY:
1. Give each team a box of long spaghetti noodles and have them line up single file behind the start line.
2. On your signal, the first player on each team lays a spaghetti noodle on the ground, touching the start line. Player then passes the box to the next player and goes to the end of the line.
3. The new player takes out a noodle, and lays it end to end with the first noodle. New player then returns to the start line, passes the box onto the next player and goes to the end of the line. Play continues.
4. With each box pass, players run farther to lay noodles end to end. The first team to have their string of noodles cross the finish line answers one of the Discussion Questions below.

TEACHABLE MOMENT:

Say: You all worked hard as a team to finish the race. The Bible talks about hard work. (*Read Proverbs 14:23.*) This verse tells us that all hard work pays off. You all worked hard, and even if your team didn't finish first, you got a lot out of your hard work. Both teams learned to work as a team and take turns. You all had to communicate with each other and experience a challenge together as a group, relying on each other. There are many ways we profit from hard work.

DISCUSSION QUESTIONS:
- What do you think would have happened if you just sat around and talked about the noodles instead of doing anything?
- Are there other things you need to work hard on in life?
- Why do you think the Bible tells us to work hard?

KEEP THAT BALLOON UP

Individual Race

OVERVIEW
Kids work to keep their balloon in the air, working against gravity the whole time.

SCRIPTURE CONNECTION:
Philippians 4:13

SUPPLIES:
- Balloons, one per child

PREPARATION:
Blow up balloons and tie a knot to secure.

TIP:
During play, children practice and reinforce learning in multiple ways that cannot be achieved by completing a worksheet.

HOW TO PLAY:
1. On your signal, kids toss their balloons up in the air.
2. The object of the game is to keep the balloon up by tapping it upward each time it descends. Players cannot hold the balloon or cradle it in their hands.
3. When a player's balloon touches the ground, that player sits down and holds their balloon.
4. Whoever can keep their balloon up the longest, answers, or chooses a volunteer to answer one of the Discussion Questions below.

TEACHABLE MOMENT:
Say: No matter how many times you bopped those balloons back up in the air, they kept falling back down. Sometimes life can seem like that too. We try and try at something, but it just doesn't work. (*Read Philippians 4:13.*) The Bible tells us that we can do all things through Christ who gives us strength. Sometimes we can get discouraged by a difficult task, but when we pray, God will give us the strength to keep on going.

DISCUSSION QUESTIONS:
- Have you ever been in a situation where it seems like nothing will ever get better?
- Have you ever worked on a project that seemed like it would never be finished?
- What did you do to keep motivated in those situations?
- Why might a kid your age ask God for help in difficult situations?

SHOE DETECTIVE

Seek and Find Game

OVERVIEW
Kids find their shoes in a race against each other. Sounds like an easy task, until the blindfolds come out!

SCRIPTURE CONNECTION:
Exodus 3:5, Joshua 5:15, Luke 15:22

SUPPLIES:
- Blindfolds, one for each child

PREPARATION:
None

REINFORCE BEHAVIORS:
Be proactive in modeling and teaching appropriate behavior Catch children being good: "Thanks for letting (Andre) go first," "Good job waiting quietly," etc.

HOW TO PLAY:

1. Kids sit in a circle. Have them take off their shoes and throw them in a pile in the center of the circle.
2. Each kid should place a blindfold on.
3. On your signal, kids find their shoes from the pile and put them on, all without removing the blindfold.
4. First child to successfully put on their own shoes answers, or chooses a volunteer to answer, one of the Discussion Questions below.

TEACHABLE MOMENT:

Say: That was a pretty funny game! Did you know the Bible talks about taking on and off shoes as well? Can anyone think of an example? Here are a few examples: Moses takes off his sandals at the burning bush (*Exodus 3:5*), Joshua took off his sandals at the Lord's command (*Joshua 5:15*), and a father gave his sandals in a parable Jesus told (*Luke 15:22*).

DISCUSSION QUESTIONS:

- Why do you think people took off their shoes in the Bible? (It was a sign of respect and reverence when they were in the presence of God or one of his angels.)
- Do we do anything like that still today? How do we show respect for God? For other people?

WHO ARE YOU?

Circle Game

OVERVIEW

Kids use disguised voices and a wrapping paper tube to try and trick the person in the middle.

SCRIPTURE CONNECTION:
Genesis 27:22

SUPPLIES:

- Blindfolds
- Empty wrapping paper tube
- Children's worship CD and player

PREPARATION:
None

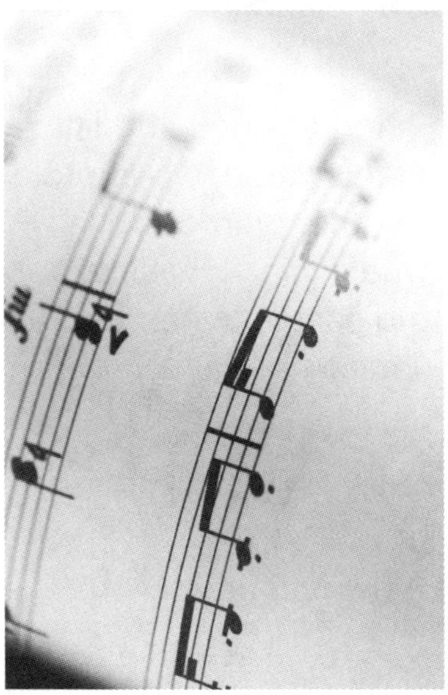

HOW TO PLAY:

1. Kids form a circle. Pick one child to be "It" and stand in the center of the circle.
2. Blindfold "It" and play the music.
3. As the music plays, the kids in the circle hold hands and rotate around the circle.
4. After five to ten seconds, stop the music. Players in the circle stop moving. Hand "It" the cardboard tube.
5. "It" lifts up the cardboard tube and points it towards the circle of friends. "It" speaks into the tube, asking, "Who are you?" The closest child answers into the tube saying, "It's me." Child tries to disguise their voice, so that "It" can't guess who is speaking. Make sure players do not yell into the tube!
6. "It" tries to guess who has answered his call. If "It" can guess correctly, he takes that child's place in the circle.
7. If "It" does not guess correctly, the child who answered the call becomes "It." Play continues as time and interest allows.

TEACHABLE MOMENT:

Say: Some of you did a good job of disguising your voice. In Genesis, there is a brother that tries to trick his father. Jacob and Esau were twins but Esau was born first so he would be the head of the family some day. Jacob wanted that so he waited until his dad was old and couldn't see well. He dressed like Esau and disguised his voice. His dad made him the head of the family. (*Read Genesis 27:22.*)

DISCUSSION QUESTIONS:

- Was it easy or hard to trick the person in the middle? Why or why not?
- How do you think Esau felt about Jacob tricking their father (Genesis 27:41)?
- Do you think it was worth it to get the blessing that way?

BALLOON RELAY

Team Race

OVERVIEW
Teams run a race, holding a balloon with two paint sticks.

SCRIPTURE CONNECTION:
Proverbs 21:5

SUPPLIES:
- Paint sticks or rulers, two for each team.
- Balloons, one for each team
- Cones or rope.

PREPARATION:
Set up cones or rope to make start and finish lines.

TIP:
Local Home Improvement stores usually give away paint stirring sticks for free.

HOW TO PLAY:
1. Kids divide into teams of three to five players. Give each team two sticks and a balloon.
2. The first player on each team holds the balloon between the paint sticks and runs to the finish line and back. They do not use their hands at any time. When they return to the start line, the player hands the balloon and paint sticks to the next player who then takes a turn.
3. If a player drops the balloon, they retrieve it with the sticks. If they pop the balloon, they return the start line to get another before continuing the race.
4. The first team to complete the race answers one of the Discussion Questions below. Repeat as time and interest allow.

TEACHABLE MOMENT:
Say: The book of Proverbs is filled with short sayings and little bits of wisdom. (*Read Proverbs 21:5.*) In this verse, we are told that steady plodding brings prosperity. In other words, slow and steady wins the race! This is often true in life as well. When we rush through things it leads to disaster. When we are slow and careful, it often leads to success.

DISCUSSION QUESTIONS:
- Can you think of a time when you rushed through a project, and it ended poorly?
- Can you think of a time when you were slow and steady on a project? How did it turn out?
- Did anyone lose their balloon in this race because they were trying to move too fast?
- Why do you think the Bible advises us to be "slow and steady?"

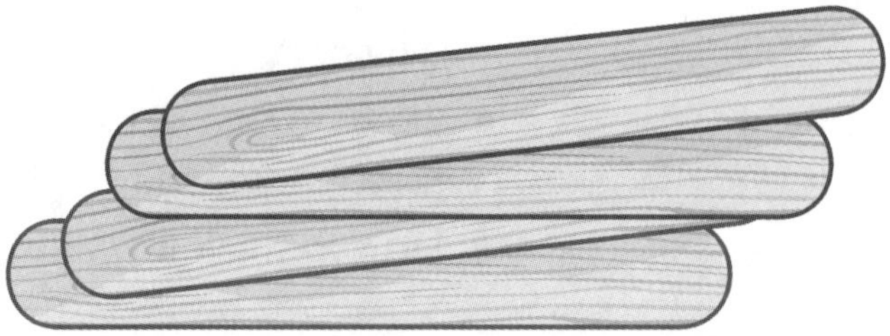

AND ONE MORE THING...

Balance Game

OVERVIEW
In this game, more and more requirements get added.

SCRIPTURE CONNECTION:
Mark 7:1-9, 23:4

SUPPLIES:
- Books
- Small balls

PREPARATION:
None

ADDITIONAL IDEAS:
- Hold the ball under the chin.
- Put the ball on the book.
- Hop on one foot.
- Spin in circles.
- Bend down to touch the ground.

HOW TO PLAY:

1. Begin by having all the kids stand in a straight line in front of you. **Say**: This game is easy to win! You just have to follow my rules. Ready?
2. Hand each child a book and tell them they need to hold it. **Say**: That's not too hard, is it? Oh, and one more thing . . .
3. Hand each child a small ball to hold as well. **Say**: That's not too hard, is it? Oh, and one more thing . . .
4. Instruct the kids to put the book on their head and balance it. **Say**: Okay, you're getting it. Oh, and one more thing . . .
5. Tell kids to stand on one foot. If at any time a player drops a book or ball, that player sits down.
6. Continue in this way, adding "one more thing" until only one or two players remain. These players tell a sentence about the day's Bible story or repeats the memory verse.

TEACHABLE MOMENT:

Say: Wow, that game ended up being pretty complicated, huh? It seemed like it was going to be easy, but I kept adding more and more rules. In Bible times, the Pharisees and teachers of the law were the same way. They not only wanted people to obey the laws of God, but also the traditions that they made up (Matthew 23:4 and Mark 7:8–9). Just like I kept adding rules. It might have seemed like I didn't want anyone to be successful. That's how it seemed with the Pharisees. Jesus told them that it didn't seem like they wanted anyone to enter the kingdom of heaven because they made it so impossible to do so with all their rules and traditions.

DISCUSSION QUESTIONS:

- What might make it difficult for a kid your age to do the right thing?
- What could a kid your age do when they have trouble obeying God? Obeying parents? Teachers?
- How could God help us do the right thing?

THE BLIND MAN GETS THE BELL

Tag

OVERVIEW
In this game, one player is left without a blindfold and ring a bell (and not get caught!

SCRIPTURE CONNECTION:
Exodus 28:35

SUPPLIES:
- Cones or long rope
- Blindfolds, one fewer than the number of players
- Small bell

PREPARATION:
Use cones or rope to define the play area. Since most of the children won't be able to see the boundaries, be sure to have enough leaders to help keep children within the boundaries

HOW TO PLAY:
1. Give one player a small bell to ring to be the bell-ringer. The bell-ringer rings the bell periodically to draw attention but tries to avoid being tagged by the remaining players.
2. Blindfold remaining children. The blindfolded children move carefully through the play area to catch the bell ringer.
3. Player who catches the bell-ringer becomes the new bell-ringer. Play additional rounds as time and interest allow.

TEACHABLE MOMENT:
Say: Did you know that the Bible talks about bells? In the Old Testament, the priest was to go to a special place called the Holy of Holies once a year. This special room was where God himself lived among the people. That's a pretty big deal! The priest had to have his heart right with God before he entered this special room. If he didn't, he would die upon entering the room. The people would tie a little bell to the bottom of the priest's robe and listen as he went into the Holy of Holies. As long as they could hear the bell jingling, they knew that the priest was still alive. If the bell stopped ringing, they knew that he had died. They had a rope tied to the priest, and if the bell stopped jingling, they would pull him out. (*Read Exodus 28:35.*)

DISCUSSION QUESTIONS:
- Was it more fun to be the bell-ringer or blindfolded? Why?
- Did you get nervous when you were blindfolded? Why or why not?
- How about when everyone was chasing after you?
- How do you think the priest felt as he entered the Holy of Holies?

STEAL THE BACON

Team Race

OVERVIEW
Numbers are called and kids race to steal the "bacon."

SCRIPTURE CONNECTION:
I Corinthians 9:24

SUPPLIES:
- Small object (shoe, bean bag, small ball, etc.)
- Optional: Washable marker

PREPARATION:
None

TIP:
Optional: Help little ones remember their number by using the washable marker to write it on their hand.

HOW TO PLAY:

1. Kids divide into two teams. Have each team stand against one wall, opposite each other.
2. Place the small object or "bacon" in the center of the room.
3. Give each player a number, making sure there are the same numbers on each side.
4. Call out a number and both students with that number rush into the middle to try and grab the bacon.
5. Once a player has picked up the bacon, they return to their wall without being tagged by the opposite player.
6. If the child holding the bacon is tagged, the opposite team gets a point.
7. If the child holding the bacon can successfully make it back to his own team wall, his team will get a point.
8. Play until all players have had a chance to run.

TEACHABLE MOMENT:

Say: Not only did you have to get the prize (bacon), you had to return to your team without getting caught. The Bible talks about running in such a way as to get the prize. (*Read 1 Corinthians 9:24.*) Paul was talking about the crowns we receive when we reach heaven, the crown that represents the work that we did for God while we are here on Earth. (*Read 2 Timothy 4:8.*)

DISCUSSION QUESTIONS:

- Have you ever competed in a hard race? In some other competition? What kind of training or practice did you have to do beforehand?
- How does practicing and training help in competition?
- How is the prize we receive for doing God's work different than a prize we might receive on Earth?

WHERE'S MY CHAIR?

Circle Game

OVERVIEW

In this twist on a classic game, kids race to find their original chairs when the music stops

SCRIPTURE CONNECTION:
Galatians 5:22-23

SUPPLIES:

- Fruit of the Spirit cards (reproducible on page 262.
- Chairs, one for every child.
- Music player

PREPARATION:

Set up chairs in a circle, with seats facing out. Make copies of the Fruit of the Spirit cards (make enough for one card to be placed on every chair). Cut the cards apart and tape one to each chair.

HOW TO PLAY:

1. Kids pick a seat and sit down. Instruct them to make a note of what fruit they are sitting on and where they are at in the circle.
2. Begin playing the music. Kids are to stand up and walk around the circle (similar to musical chairs). When the music stops, kids are to race back to their original chair.
3. The LAST child to sit down is out for the round. You may need to designate an adult to be the official referee on this one!
4. When a child is out, they remain seated in their chair as the game continues.
5. Play until there is one child left. Declare a winner!

TEACHABLE MOMENT:

Say: You might have noticed that the words on your chairs were familiar. They come from the book of Galatians. These fruits are the things that show up in our lives when we chose to follow God. The Holy Spirit makes these things grow in our lives just like fruit grows on real trees. (*Read Galatians 5:22–23.*)

DISCUSSION QUESTIONS:

- Which one of these fruits is the easiest for you to practice?
- Which one is the hardest?
- Was it difficult to find your way back to your chair?
- Which fruit do you wish you could improve in your life? Let's pray about that.

BALLOON HOCKEY

Team Race

OVERVIEW

In this fun twist on hockey, kids bat around a balloon instead of the traditional hockey puck.

SCRIPTURE CONNECTION:
2 Chronicles 15:7

SUPPLIES:

- Pool noodles
- Balloon
- Soccer nets or cones to designate goal area
- Large space to play, such as a gym.

PREPARATION:
Set up goals on each side of the room.

HOW TO PLAY:

1. The object of the game is for kids to get the balloon into the opposing team's goal.
2. Kids divide into two evenly numbered teams. Each team selects one player to be the goalie and standing near the goal to protect it.
3. Everyone else will move the balloon up and down the playing area by hitting it with their pool noodle. They can hit it when the balloon is high in the air or low on the ground, but they cannot ever touch the balloon with their hands (not even the goalie).
4. The first team to score five points wins (or you may wish to set the timer for ten to fifteen minutes instead).

TEACHABLE MOMENT:

Say: This was a pretty exhausting game. Not only did you have to do a lot of running around, but that balloon was mighty unpredictable! Sometimes life can feel like this, too. Things don't go the way we expect (or want!), and it might seem like we are running around all over the place for nothing. However, God has a special plan and a purpose for our life. He wants us to continue working for his kingdom, following his commands and spending time with him. He promises that if we do not give up, we will be rewarded (*Read 2 Chronicles 15:7.*)

DISCUSSION QUESTIONS:

- What kind of reward do you usually get in a game like this?
- What kind of reward do you think God is talking about in 2 Chronicles 15:7?
- Why might kids your age feel like giving up?
- What can a kid do to stay motivated when times get tough?

THE BLOB

Tag

OVERVIEW
You better move quick in this rapidly morphing game, or else you will become part of the blob!

SCRIPTURE CONNECTION:
Psalm 40:12

SUPPLIES:
None

PREPARATION:
None

DISRUPTIVE BEHAVIORS:
- Anticipate early stages of agitation (i.e. self-talking isolating, deep breathing, etc.)
- Provide frequent and continuous verbal reinforcements
- Instruct the child to take deep breaths or count to 10
- Provide means for encouraging child to regain self-control by offering one or two specific options
- Redirect to alternative activity to regain appropriate behavior

HOW TO PLAY:
1. Select one player to be "It." The game is played almost like the traditional game of tag, but when "It" tags someone, they join hands and continue the game together.
2. Each time a child is tagged, they will join hands or link elbows with "It" to form a blob. The blob continues to chase the remaining kids, all the while staying connected. If someone breaks contact, everyone has to pause for the blob to come back together.
3. Last player free of the blob answers, or chooses a volunteer to answer, one of the Discussion Questions below.

TEACHABLE MOMENT:
Say: That game started out looking pretty easy, but the bigger the blob got, the harder it was to avoid being tagged! Sometimes life takes us for a turn like that too. One day, everything seems to be going fine, and the next day, it seems like disaster has overtaken us. King David felt just that way when he wrote Psalm 40. (*Read Psalm 40:12.*)

DISCUSSION QUESTIONS:
- Why do you think David was so upset?
- What could kids your age do if they felt their troubles or sins are overtaking them?

THE NUMBER GAME

Team Race

OVERVIEW
Kids must be quick thinking and quick moving to succeed at this game!

SCRIPTURE CONNECTION:
Genesis 18:24-26

SUPPLIES:
- Construction paper

PREPARATION:
On separate construction-paper sheets, print a number from one to nine to make one set. Make one set of sheets for each team of nine players.

HOW TO PLAY:

1. Kids divide into evenly numbered teams of six to nine. If teams have fewer than nine players, some players hold two numbers.
2. Give each child one piece of construction paper.
3. Call out a three digit no repeating numbers (for example 234, 546, 872, 934). Kids assemble themselves while holding their construction paper in the right order to make the number you call out. Whichever team assembles the fastest gets a point.
4. The first team to score ten points tells a sentence from the Bible story or recites the memory verse.

TEACHABLE MOMENT:

Say: In this game, we were just making up random numbers, but in the Bible, the numbers that are mentioned are very important. In one particular case, the fate of an entire city rested on the number of righteous people in it. One day, an angel of the Lord came to visit a man named Abraham. He told Abraham that the cities of Sodom and Gomorrah were so evil that God was going to destroy them. Let's see how Abraham responded. (*Read Genesis 18: 24–26.*) That was a pretty bold move of Abraham. What is even crazier is that Abraham kept asking for a lower and lower number. Finally, the Lord agreed that if even ten righteous people could be found in the city, God would spare it. But sadly, there were not enough righteous people found to save the city.

DISCUSSION QUESTIONS:

- What is a righteous person?
- Why did Abraham care so much about those cities?
- Are there ten righteous people in our city? How about in your school?

LIMBO

Individual Game

OVERVIEW
This classic game is easy to set up and fun for all ages!

SCRIPTURE CONNECTION:
I Kings 18:39

SUPPLIES:
- Large stick (broomstick, pool noodle, etc.)
- Music player

PREPARATION:
None

HOW TO PLAY:
1. Designate two people to hold the pole (leaders or older kids). Helpers hold the pole above the heads of the kids.
2. Play the music as the kids walk under the pole. When everyone has gone under the pole, have the helpers lower it.
3. Kids again walk under pole. They may have to duck or lean backward to avoid touching the pole but they can't lean forward.
4. If a child touches the pole as they pass under it, they are out for that round. They can touch the ground with their feet only.
5. Continue lowering the pole every time the line of kids passes under the pole. The last player, or a volunteer they choose, tells a sentence about the Bible story or recites the memory verse.

TEACHABLE MOMENT:
Say: You got lower and lower for fun. In the Bible, people would lower their bodies as a sign of respect or repentance. (*Read 1 Kings 18:39.*) Right before the people said this, they saw fire fall from heaven. A man named Elijah had prayed and asked God to show the people just how powerful the one true God was. The people were beginning to stray away from God and worship false gods and Elijah wanted to show them the truth. The people fell to the ground to show that they were sorry for their actions.

DISCUSSION QUESTIONS:
- Were the people truly sorry for worshiping fake gods?
- Can you think of other instances in the Bible when someone lay flat on the ground?
- What do we do to show respect? To show repentance?

OUTDOOR GAMES

CAT AND MICE

Tag

OVERVIEW
Watch out! Each mouse must find their own mouse hold to hide from the cat.

SCRIPTURE CONNECTION:
Psalm 32:7

SUPPLIES:
- Hula hoops and/or flying discs
- Large field

PREPARATION:
Scatter hula hoops and/or flying discs around play area.

$TIP:
Don't have enough hoops or flying discs? Use paper tape or chalk to mark off holes on the ground.

HOW TO PLAY:

1. Select one player to be the cat. All the other children are mice. The toy hoops and/or flying discs are the mouse holes.
2. On your signal, the mice scatter and try to make it to a "mouse hole." Only one child per mouse hole! There should be fewer mouse holes than there are children.
3. The cat chases the mice and tries to catch them. When the cat catches a mouse, the mouse sits on the ground.
4. You may need to remove mouse holes as the game continues to make sure there are still fewer holes than mice.
5. From time to time, yell "Cheese time!" When you yell this, all mice leave their current holes to find new ones.
6. The game continues until there is only one mouse left.

TEACHABLE MOMENT:

Say: Mice naturally want to hide from cats–otherwise, they might get eaten! That certainly gives them a reason to be afraid. You might be afraid of some things in life–new experiences, mean kids at school, scary noises. Did you know that God is with us wherever we go? In the book of Psalms, we are told that God will be our hiding place. (*Read Psalm 32:7.*) Just like you had a safe place to hide in this game (the mouse holes), God himself is a safe place for us in life.

DISCUSSION QUESTIONS:

- What kinds of things are most people afraid of?
- Is it easy to trust in God? Why or why not?
- Where do you feel very safe (like a mouse in his mouse hole)?

SPIDER WEB TAG

Tag

OVERVIEW

A giant chalk spider web serves as the boundary lines in this game of tag and chase.

SCRIPTURE CONNECTION:
Job 8:13-15

SUPPLIES:

- Sidewalk chalk
- Large area of pavement

PREPARATION:
Draw a giant spider web on the pavement with at least eight to ten rings on it.

HOW TO PLAY:

1. Have a child stand in the middle of the web as the spider the other children stand on the outer ring of the web as flies.
2. On your signal, the flies will run away from the spider, but they keep their feet on the spider web at all times. When the spider catches a fly, that fly leaves the webs and sits until the round is over.
3. Play until there is only one fly left. This player answers, or chooses a volunteer to answer, one of the Discussion Questions below.

TEACHABLE MOMENT:

Say: Did you know that the Bible talks about spider webs? In the book of Job, some friends are talking to Job about people who live without God. They explain that when we trust in things other than God, it's like trusting in something as fragile as a spider web. (*Read Job 8:13–15.*) When we trust in God, we can be sure that we are trusting in someone solid and good.

DISCUSSION QUESTIONS:

- What are some things that people might trust in other than God?
- How are these things as fragile as a spider web?
- What are some things you can do to help you trust in God?

GOLD HUNT

Seek and Find Game

OVERVIEW
Kids search high and low to find a great treasure.

SCRIPTURE CONNECTION: Exodus 39 (various verses)

SUPPLIES:
- Gold spray paint
- Small rocks, at least three for each child
- Timer

PREPARATION:
Gather small rocks and spray paint them gold. Allow them to dry. Before the kids arrive, hide the rocks throughout the play area. If you have trees, try to hide a few in the nooks of the trees, just for fun. Save one rock to show the kids.

HOW TO PLAY:

1. Gather everyone together and explain that you have hidden many golden rocks in the play area (show them the sample rock).
2. Set the timer for five minutes. Kids go on a treasure hunt to find as many golden rocks as possible.
3. After the time is up, gather them back together and count the rocks. Whoever has found the most gold answers, or chooses a volunteer to answer, one of the Discussion Questions below.

TEACHABLE MOMENT:
Say: Gold is mentioned many times in the Bible. In *Exodus 39*, it is mentioned in almost every single verse! In this passage, God is giving the Israelites instructions on how to build the tabernacle (read a few verses to the kids). The tabernacle was the place where God lived among the people. It was the place where they worshipped God. It was God's home. God instructed the Israelites to do their best and give their best when constructing the tabernacle. God was worth the very best. Overlaying things with gold was a way of showing how valuable and important God was.

DISCUSSION QUESTIONS:

- What do we use gold for these days?
- Does gold still signify something important?
- How can we show God that he is important in our lives (without using gold)?
- How do we show others that God is important in our lives?

SCAVENGER HUNT

Seek and Find Game

OVERVIEW

A classic scavenger hunt is sure to have kids running around and having fun!

SCRIPTURE CONNECTION:
Jeremiah 29:13

SUPPLIES:

- Scavenger Hunt List, page 287
- Large play area
- Timer

PREPARATION:
Photocopy one Scavenger Hunt List for each team.

SAFETY FIRST!
Set up boundaries for the hunt and have your volunteers surround the area. You can change the suggested items to what you have on hand. Create a visual list for little ones by taking pictures, placing the images on a sheet, and making copies.

HOW TO PLAY:

1. Kids divide into teams of three or four players.
2. Give each team a scavenger hunt list.
3. Set the timer for 10 minutes and send the kids off searching for the items.
4. The first team to find all the items wins.
5. If kids are still searching after 10 minutes, bring them back and count the items. Whoever has the most items wins.

TEACHABLE MOMENT:

Say: Nice job on the searching guys! Some of you were looking hard and found a lot of stuff. A few of you didn't seem like you were searching quite as urgently. The Bible has a verse that reminds me of this situation. In the book of Jeremiah, the prophet Jeremiah is giving the people a message from God. Some of God's people were not trying to follow God. They were not seeking him with all their heart. As a result, they did not feel close to him. They did not find him. When we want to be close to God, we need to seek after him, just like you searched for the things on your lists.

DISCUSSION QUESTIONS:

- What was the easiest thing to find on your list?
- What was the hardest thing to find on your list?
- How is seeking after God like searching for the things on your list?
- How is one way that you seek after God?

HUMAN BOARD GAME

Individual Game

OVERVIEW
Kids are the game pieces as they hop, skip, and make their way through the game board.

SCRIPTURE CONNECTION:
Proverbs 12:28

SUPPLIES:
- Optional: Human Board Game, page 288
- Optional: Bean Bags and Number Cubes, page 308
- Sidewalk chalk
- Large play area
- Large number cube

PREPARATION:
Draw a large game board on the pavement using chalk. The board should have three times more spaces than players. Optional: Use Human Board Game sheet as a reference. In some of the spaces write instructions for players to do when they land on that space. Some examples: Move back three spaces, jump up and down until your next turn, etc. Optional: Make a number cube using the instructions on page 308.

HOW TO PLAY:
1. To begin, have all the kids stand near the start space. Have the youngest player roll the dice and move forward that many spaces. They should follow the instructions on the space (if applicable).
2. Continue with the next youngest player rolling the die and advancing accordingly.
3. Play this way, with players taking turns until someone reaches the end of the path.

TEACHABLE MOMENT:
Say: This was a pretty crazy game! It was different to be the playing pieces. In this game, there was a specific path you were to go on. There might have been some back and forth (and some crazy actions), but you always stayed on the same path. Life isn't always this simple, is it? There are all kinds of choices we can make in life–some that lead down the path of righteousness (God's way), and some that lead us into sin. It isn't always easy to make the right choices. The more we read the Bible and pray, the easier we will be able to make good decisions along the path of life.

DISCUSSION QUESTIONS:
- In our key verse (Proverbs 12:28), it talks about a path of immortality. What do you think that means?
- How does a person gain immortality? God wants us to live forever with him. That's why he offers us the gift of eternal life.
- Do you think it's easy or difficult to walk the path of righteousness?

NOODLE SOUP

Team Race

OVERVIEW

Players on each team try to steal some soup while the crazy chefs try to swat the players away with pool noodles.

SCRIPTURE CONNECTION:
Acts 2:44

SUPPLIES:
- Cones
- Pool noodles cut into small pieces
- Pool noodles (uncut)
- Timer
- Optional: Baby pool

PREPARATION:
Place the piles of small noodle pieces in the middle of the play area. Optional: Put noodle pieces in a baby pool to keep them corralled. Set up four cones to serve as each team's base. Place the cones about twenty feet away from the pile of noodle pieces.

HOW TO PLAY:
1. Split the group into four equal teams.
2. Pick two students as the "crazy chefs" and have them stand near the baby pool, each holding one of the long pool noodles.
3. Begin with the teams standing near their cones.
4. On your signal, one player from each team runs to the soup bowl and tries to grab one of the noodle pieces. The crazy chefs try to protect their soup by swatting at incoming players with their long pool noodles.
5. If a player is hit with the noodle, they return to their team empty-handed and the next player in line can have a turn.
6. If a player successfully grabs a noodle piece, they race back to their team and allow the next player in line to try.
7. The game continues for three or four minutes (each player should have two or three turns to grab soup/noodle pieces).
8. When the timer beeps, count the noodle pieces and declare a winner (the most pieces win).

TEACHABLE MOMENT:

Say: When the church was first getting started, early Christians often met and ate together. (*Read Acts 2:44.*) They shared food they had so that no one was without. In our game, the crazy chefs were the opposite of the early Christians–they didn't want to share with anyone!

DISCUSSION QUESTIONS:
- Do you ever feel like the crazy chefs wanting to keep the things you have to yourself?
- Why is it good to share?
- Why is it hard to share?
- Did the early Christians had a hard time sharing all they had?

BLIND MAN'S PASS

Tag

OVERVIEW

One group of kids form a wall while another group of kids tries to sneak past undetected.

SCRIPTURE CONNECTION:
Acts 12:7

SUPPLIES:
- Blindfolds, enough for half the kids

PREPARATION:
None

HOW TO PLAY:

1. Kids divide into two groups. Have one group stand in a straight line, about arms width apart. Have this group put on blindfolds.
2. Have the second group stand behind the first group.
3. The second group's goal is to make it past the blindfolded kids. They walk in between two blindfolded players (no going around the ends of the line). They can crawl if they want.
4. As the second group tries to sneak past, the blindfolded players can wave their arms up and down trying to tag them.
5. Whoever makes it past the blindfolded players is the winner.
6. Kids switch places and play again.

TEACHABLE MOMENT:

Say: Even though the players were blindfolded, it was still tough to make it past them. Peter, a disciple of Jesus, found himself in a difficult situation like this one as well. Peter had been put in prison and chained to four guards. It seemed like there was no way he could escape! However, the night before Peter's trial, his friends prayed for him. We are told that an angel of the Lord came to Peter and set him free. (*Read Acts 12:7.*) Even though it seemed like it was impossible for Peter to get out of prison we know that with God, all things are possible.

DISCUSSION QUESTIONS:

- What time have you seen God change an "impossible" situation into a "possible" one?
- How has God helped you through hard times?
- How did Peter's friends prayers make a difference for him?

LEAF BLOW

Individual Race

OVERVIEW

Kids pick a leaf and get down on the ground, huffing and puffing to get their leaf cross the finish line first!

SCRIPTURE CONNECTION:
Leviticus 23:40;
Isaiah 55:12

SUPPLIES:
- Chalk
- Section of pavement (the flat ground will work too, but leaves might be harder to blow).
- One leaf per child (dry, warped leaves are best).

PREPARATION:
Use chalk to draw a long start line (big enough for all the players to kneel on the ground behind it). About fifteen to twenty feet away, draw the finish line.

TIP:
This would be a good opportunity for a nature walk. Take the kids out and try and find all the ways nature praises God.

HOW TO PLAY:

1. Hand each player a leaf and line up behind the start line, on their hands and knees.
2. On your signal, they will begin blowing on their leaf in an attempt to get it all the way to the finish line (no touching with the hands!)
3. First to cross the finish line wins.

TEACHABLE MOMENT:

Say: We don't think about leaves being an important part of the Bible, but they are mentioned a few times! In Leviticus, God gives his people special instructions on how to use leaves to worship him. (*Read Leviticus 23:40.*) The book of Isaiah talks about the trees praising God by "clapping their hands." Of course, this is poetry. Trees don't clap their hands, but it does kind of look like that when the leaves move in the wind.

DISCUSSION QUESTIONS:

- What do you think about praising God by waving leaves and branches in the air?
- How do you think nature praises God?
- What are some other ways we can worship God and praise him?

OUTDOOR GAMES | AGES: 6–10 | TIME NEEDED: 8 MIN

BEAN BAG RELAY

Team Relay

OVERVIEW
Kids race back and forth, passing off a bean bag as they go, to win this race.

SCRIPTURE CONNECTION:
2 Timothy 2:2

SUPPLIES:
- Six cones
- Three bean bags
- Large play area

PREPARATION:
Set up three sets of cones, with each set about ten feet apart from each other (see sketch).

TIP
Adjust the number of teams, and the number of players according to the number of kids in your group. Just be sure to have two cones, and one bean bag for each team.

HOW TO PLAY:
1. Kids divide into three teams of four or six players. The goal of this game is to pass the bean bag as quickly as possible from one half of the team to the other half.
2. Put half of each team behind the left set of cones. The other half of each team lines up behind the cones on the right. (See diagram.)
3. Give a bean bag to the first person on the left side of each team. On your signal, the first player on each team goes to their teammate at the opposite cone, passes the bean bag, and then sits down.
4. The second player repeats action to pass bean bag to the third player. This continues until everyone has a turn.
5. The first team to finish the relay answers one of the Discussion Questions below.

TEACHABLE MOMENT:
Say: We passed off the bean bag to each player so we could all work together to complete the race. The Bible talks about passing on something—the things we learn in the Bible. In the early days of Christianity, the only way to spread the good news of Jesus was by telling someone else. The complete Bible didn't exist. So one person would tell a friend who would tell someone else. Just like we passed on the bean bag to our friends, we can pass the news of Jesus to our friends. (*Read 2 Timothy 2:2.*)

DISCUSSION QUESTIONS:
- Was it easy or hard to pass the bean bag to a friend in this game?
- Do you think it is easy or hard to pass on the gospel to others?
- Tell a way we can tell others about the good news of Jesus.

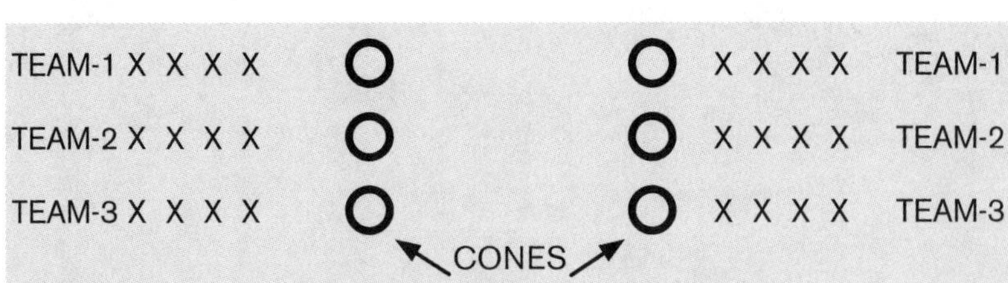

FIND THAT TREASURE

Individual Race

OVERVIEW
Kids use stealth and speed to find the treasure and make a break for it!

SCRIPTURE CONNECTION:
Proverbs 16:16

SUPPLIES:
- Sidewalk Chalk
- Bean bags, one of which is gold
- Large play area of cement or pavement

TIP:
If you're playing on the grass instead of pavement, you can use a toy hoop, rope, or cones to mark off the play area.

PREPARATION:
Draw a three-foot-wide circle on the pavement. Draw a circle about twelve feet across around the inner circle. Place the golden bean bag in the inner circle and pile the rest of the bean bags on top of it.

HOW TO PLAY:

1. Choose one child to be the guard. Station them in the outer circle. The rest of the children stand outside of the outer circle.
2. On your signal, kids try to sneak into the inner circle to steal the golden bean bag without being caught by the guard. The guard tags any child in the inner circle.
3. When a child is tagged, they are turn into a guard and help to protect the inner circle and the golden bean bag.

TEACHABLE MOMENT:

Say: Wow, there was some pretty fierce competition for that golden bean bag! Gold has been a precious commodity since the beginning of time. God had the Israelites use gold to build his tabernacle. Kings always used gold and precious jewels to build their palaces. Did you know that there is something even more precious than gold? The Bible tells us that wisdom is more precious than gold. (*Read Proverbs 16:16.*)

DISCUSSION QUESTIONS:

- Why do you think the Bible says that wisdom is even more valuable than gold?
- What do you think people value these days?
- What are some things that people today value as much as gold?
- What are some ways to find wisdom?

PILLOWCASE RACE

Team Race

OVERVIEW

In this updated version of the potato sack race, kids get to the finish line by hopping inside a pillowcase.

SCRIPTURE CONNECTION:
Leviticus 11:21

SUPPLIES:

- For fewer than five kids, one pillowcase
- For more than five kids, one pillowcase for each team
- Cones or rope

PREPARATION:

Set up cones or rope to mark start and finish lines about twenty yards apart.

HOW TO PLAY:

1. If you have less than five kids, have them line up at the start line. On your signal, they hop inside the pillowcase to the finish line and back.
2. If you have more than five kids playing, divide them into evenly numbered teams that line up at the start line. On your signal, the first player from each team climbs inside a pillowcase, hops to the finish line, climbs out of the pillowcase, and returns to their team.
3. Players hand the pillowcase to the next player in line who takes a turn. Play continues until all players have a turn.
4. The first team to complete the race says a sentence about the Bible story or recites the memory verse.

TEACHABLE MOMENT:

Say: We don't usually hop. What are the names of some animals or bugs that hop? The Bible talks about all kinds of things. In the Old Testament, God laid out some pretty detailed rules for his people–including what they could and couldn't eat. Did you know that hopping bugs were on the menu? (*Read Leviticus 11:20–22.*)

DISCUSSION QUESTIONS:

- Were you surprised that God suggested eating grasshoppers?
- Have you ever eaten a bug like this?
- Can you think of a person in the Bible who regularly ate locusts? (John the Baptist)
- Do you think you would eat bugs if you lived during Bible times?

DRAGON TAIL

Team Race

OVERVIEW
You've got to stick together in this twisty-turny game to catch the dragon's tail!

SCRIPTURE CONNECTION:
Revelation 12:7

SUPPLIES:
• Bandana

PREPARATION:
None

SAFETY FIRST:
This game is played in close quarters and includes a lot of motion. Be sure kids know the rules and boundaries. Be sure to point out kids that are being careful and kind.

HOW TO PLAY:

1. Have all the kids line up in a single file line.
2. Instruct each child to hold onto the shoulders of the person in front of them.
3. Tuck a bandana into the pocket or waistline of the last person in line.
4. The first person in line (the "dragon head") will try to grab the bandana (the "dragon tail") from the last person. Everyone stay connected in the game–no letting go of the person in front of you!
5. The middle and end of the line can try their best to stay away from the head as long as they stay connected.
6. If the bandana is caught, the game is over. Scramble the kids up and begin again.

TEACHABLE MOMENT:

Say: Wow, that was a seriously tangled up dragon! Even though this game was fun, I bet we would not be laughing if a real dragon was here! Did you know that in the end times, there will be a battle with a great dragon? (*Read Revelation 12:7–8.*) Usually we think of angels as sweet creatures floating through the air–but in this passage, we see that they are mighty warriors.

DISCUSSION QUESTIONS:

- What do you think of when you think of angels?
- What do you think the dragon in this battle will look like?
- How do you feel to know that angels can be warriors, too?

BACK TO BACK

Partner Race

OVERVIEW
Partners balance a ball between then as they run this race.

SCRIPTURE CONNECTION:
Proverbs 18:24

SUPPLIES:
- Two large beach balls
- Cones

PREPARATION:
Set up cones in two straight lines, about five cones each. Make sure they are spaced far apart enough for the partners to run around them.

TIP:
Some kids get frustrated when they are unable to accomplish a task. They don't want to appear incapable in front of their peers. Preload this game with plenty of talk about how fun it is even when the ball falls. Set them up to laugh off any inability that may surface to get to the end.

HOW TO PLAY:
1. The object of the game is to run in and out of the cones with the ball held firmly in place by the pair. Kids form pairs and give each two pairs a large beach ball to begin.
2. Have the kids stand back to back and position the beach ball between them and against their backs. Partners will move sideways, so that neither has to run backward.
3. Whichever pair makes it through the cones and back first wins. If the ball falls as they are racing–they should stop where they are (one person can retrieve the ball), reposition the ball and continue. They cannot move without the ball held between their backs.

TEACHABLE MOMENT:
Say: That game is a lot harder than it looks! You had to stick close and communicate well to make sure that ball stayed in place! This game reminds me a lot of a verse in the Bible. Let me read it to you. (*Read Proverbs 18:24.*)

DISCUSSION QUESTIONS:
- Do you have a friend who sticks close to you as this verse describes?
- What are reasons a kid your age might be an unreliable friend?
- What should a kid your age do if they realize they have an unreliable friend?
- Is it hard to be a friend that "sticks closer than a brother?"
- What do you think makes a good friend?

TWISTS AND TURNS

Individual Race

OVERVIEW
Kids follow a twisty trail and try to keep their feet on the line.

SCRIPTURE CONNECTION:
Psalm 17:5

SUPPLIES:
- Sidewalk chalk
- Large play area of cement or pavement
- Stopwatch or timer

PREPARATION:
Use the sidewalk chalk to draw a very squiggly and long line on the concrete. Make several twists and turns, spirals, and even cross over the line. Mark a start spot and a finish spot. If you want to make it more complex for older kids, draw two lines the same length in different colors for kids to race on.

HOW TO PLAY:

1. When the kids arrive, ask for a volunteer. The volunteer will walk along the line as fast as they can, being careful not to step off the line. Time them as they race through the course.
2. Allow everyone a chance to finish the course, keeping track of times. Declare a winner based on the fastest time.

TEACHABLE MOMENT:

Say: This path was full of twists and turns. It was hard to predict where that line was going to head next. Sometimes life can be a lot like this maze. It seems like we go through a lot of twists and turns just to end up kind of close to where we began! Thankfully, we don't have to worry about where our path will end up. We know that, as Christians, God has a very special plan for our lives. (*Read Psalm 17:5.*) When we pray and seek his guidance, he will direct our path.

DISCUSSION QUESTIONS:

- Have you ever felt lost in life? Why did you feel that way?
- How do you think God helps us know which way to go in life?
- Have you ever had to make a hard decision and you didn't know what to do?

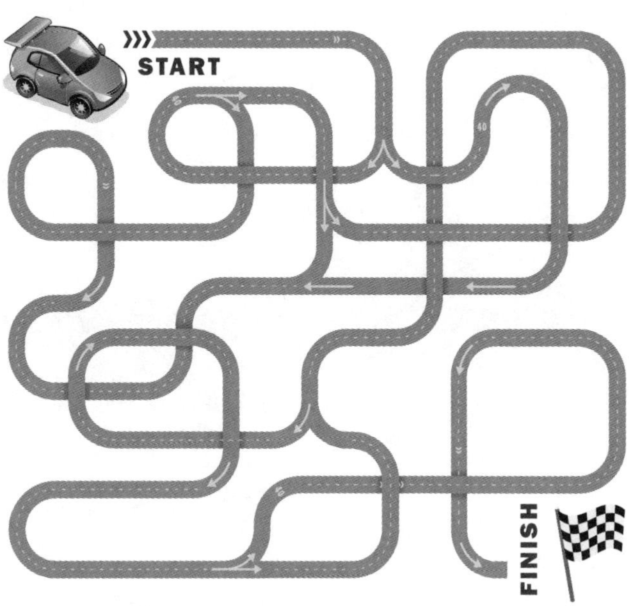

LAWN TWIST

Individual Race

OVERVIEW
Twister goes outdoors!
With a little prep work, your kids will be laughing and falling all over themselves!

SCRIPTURE CONNECTION:
Psalm 37:23-24

SUPPLIES:
- Spray paint: Red, Green, Blue, Yellow
- Poster board
- Medium size bowl
- Scissors
- Pencil or pen
- Spinner from a twisting game or cards from page 265

PREPARATION:
To begin, trace a medium sized bowl onto some poster board twice and cut it out to create a template. Take your template out to the yard and start spraying inside those holes. You will need six of each color, all in a straight line.

TIP:
You could create several game boards to accommodate more kids at once.

HOW TO PLAY:
1. When the kids arrive, have them stand on the side of the game board. Draw a card or use the spinner to call out a direction.
2. Kids follow the called instructions. They cannot move a hand or foot once it is on the board. They will get twisted up quickly!
3. If anyone falls (or if any part of their body besides hands and feet touch the ground), they are out. The game continues until there are two or three players left. These kids answer one of the Discussion Questions below.

TEACHABLE MOMENT:
Say: It was hard to stay steady in this game, wasn't it? The Bible talks about stumbling and falling, but it has a bit of a different meaning. (*Read Psalm 37:24.*)

DISCUSSION QUESTIONS:
- What is this verse talking about?
- God has provided the Bible to show us how to make good decisions and keep ourselves from falling into sin. What are ways we can keep from stumbling and falling?
- When is a regular time when you read the Bible? Talk with others about the Bible?

ONE-MAN TUG OF WAR

Individual Race

OVERVIEW
To make the tugging and pulling even more challenging, kids do this on their own.

SCRIPTURE CONNECTION:
I Corinthians 10:13

SUPPLIES:
- Long, sturdy rope
- Two large pieces of cardboard

PREPARATION:
Place the pieces of cardboard a few feet from each other.

SAFETY FIRST:
Be sure to station a volunteer near each piece of cardboard.
If a child begins to fall over, spot them to keep them upright and avoid any injury.

HOW TO PLAY:
1. To begin, kids line up in height order. Select the two smallest players. These players each stand on one of the pieces of cardboard. Hand each player an end of the rope.
2. On your signal, players pull on the rope, tug-of-war style, trying to yank the other player off their piece of cardboard. If a player's foot (or any other part of their body) touches the ground, they are eliminated and sit down.
3. Select the next smallest child to take the eliminated player's place. Continue play until each child has had a turn. The last player standing answers, or chooses a volunteer to answer, one of the Discussion Questions below.

TEACHABLE MOMENT:
Say: This was a tough game! Especially with someone else trying to pull you off your feet! Sometimes in life, friends will try to get us to do the wrong thing. It can feel a lot like this game. You're trying to stand strong and do the right thing, but it feels like you're getting tugged hard. The Bible promises that God will help us stand firm. God will help you escape temptation or fight against it. (*Read 1 Corinthians 10:13.*)

DISCUSSION QUESTIONS:
- What kind of temptations do kids your age face?
- How can we escape temptation?
- Who is a someone in the Bible who escaped temptation?
- How is this game like being pulled to do the wrong thing in life?

BALLOON STOMP

Individual Race

OVERVIEW
Kids run towards others to pop balloons, but they have to guard their own at the same time!

SCRIPTURE CONNECTION:
I Peter 5:8

SUPPLIES:
- Balloon, one for each player plus extra
- Yarn
- Scissors

PREPARATION:
Inflate the balloons before the kids arrive and tie each one to a piece of yarn (about 1' long).

HOW TO PLAY:
1. Tie a balloon to each kid's ankle.
2. On your signal, kids run around the yard trying to stomp on everyone else's balloon. They have to be careful and keep an eye on their own balloon so it doesn't get popped.
3. Children whose balloon is popped sit to the side. The last player standing answers, or chooses a volunteer to answer one of the Discussion Questions below.

TEACHABLE MOMENT:
Say: There were two important tasks you had in this game. First, you had to keep your balloon safe. Second, you had to pop everyone else's balloon. I bet it's a lot more interesting to pop everyone else's balloon than to focus on your own, isn't it? Life is like that. We get so focused on looking at the lives of others around us, that we forget to protect our own. We fall into temptation or make bad choices because we distract ourselves with what everyone is doing. This is just what Satan wants. The Bible tells us that he prowls around like a lion looking for someone to devour. (*Read 1 Peter 5:8.*)

DISCUSSION QUESTIONS:
- Why do you think Satan prowls around like a lion looking for someone to devour?
- In what ways do you see Satan attacking your life?
- How can we be alert and watch out for our enemy Satan? How can we fight Satan?

WET AND WILD WATER GAMES

PING-PONG FLOAT

Team Race

OVERVIEW
Kids race against each other to fill a bucket and get their Ping-Pong ball to float up and out!

SCRIPTURE CONNECTION:
Romans 15:13

SUPPLIES:
- Empty buckets, one for each team
- One larger bucket
- Nearby water source
- Paper or plastic cups
- Ping-Pong Balls, one per team

PREPARATION:
Fill up larger bucket with water. Place water bucket at one end of the play area, near a water source.

HOW TO PLAY:

1. Kids divide into two teams of four to six players each. Teams stand in single-file lines with the filled water bucket between them.
2. Place the empty team buckets several feet away from the first. Place a Ping-Pong ball inside each bucket.
3. You may need to refill the water bucket as the game progresses. If you do, call out "Freeze!" All players freeze in position until you return with the filled water bucket and call, "Unfreeze!" Play then continues.
4. Hand a paper or plastic cup to the first player on each team. On your signal, the first player on each team scoops up a cup of water and runs to the Ping-Pong bucket, dumps in the water, returns to team, and hands cup to the next player.
5. The next player takes a turn, and play continues until there is enough water in the Ping-Pong bucket to overflow and cause the Ping-Pong ball to move out of the bucket.
6. The first team to get their Ping-Pong ball out of their bucket by raising the water level wins.

TEACHABLE MOMENT:

Say: You may have heard the phrase "be a bucket filler". This means we should pour good things into the lives of others. Do you know who the ultimate bucket filler is? God is! God fills up our lives with love, peace, and joy so that we can pour good things into the lives of others. (*Read Romans 15:13.*)

DISCUSSION QUESTIONS:

- How can you be a bucket filler?
- Do you think the same is true in life?
- Do you need a lot of people to help fill up your bucket? **Say:** In life, we often look to others to for encouragement and to help us feel good, but only God can fill up our lives with peace and goodness.
- How do you think you can tap into the peace that only God can give?

PLASTIC BAGGY TOSS

Partner Game

OVERVIEW

This classic game comes with a twist. Toss the bags and don't get wet.

SCRIPTURE CONNECTION:
Psalm 68:9
Deuteronomy 11:17
I Kings 18:1

SUPPLIES:
- Sandwich-sized resealable plastic bags, one for each pair of partners plus extras
- Water source

PREPARATION:
Fill up sandwich bags with water, remove as much air as possible and seal.

HOW TO PLAY:
1. Group divides into pairs. Give each pair a water-filled sandwich bag.
2. Partners stand about one foot apart and toss the bag once. If the toss is caught, one partner takes a step backward. If the toss is not caught, partners sit down and wait for next round.
3. Pairs toss the sandwich bag again. Play continues until there is one pair left. This pair answers one of the Discussion Questions below.

TEACHABLE MOMENT:

Say: Playing with water is fun! When your bag broke open, it was probably refreshing to get a splash of water on you. Did you know that rain was often a sign of God's blessing in the Bible? If the people were disobedient to God, he would often withhold rain from the land. (*Read Deuteronomy 11:17* and *1 Kings 18:1.*) It was considered a blessing when God sent rain to the land. (*Read Psalm 68:9.*)

DISCUSSION QUESTIONS:
- How do people today feel about rain?
- How did not having rain or water help the people turn to God?
- What are things that we consider blessings in our lives today?

HOLE IN THE BUCKET

Team Relay Game

OVERVIEW

Kids try to fill a large bucket with water by transferring water in a coffee canister full of holes.

SCRIPTURE CONNECTION:
I Kings 18

SUPPLIES:

- Five-gallon buckets, one for each team
- Empty plastic thirty-ounce coffee canisters, one for each team
- Drill or nail and hammer
- Water source
- Container of water larger than five-gallon buckets

PREPARATION:
Make five to ten holes in the coffee canisters with either the drill or the nail and hammer. Fill the large container of water and keep near a water source.

HOW TO PLAY:

1. Kids divide into teams of four to six players.
2. Place the five-gallon buckets about twenty to thirty feet away from the large container of water. Make sure each team knows which one is their bucket.
3. Hand the empty coffee canister to the first person on each team. Players dip canisters into the large container of water and run to their five-gallon bucket to pour the water in bucket before it all leaks out!
4. You may need to refill the water bucket as the game progresses. If you do, call out "Freeze!" All players freeze in position until you return with the container filled with water and call, "Unfreeze!" Play then continues.
5. After they emptying canister, players will return to their team, and pass canister to the next person. The game continues this until one team fills their five-gallon bucket.

TEACHABLE MOMENT:

Say: That took some effort to fill up those buckets. Do you think it would have been a little easier if there weren't so many holes in your canisters? There is a story in the Bible where people had to carry a lot of water as well. (*Read 1 King 18:33–35.*) Elijah, the prophet, wanted to show the people who the one true God was, so he set up an altar and asked God to send fire from heaven. But first, he drenched the altar in water. The people had to carry a lot of water to soak the altar, but it certainly proved how powerful God was!

DISCUSSION QUESTIONS:

- How do you think the people felt getting all that water for Elijah to soak the altar?
- Did carrying a leaky bucket seem like an impossible task? Why or why not?

SPONGE BUCKET RELAY

Team Relay Game

OVERVIEW
Kids race against the clock to fill a bucket as full as they can. Their only tool? A soaking wet sponge.

SCRIPTURE CONNECTION:
Mark 16:15

SUPPLIES:
- Buckets, two per team
- Large car-washing sponges, one per team
- Timer
- Ruler

PREPARATION:
Fill one of each team's buckets with water. Place on one side of the play area. Place the empty buckets far from the full bucket on the opposite side of the play area.

PRESCHOOL TIP:
To help little ones, color coordinate buckets for each team and place buckets closer together.

$ TIP:
You can use washcloths if you don't have sponges or use two of the biggest sponges you have and have players carry one sponge in each hand.

HOW TO PLAY:
1. Kids divide into evenly numbered teams and line up behind their bucket filled with water.
2. Set the timer for three minutes. Signal teams to start.
3. The first player on each team dips the sponge in the water, gets it soaking wet, and runs to the empty bucket, squeezes the water into the empty bucket.
4. They then return to team, pass on the sponge to the next player in line, and goes to the end of the line. Play continues until the timer goes off.
5. Measure the height of the water in the buckets to see which team has the most water. This team answers one of the Discussion Questions below.

TEACHABLE MOMENT:
Say: One of our jobs as a Christian is to share the good news of the gospel with others. (*Read Mark 16:15.*) We can't share the Bible with others if we don't know it ourselves! That's why it's important to soak up God's word. Just like we soaked these sponges in water, we should soak ourselves in God's word. Then we can run to others and squeeze out goodness and love because we have spent time with God ourselves.

DISCUSSION QUESTIONS:
- Do you think it is easier to be kind to someone after you have spent time praying and reading the Bible? Why or why not?
- What do you do to soak up God's word like a sponge?

WATER BALLOON OBSTACLE COURSE

Individual Race

OVERVIEW
Kids race through an obstacle course holding two water balloons while completing the course.

SCRIPTURE CONNECTION:
James 1:12

SUPPLIES:
- Water Balloons, two for each child plus extras
- Timer or stopwatch
- Objects; see Water Balloon Obstacle Course Ideas on page 290

PREPARATION:
Set up the obstacle course ahead of time. Fill water balloons so there are at least two balloons per child

TIPS:
- For a small group, kids race against the clock, watching each other as they wait.
- For a larger group, let several kids go through the obstacle course at once, spacing out start times by about thirty seconds.

HOW TO PLAY:
1. Demonstrate how to go through the obstacle course without balloons.
2. Pass out two balloons to each player to carry as they complete the course.
3. If kids breaks a water balloon along the way, they go back to the beginning of the course and are given a replacement balloon.

TEACHABLE MOMENT:
Say: Sometimes in life, we face obstacles as well. They don't look like the ones in this race, of course, but they could be a problem we are trying to solve, or something we are discouraged about or worried about. The Bible tells us to keep going when things get tough. (*Read James 1:12.*) God will reward our effort.

DISCUSSION QUESTIONS:
- What did you think about this obstacle course?
- What was the hardest part?
- How did it feel to have to start back at the beginning?
- The Bible tells us "Blessed is the person who keeps on going when times are hard." This means we are to keep working hard, even when we get discouraged. Did anyone feel discouraged about this obstacle course? Why or why not?

Bonus:
To drive the Scripture home, have crowns prepared for the kids to reward them for finishing the obstacle course.

DRIP, DRIP, DROP

Circle Game

OVERVIEW

This game takes a wet spin on the classic Duck, Duck, Goose. Even older kids will want to play when they learn they can pour water on a friend's head!

SCRIPTURE CONNECTION:
Psalm 63:1

SUPPLIES:
- Water source
- Small paper or plastic cups
- Grassy area to play

PREPARATION:
Fill a cup. Have your water source nearby for refills.

TIP:
Not every child will like having water thrown on them. Be sure to find another way they can be part of the fun. Can they be the cup filler or give them a towel to hide behind?

HOW TO PLAY:
1. Kids sit in a circle on grass.
2. Give one child a small cup filled with water. They will be "It" for the first round.
3. Explain that the game is played like Duck, Duck, Goose. "It" will go around the circle, saying "Drip, drip, drip" on each child's head. When they choose someone to tag, they yell "Drop!" and dump the cup of water on their friend's head.
4. "It" then races around the circle, being chased by their now-wet friend. If "It" makes it back to the open space, they are safe. If not, they go in the middle. The chaser becomes the new "It," and play continues until everyone has a turn.

TEACHABLE MOMENT:

Say: It's not always fun to get water dumped on your head, but on a particularly hot day, it feels great, doesn't it? In the book of Psalms, David talks about thirsting after God like a person who is in a dry and hot land where there is no water. (*Read Psalm 63:1.*) David longed to be close to God—like how we long to be cooled off by a cup of water on a hot day.

DISCUSSION QUESTIONS:
- Have you ever thirsted after God in this way?
- What are some things you can do to feel closer to God?
- What is your favorite way to draw closer to God?

SPONGE THROW TARGET PRACTICE

Individual Game

OVERVIEW

Kids toss wet sponges at a target to hit a bulls-eye and score points for their team.

SCRIPTURE CONNECTION:
Colossians 3:23

SUPPLIES:
- Large sponges, soaking in buckets of water
- Sidewalk chalk
- Optional: Paper and pen to keep score

PREPARATION:
Draw a very large target on the pavement (see sketch). Assign point values:
- Outer ring = 10 points
- Next ring = 20 points,
- Center = 50 points

Draw a start line a few feet from the target.

TIP:
If you have more than ten kids, draw two targets and assign an adult leader to each to enforce the rules and keep track of the score.

HOW TO PLAY:
1. Kids divide into teams if you wish (boys verses girls is always fun).
2. Kids stand behind the line. Set the bucket of water and sponges next to throwing line.
3. Kids throw three sponges at the target, aiming for the middle.
4. Add up points and keep track of the score, declaring a winner after everyone has had a chance to throw.

TEACHABLE MOMENT:
Say: It wasn't always easy to hit the bull's eye—especially when you first started, but the more you practiced, the more accurate you became. This is how God wants us to treat everything in our life. When we work at something, he wants us to work at it with all our hearts. (*Read Colossians 3:23.*) When we are diligent and hard-working, God will help us reach our goal (or hit the target). Let's remember that everything we do is for God's glory and we should try our best on all our tasks.

DISCUSSION QUESTIONS:
- What would have happened if you threw the sponge without looking or trying?
- What are some things in life that you had to practice before you got good at them?
- Why do you think it brings God glory when we try our best at something?

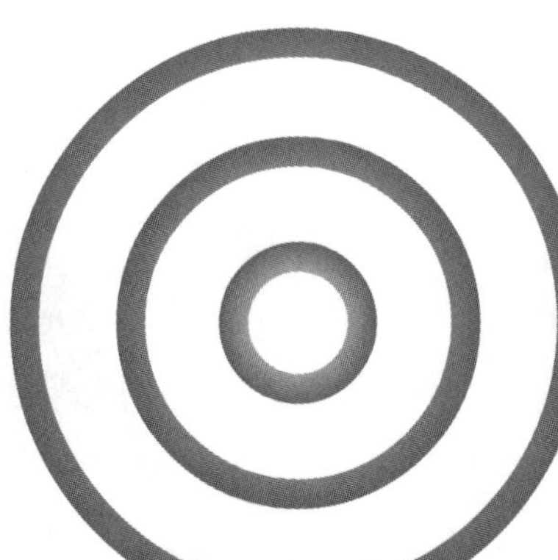

SPONGE PARTNER TOSS

Partner Game

OVERVIEW
Kids soak a large sponge in water and then toss it to their partner. The distance between partners increases with each toss until the sponge is dropped.

SCRIPTURE CONNECTION:
John 7:37-39

SUPPLIES:
- Large sponge (one for each pair of kids)
- Buckets
- Large field or play area
- Timer

PREPARATION:
Fill up half the buckets with water.

TIP:
You can also play this game with water balloons. Use Bunch of Balloons (available online and in stores) for super-fast filling!

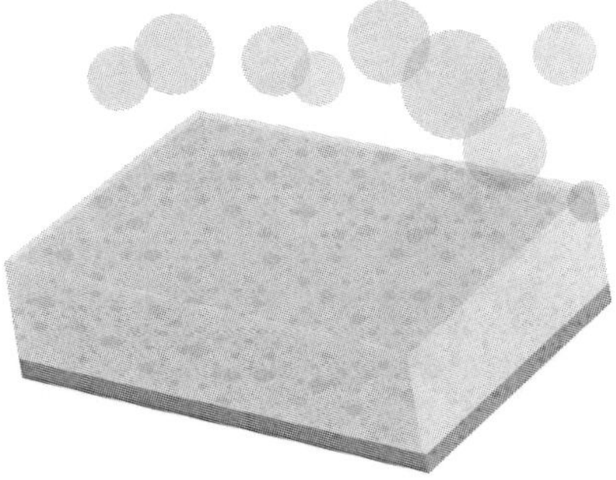

HOW TO PLAY:
1. Kids divide into pairs and stand a few feet away from each other.
2. Give each pair one empty bucket, one bucket of water, and one sponge.
3. One child in each pair dips the sponge in water and then tosses it to their partner who wrings it out into their empty bucket and then tosses it back to their partner.
4. This process continues for one minute, and then the partners switch places and roles (so each player can get equally soaked).
5. Continue the game for another minute and then have everyone stop.
6. Examine the freshly filled buckets and determine which has the most water in it. That pair answers, or chooses a volunteer to answer, one of the Discussion Questions.

TEACHABLE MOMENT:
Say: Did you know water is mentioned in the Bible? Jesus told people that if they were thirsty, they should come to him and drink. He promised that whoever believes in him would have rivers of living water flowing from inside them. (*Read John 7:37–39.*) It sounds crazy, but it was a way of saying that the Holy Spirit would live in the lives of people who believed in Jesus.

DISCUSSION QUESTIONS:
- Why do you think Jesus used the expression "living water?"
- Do you ever hear people using the expression "thirsty for . . ." these days? We all thirst for something spiritually–because we were created for eternity.
- What are some things people might try to satisfy their thirst?

SOAKING WET TRAFFIC LIGHT

Individual Race

OVERVIEW
Red Light, Green Light gets a twist when kids run through a sprinkler to get to their goal.

SCRIPTURE CONNECTION:
Philippians 3:14

SUPPLIES:
- Lawn sprinkler
- Water source, hose
- Large field

PREPARATION:
Place the sprinkler in the middle of the playing field and turn it on.

SAFETY FIRST:
Have a policy of sunscreen for each child before they play in the sun. Be careful to only help kids apply with other adults around. Ideally, have parents put on sunscreen before they drop off their child.

HOW TO PLAY:
1. Kids line up in a straight line. Pick one person to be the traffic controller and stand on the other side of the play area with their back turned.
2. Traffic controller yells, "Green light" and kids run through the sprinkler water towards them.
3. After a moment, traffic controller yells, "Red light," and everyone stops immediately.
4. Traffic controller yells, "Red light" and spins around and to see if anyone is moving. Anyone who moves starts back at the start line.
5. Whoever reaches the controller first wins and can serve as the next controller.

TEACHABLE MOMENT:
Say: This was a wet and wacky way to play Red Light, Green Light! Everyone was working towards the goal of reaching the traffic controller. That reminds me a lot of a verse in Philippians. (*Read Philippians 3:14.*)

DISCUSSION QUESTIONS:
- What was your goal in this game?
- What is our goal in the Christian life?
- What are some things that get in the way of our goals to be good Christians?
- What helps us stay focused on our goals?

SPLASH TIME

Partner Game

OVERVIEW
When their numbers match, kids get a surprise splash!

SCRIPTURE CONNECTION:
Mark 8:31

SUPPLIES:
- Plastic cup
- Bucket of warm water
- Numbered cards, one fewer than the number of players
- Empty bucket

PREPARATION:
Put numbered cards in empty bucket.

HOW TO PLAY:

1. Select one volunteer to be "It." "It" draws a number, memorizes it, and keeps it a secret! "It" then puts the number back in the bucket.
2. All the other players will then draw a number, hold it in their hand, and keep it a secret. They form a circle around "It." Fill a cup with warm water and hand to "It."
3. Starting with the youngest player, each player goes around the circle saying aloud the number written on their card. When "It" hears the same number that they chose, "It" throws the water from the cup at that person.
4. The player who got doused with water becomes "It." Continue play as time and interest allow.

TEACHABLE MOMENT:

Say: Even though you knew what was going to happen, it still surprised some of you. There were a few times in the Bible like this, too, like Jesus dying on the cross. Jesus had told his disciples that he was going to die and rise again, but it still surprised some of them. (*Read Mark 8:31.*) They couldn't believe he died and many didn't believe that he rose again!

DISCUSSION QUESTIONS:

- Why were the disciples were surprised by Jesus' death and resurrection?
- If you lived in Bible times, why might it be hard to believe Jesus rose from the dead?
- What other surprising stories are in the Bible?

FROZEN TOES

Individual Game

OVERVIEW

Toes will get mighty cold as kids attempt to transfer ice cubes from a kiddy pool to their own cups.

SCRIPTURE CONNECTION:
Genesis 43:24

SUPPLIES:
- Ice cubes
- Kiddie pool
- Cup or bowl for each player
- Timer

PREPARATION:
Fill the kiddie pool with ice cubes.

HOW TO PLAY:

1. Set the timer for one minute.
2. Have all the kids sit around the pool with their feet resting on the edge. Have them hold their cup or bowl in their hand.
3. On your signal, kids put their feet into the ice and try to pick up an ice cube and transfer it to their bowl or cup (using ONLY their feet).
4. When the timer beeps, kids remove their feet and count the number of ice cubes in each cup.
5. Whoever has the most cubes at the end of time wins.

TEACHABLE MOMENT:

Say: Did you know that is was traditional for people to wash their feet whenever they came into a home during Bible times? It is mentioned both in the New Testament and the Old Testament. You may remember when Jesus' washed his disciples' feet. Let's read another verse about it from Genesis. (*Read Genesis 43:24.*) The roads were very dusty back then and people usually wore sandals. Washing your feet was a way of keeping the house clean.

DISCUSSION QUESTIONS:

- Why do you think people stopped washing their feet when they came into houses?
- What is something we usually do instead?
- What was your favorite part of this game?
- What was your least favorite part?

WATER BALLOON BASEBALL

Individual Game

OVERVIEW
Kids try to pop a water balloon with a baseball bat so that they can run the bases.

SCRIPTURE CONNECTION:
John 4:10

SUPPLIES:
- Large supply of water balloons
- Plastic baseball bat
- Four bases
- Large grassy field to play in

PREPARATION:
Set up the bases like a baseball diamond, keeping in mind the ages of your kids as you set up the distance between the bases.

TIP:
Have a smaller area to serve as your field. Water balloons don't travel far. For added challenge and a refreshing twist, have them use their hand as a bat.

HOW TO PLAY:
1. Divide the kids up into two even teams.
2. The game is played similarly to baseball. Ask an adult helper to be the pitcher. The pitcher throws a water balloon at each batter.
3. Kids line up to take turns at bat. If batter hits the balloon and pops it, batter runs the bases.
4. If batter misses the balloon, pitcher throws another balloon. If batter misses three balloons, their turn is over.
5. Continue until each player has a turn at bat.

TEACHABLE MOMENT:
Say: This was a fun game! Water balloons are a ton of fun to use, but it always seems like the run out too quickly! This reminds me of a verse! (*Read John 4:10.*) In this verse, Jesus wasn't talking about the water we put in our balloons. He was talking about the Holy Spirit.

DISCUSSION QUESTIONS:
- Why do you think Jesus used the term "living water?"
- Have you ever been super thirsty and in need of a drink?
- Do you think we can be thirsty spiritually as well as physically?

CAR WASH

Group Activity

OVERVIEW

While not exactly a game, this wet activity is a great way for kids to have fun and serve at the same time!

SCRIPTURE CONNECTION:
Matthew 20:28

SUPPLIES:
- Buckets of warm soapy water
- Sponges
- Hose
- Cars to wash!

PREPARATION:
Announce at church that the kids will wash cars during service. Make sure kids dress appropriately for getting wet.

WHAT ARE SCHOOL-AGE CHILDREN CAPABLE OF LEARNING ABOUT GOD:
- Discovering the power of the Bible
- Understanding the power of prayer
- Understanding Spiritual gifts
- Serving the world with their time and talents
- Learning to share their faith
- Choosing healthy friendships and boundaries

HOW TO PLAY:
1. People who would like their car washed park in an area that you designate.
2. Help the kids spray down a car and then scrub it with soap and water until it shines!
3. Hose down the car again and allow it to dry in the sun.

TEACHABLE MOMENT:

Say: It's a lot of fun to wash a car, and it's a big help to people as well. Did you know that God loves it when we serve? (*Read Matthew 20:28.*) Jesus served many people during his time here on Earth. Jesus is powerful and God's Son. He could have easily thought he was "too good" to help others, but that's not what he did. Jesus spent his life helping other–healing, teaching, and feeding them. Then, he showed us what ultimate service is by giving up his own life so that we can be free from the penalty for our sins.

DISCUSSION QUESTIONS:
- Why do you think Jesus spent his life serving others?
- Who do you know that serves a lot? How do they serve God and others?
- What are some ways you can serve at home? At school?

TUG OF WAR SPLASH

Individual Game

OVERVIEW

This old-school game gets a makeover as kids stand on crates and try not to get pulled into a pool of water!

SCRIPTURE CONNECTION:
I Corinthians 10:13

SUPPLIES:
- Long, sturdy rope
- Inflatable wading pool

PREPARATION:
Place wading pool in the middle of play area and fill with water.

HOW TO PLAY:

1. Players line up in height order. Select the two of smallest players and have each player stand on either side of the wading pool.
2. Hand each player an end of the rope.
3. On your signal, players pull on the rope, trying to yank the other player into the pool. A player is eliminated as soon as they touch any of the water in the baby pool.
4. After one player is eliminated, select the next smallest child to take the eliminated player's place.
5. Play continues until all children have had a turn.

TEACHABLE MOMENT:

Say: This was a pretty tough task–staying out of the water! Especially with someone else trying to pull you in! Sometimes in life, friends will try to get us to do the wrong thing. It can feel a lot like this game. You're trying to stand strong and do the right thing, but it feels like you're getting tugged hard. The Bible promises that God will help us stand firm. God will help you escape temptation or fight against it. Let's read our verse together. (*Read 1 Corinthians 10:13.*)

DISCUSSION QUESTIONS:

- How is this game like being pulled to do the wrong thing in life?
- What kind of wrong things are kids your age sometimes tempted to do?
- How can we escape temptation?
- Can you think of a person in the Bible that escaped temptation?

WATER GUN SOCCER

Team Race

OVERVIEW
The goalies are armed with intense water guns in this soccer game!

SCRIPTURE CONNECTION:
Proverbs 4:23

SUPPLIES:
- Four cones or two soccer nets
- Beach ball for soccer
- Two squirt guns

PREPARATION:
Set up cones or nets about 50 feet away from each other. Fill squirt guns with water.

$TIP:
Use water hoses instead of squirt guns.

SCHOOL AGE CHILDREN ON THE MOVE:
- Owning their own beliefs
- Moving faith from fiction to fact
- Having faith become more personal
- Moving from wanting adult approval to participating because they are capable
- Questioning instead of accepting things at face value

HOW TO PLAY:
1. Kids divide into two evenly numbered teams. Assign a goal to each team.
2. Select one or two goalies for each team and have them stand directly in front of the goal. Give each goalie a prepared squirt gun. Goalies are allowed to fire at will when the opposite team approaches.
3. Kids gather in the center of the field. Toss the beach ball into the middle of the kids.
4. Each team will try to kick the ball into the opposite team's goal. No hands allowed!
5. The first team to score five goals answers one of the Discussion Questions below.

TEACHABLE MOMENT:
Say: This was no ordinary game of soccer, was it? It certainly was harder to score a goal with water flying at you. Those goalies did a great job guarding what was important. That reminds me of a verse in the Bible. Let's read it together. (*Read Proverbs 4:23.*)

DISCUSSION QUESTIONS:
- Why do you think we should guard the heart?
- How would you guard your heart?
- Have you ever had your heart hurt? How did you recover?

MELT A CUBE

Individual Game

OVERVIEW
Kids race to be the fastest to melt their ice cubes.

SCRIPTURE CONNECTION:
Isaiah 6:6-7

SUPPLIES:
- Ice cubes, one for each kid plus extras for additional rounds
- Tray

PREPARATION:
Place ice cubes on tray.

TIP:
If you have a small group and want to get crazy, make some big ice cubes by using Tupperware storage containers. Spray containers with cooking spray first.

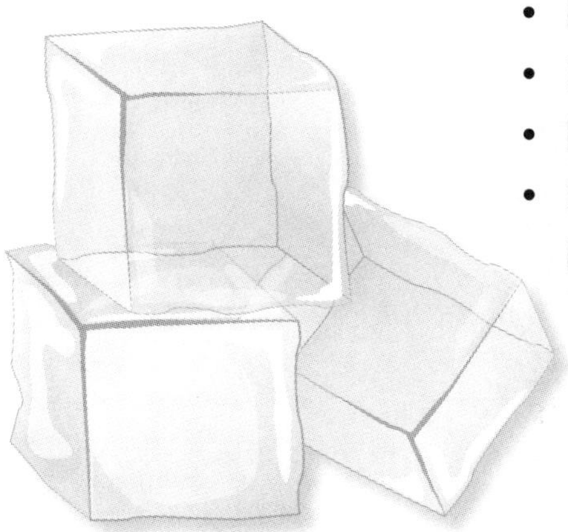

HOW TO PLAY:
1. On your signal, each child takes an ice cube and uses their hands to press in on the ice cube or rub it between their hands to melt it.
2. Whoever completely melts their ice cube first answers, or chooses a volunteer to answer, one of the Discussion Questions below.

TEACHABLE MOMENT:
Say: Are your hands feeling pretty cold right now? Ice is one of the coldest things we can handle. What do you think is one of the hottest things we can handle? You should never touch one, but a burning coal is something that's very hot. In the Bible—a man named Isaiah was touched with a burning coal on his lips. Ouch! An angel did it to Isaiah to show that his sins were forgiven. I bet he would have liked having an ice cube right then. (*Read Isaiah 6:6–7.*)

DISCUSSION QUESTIONS:
- Why do you think the angel did that to Isaiah?
- Isaiah was distraught because of his sin and the sins of others. He was very repentant.
- Have you ever felt repentant like Isaiah?
- What did you do to ask for forgiveness?

HOW THE VOLUNTEER CAN HELP:
- Pray for the children, and the movement of the Holy Spirit to move in the lives of kids, leaders, and other volunteers.
- Prepare the lesson and memorize key learning points.
- Empower the children to think independently.
- Promote and praise each child.
- Find real-life application for lessons, modeling and sharing personal (and appropriate) stories from their faith.

SPONGE DODGE BALL

Team Race

OVERVIEW

This classic game gets a wet and wild twist when the balls are replaced with water-soaked sponges.

SCRIPTURE CONNECTION: Matthew 26:41

SUPPLIES:

- Large sponges, at least ten for each team
- Several buckets
- Large outside play area

PREPARATION:

Fill buckets with water and line them up in a straight line in the middle of the play area to serve as a dividing line.

HOW TO PLAY:

1. Kids divide into two evenly numbered teams. Give each team ten sponges. Kids to wet sponges in water bucket. Kids are welcome to fill up the sponges with water again throughout the game, but they have to be careful not to get hit!
2. On your signal, kids throw their sponges at the other team without passing the dividing line of buckets.
3. Players hit with a sponge sit on the ground or move to the side.
4. Kids continue throwing and hitting each other until there are only one or two kids left in the game. Player(s) answer, or choose a volunteer to answer, one of the Discussion Questions below.

TEACHABLE MOMENT:

Say: That was some wet and wild fun! While it might have been tempting to get your sponge wet at the buckets, you had to be super careful while you were up there. You weren't exactly "watching and praying" when at the buckets, but it does remind me a little bit of Matthew 26:41. Let's read it together.

DISCUSSION QUESTIONS:

- How do you think watching and praying keeps us out of temptation?
- What does the verse mean when it says "The spirit is willing, but the body is weak?"
- Sometimes, when people want to do the right thing but some temptation was just too hard, it almost can feel like your body has a mind of its own. How do you think we can avoid tempting situations like that?

SHIVERING ICE AND SNOW GAMES

LOST PING-PONG BALLS

Individual Game

OVERVIEW

Just like an Easter egg hunt, kids hunt for Ping-Pong balls in the snow.

SCRIPTURE CONNECTION:
Luke 15:8

SUPPLIES:
- Ping-Pong balls (at least three to five for each player)
- Field of snow

PREPARATION:
Scatter the Ping-Pong balls throughout the snow. You may wish to throw them out to prevent footprints. You might even try to hide them the night before and hope that fresh snow falls on the ground!

HOW TO PLAY:

1. Kids search for and gather the Ping-Pong balls.
2. The person who finds the most Ping-Pong balls at the end of the time answers, or chooses a volunteer to answer, one of the Discussion Questions below.

TEACHABLE MOMENT:

Say: It was pretty tough to find those Ping-Pong balls, wasn't it? There is a parable in the Bible that talks about finding lost things. In Luke 15, we read about a woman who loses a valuable coin in her home. (*Read Luke 15:8.*) She sweeps and cleans until she finally finds it. She'll stop at nothing to get that coin back! Did you know God feels the same way about us? God cares about lost people. He wants them found. He wants them to be a part of his family.

DISCUSSION QUESTIONS:

- What do you think it feels like to be lost?
- If you ever felt like one of those Ping-Pong balls–all alone in the snow–what can you do?
- Did you know that God wants you to be a part of his family? How does that make you feel?
- What does it mean to be a part of God's family?

BUCKETS OF SNOW

Team Race

OVERVIEW
Kids toss snowballs into buckets to win this game.

SCRIPTURE CONNECTION: Philippians 3:14

SUPPLIES:
- Buckets, one for each team
- Snowy play area
- Timer

PREPARATION:
For each team set a bucket in the play area. Draw a circle in the snow a few feet around the bucket on all sides.

HOW TO PLAY:
1. Kids divide into teams of five to ten players and stand near their bucket, outside of the circle you prepared.
2. On your signal, kids make snowballs and try to toss their snowballs into the bucket. They do not cross the circle around the bucket.
3. After a few minutes, signal teams to stop playing. Count the number of snowballs in each bucket. Only formed snowballs count—loose snow does not. Whichever team has the most snowballs answers one of the Discussion Questions below.

TEACHABLE MOMENT:
Say: This game was a little more complicated than just tossing a ball into a bucket. We had to be careful not to break the snowballs, or they would not count. The Christian life can be a little tough, too. Sometimes it seems like everyone else has an easier life than us. We have a big goal—to live like Jesus Christ. Sometimes, it might seem impossible—like tossing a snowball into a bucket without it breaking—but with God's help, we can press on towards the goal. (*Read Philippians 3:14.*)

DISCUSSION QUESTIONS:
- What is the hardest part of being a Christian?
- What is the best part of being a Christian?
- Does it ever seem like the things God asked us to do are too much?
- What things have you faced that felt impossible?

FOLLOW THE FOOTSTEPS

Individual Game

OVERVIEW
In this Follow the Leader game, kids follow in the footsteps of someone who has gone before.

SCRIPTURE CONNECTION:
Psalm 119:105

SUPPLIES:
- Snow boots for you to wear
- Snowy play area
- Stopwatch

PREPARATION:
Stomp through the field, leaving deliberate tracks. Make sure to do some fun loopy-loops, hopping steps, or cross your path to add confusion.

TIP:
Be aware of your stride. Be sure you don't make the steps too wide for a child to step in.

HOW TO PLAY:

1. Kids follow in your footsteps in a single file line. Time them to see how long it takes.
2. Kids complete the path again (if you're not freezing yet!) and time them to see if they complete it faster.

TEACHABLE MOMENT:
Say: This was a different way to follow the leader, wasn't it? Instead of following a person, you followed a person's footsteps. God has given us a path to follow as well. Even though we can't see God like we can see other people, we can be directed by the Bible. (*Read Psalm 119:105.*)

DISCUSSION QUESTIONS:

- Was it easier to go through the path a second time? Why?
- Do you think it was it easier to go through the path at the very front of the line or the end of the line?
- Do you think the history that we read about in the Bible helps guide us? How?
- How can we use the Bible to direct our path?

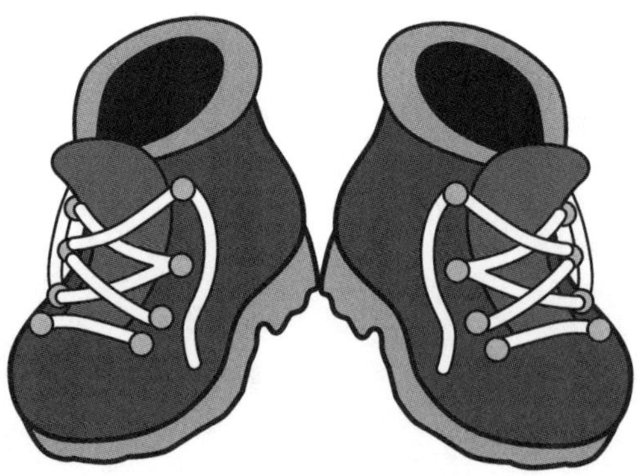

LONG JUMP

Individual Game

OVERVIEW
In this winter version of the Olympic game, players use the snow to mark their jumps.

SCRIPTURE CONNECTION:
Isaiah 40:31

SUPPLIES:
- Smooth ground that is covered in snow

PREPARATION:
Mark a line in the snow about 5 feet across. This is the jumping line.

HOW TO PLAY:

1. Kids run towards the jumping line and jump when they reach it. Their footprints will show how far they jump. Keep track of the furthest jump as you go.
2. Allow each child to have a turn and declare a winner based on the longest distance jumped.

TEACHABLE MOMENT:

Say: This was a pretty intense jumping game. You probably don't usually concentrate on jumping that far on a regular basis. I wonder how far you could jump if you had a pair of wings to help you? In the Bible, there is a verse that talks about soaring like an eagle. In this verse, we are told that God will renew our strength when we grow weary. (*Read Isaiah 40:31.*)

DISCUSSION QUESTIONS:

- What would it be like to have wings?
- What would it be like if you could run and not grow weary?
- Do you think this verse is talking about physically running? If not what is it talking about?

SNOWBALL BOCCE

Team Game

OVERVIEW
This timeless backyard game can be played in the snow, with a few minor variations.

SCRIPTURE CONNECTION:
James 4:8

SUPPLIES:
- Large field filled with packable snow
- Spray bottles filled with colored water (one color for every four players)
- Cone
- Rope

PREPARATION:
Set up a cone and use rope to make a boundary line about fifteen feet from the cone.

TIP:
Don't want to be bothered with the snowballs and colored water? Use a standard Bocce ball set instead. It will still be a unique playing experience because of the snow, but a lot less work!

HOW TO PLAY:

1. Kids divide into teams of four. Have each team member make a snowball and then spray it with their team's color (using water-filled spray bottles).
2. Allow kids to throw (or roll) their colored snowballs towards the cone, one at a time. Give each team one turn until everyone has had a turn.
3. The object of the game is to get as close to the cone as possible without actually touching it.
4. Measure the distance and determine the closest colored snowball. That team answers one of the Discussion Questions below.
5. Play again as time and interest allows.

TEACHABLE MOMENT:

Say: This was a little bit tricky, wasn't it? You wanted to get close to that cone, but not too close! The interesting thing about this game is that the cone stayed still. You couldn't talk the cone into coming closer to your ball or persuade it to take a few steps closer to the boundary line. Thankfully, God is not like this cone! The Bible tells us that if we come close to God, he will come close to us. (*Read James 4:8.*) The more we spend time with God, the closer he moves towards us.

DISCUSSION QUESTIONS:

- How do you draw close to God?
- How can you tell if God is drawing close to you?
- When do you feel the closest to God?
- When do you feel the furthest?
- Do you think our verse (James 4:8) offers us any more clues about why we might feel far from God?

BIGGEST SNOWBALL

Team Game

OVERVIEW
Kids work together as a team to make the biggest snowball.

SCRIPTURE CONNECTION:
James 1:15

SUPPLIES:
- Large field filled with packable snow
- Timer
- Optional: Camera
- Optional: Measuring tape

PREPARATION:
None

HOW TO PLAY:
1. Kids divide into teams of three to five players. The purpose of the game is to create the largest snowball possible by rolling a little snowball on the ground to make it bigger.
2. Set the timer for a few minutes and let the kids get rolling!
3. At the end of the time, and vote on who has made the largest snowball. Optional: Take photos of snowballs and kids. Use measuring tape to measure snowballs.
4. If you're feeling especially adventurous, bring all the snowballs together to make a super huge snowman!

TEACHABLE MOMENT:
Say: It's hard to believe that you were able to create such huge snowballs when all you started out with was a tiny bit of snow. That reminds me of something else in life–sin. When we allow sin to grow in our life, there's no telling how big and destructive it will grow. (*Read James 1:15.*) This verse tells us that when sin is allowed to grow, it brings death and destruction. We know that the eternal punishment for sin is death, but sin also can bring deadly consequences here on Earth. It can kill relationships, ruin trust, hurt others, and all kinds of things. Don't let sin grow in your life like these snowballs! Ask God to rid your life of sin as soon as you notice something is not right.

DISCUSSION QUESTIONS:
- Why do you think it is so easy for sin to grow in our lives?
- How can we tell when there is sin in our lives?
- How can we get rid of the sin in our lives?
- What kind of damage might sin do if we continue to allow it to grow?

PAINTING IN THE SNOW

Individual Game

OVERVIEW
Pass out the spray bottles and watch as kids transform snow into works of art.

SCRIPTURE CONNECTION:
Romans 1:20

SUPPLIES:
- Snow covered field or mounds of snow; a freshly plowed parking lot is perfect!
- Spray bottles, one for each child
- Food coloring or liquid watercolors.

PREPARATION:
Fill each bottle with water and put one or two teaspoons of liquid watercolor or a few drops of food coloring in each bottle. Put spray lid back on bottle.

HOW TO PLAY:

1. Give spray bottles and encourage them to spray the colored water to create works of art in the snow. They may exchange bottles with each other to create a complete masterpiece.
2. After several minutes, gather the kids for discussion.

TEACHABLE MOMENT:

Say: These works of art are amazing. I love all the colors and the patterns. Of course not! Someone spent time on these things. I can even parts of your personalities reflected in the art. The same is true of creation. The things you see all around–trees, plants, animals–they didn't just fall from the sky one day. God spent time creating them and filling in all the details. We can see evidence of God in the things he created. Just like we can see evidence of you in the art you made today. Romans 1:20 tells us that creation shows us that God is real. (*Read Romans 1:20.*)

DISCUSSION QUESTIONS:

- Have you ever heard someone say that the world just showed up one day? That God didn't have anything to do with it? That's such a crazy idea. Of course, someone created the earth–all the wonders around us couldn't just show up on their own.
- Where can we read more about how God created the earth?
- What is one of your favorite parts of creation?

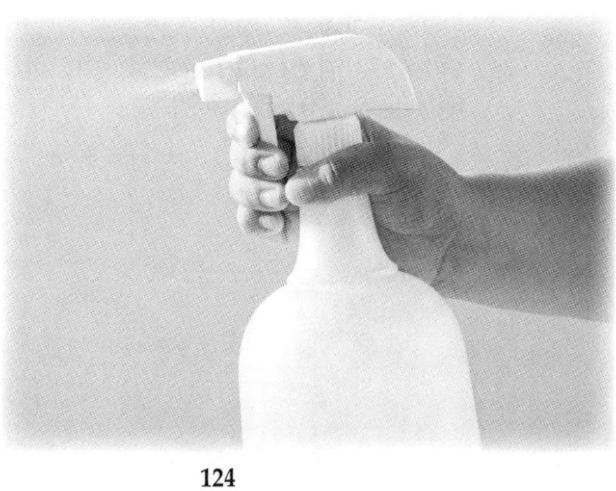

TUG OF WAR

Team Race

OVERVIEW
In this classic outdoor game, kids will have to battle slippery snow to win!

SCRIPTURE CONNECTION:
Romans 7:22-23

SUPPLIES:
- Cone
- Large, heavy duty rope

PREPARATION:
Set the rope in the middle of an open area outside and set the cone in the middle of the rope (lengthwise).

TIP:
Allow the children an opportunity to reflect on any sin they need to confess. You can have them write it on paper and then do something symbolic with the papers after a time of prayer. Suggestions could be: run papers through a shredder, rip them up, write "forgiven" on them and throw them in the trash, etc.

HOW TO PLAY:
1. Divide the children up into two teams.
2. Have teams line up on either side of the cone, facing each other, and hanging onto the rope.
3. On your signal, kids will pull against the other team, trying to get the front person on the team to cross past the cone.
4. If a team passes the cone, they lose.

TEACHABLE MOMENT:
Say: It was back and forth there! This was a hard enough game on the regular ground, but the snow makes it even trickier! This game reminds me a lot of a passage in the Bible–Romans 7. In this passage, Paul talks about his back and forth struggle with sin. He says that he wants to do the right thing, but sin keeps tugging back and making him slip. (*Read Romans 7: 22–23.*)

DISCUSSION QUESTIONS:
- When have struggled with doing the right thing?
- What sins do you think can trip up or make a kid your age fall?
- How can we protect ourselves against sin?
- How does this game remind us of the struggle we have with sin?

STACK THAT SNOW

Team Game

OVERVIEW
Kids work together as a team to make a giant pyramid of snow.

SCRIPTURE CONNECTION:
Genesis 11:4

SUPPLIES:
- Plenty of snow
- Timer
- Optional: Measuring tape

PREPARATION:
None

HOW TO PLAY:
1. Kids divide into two teams and set the timer for a few minutes.
2. Kids to work together to make a pyramid of snowballs.
3. When the timer beeps, kids can no longer speak to each other.
4. Set the time for a few minutes more. When the timer beeps, group votes which pyramid is the tallest. Optional: Measure pyramids to determine the tallest.

TEACHABLE MOMENT:

Say: This activity reminds me of an account from the Bible. In the early days of the earth, the people all worked together to try and build a tower that reached all the way to the sky. (*Read Genesis 11:4.*) We were building for fun, but these people were building to make a great name for themselves. God did not like the motivation behind their actions, so he did something to stop the work. He made them all speak different languages! After that, the people gave up the work and went their separate ways.

DISCUSSION QUESTIONS:
- How difficult would it have been to build these pyramids if you were speaking different languages?
- How long would it take us to build a pyramid to the sky?
- Why do you think the people wanted to build such a tower?

FROZEN DODGEBALL

Team Game

OVERVIEW

In this classic playground game, kids toss snowballs at each other instead of balls. When you are hit, you sit.

SCRIPTURE CONNECTION: Ephesians 6:16

SUPPLIES:

- Plenty of snow
- Timer
- Rope or cones to mark the boundaries of the game

PREPARATION:

Use rope or cones to divide the play area into two sections. Each team stays on their side.

HOW TO PLAY:

1. Kids divide into two teams. The object of the game is to get all the other team's players out before the end of the round.
2. Set timer for a few minutes.
3. On your signal, kids form snowballs and throw them at the opposite team. **Say:** If you are hit you are out and sit until the end of the round. You can make snowballs from your sitting position for your teammates to use.
4. The team with the most players still standing at the end of the round wins.

TEACHABLE MOMENT:

Say: It seemed like snowballs were coming from every direction in that game! At first, it was hard not to get hit, but as the numbers dwindled, it became a little easier to stay in the game. Did you know, that Satan likes to attack us too? The Bible tells us that he throws fiery arrows at us. These aren't real arrows, they are spiritual. They are arrows of fear, doubt, jealousy, and other kinds of feelings that might lead us into sin. (*Read Ephesians 6:16.*) We don't have to be afraid of Satan and his attacks though. God has given us protection from Satan's attacks–it is called the Armor of God!

DISCUSSION QUESTIONS:

- What are the parts of the Armor of God?
- What is your favorite piece of God's armor?
- When you feel like everything is falling apart, what makes you feel safe?

CAPTURE THE FLAG

Team Tag

OVERVIEW

Kids hide a flag on their side of the playing field. The other team must capture the flag without getting captured themselves!

SCRIPTURE CONNECTION:
Deuteronomy 4:29

SUPPLIES:

- Timer
- Two brightly colored pieces of fabric
- Rope or cones to mark the boundaries of the game

PREPARATION:

Set up clear boundaries and divide the play area in half, one for each team. Post a leader near the outer boundaries to make sure kids don't wander too far away. Set up a designated place for the jail. Post a leader in the jail with a timer.

HOW TO PLAY:

1. Divide the kids up into two equal teams. Give each team a piece of fabric and a few minutes to hide their flag. If the ground is very snowy, they may wish to create some diversion tracks by sending various team members in opposite directions.
2. The flag must be partially visible.
3. Once the flags are hidden, everyone returns to the dividing line, and the game begins. Teams cross into enemy territory to try and find the opposing team's flag. If they are caught (tagged by the opposite team) when on enemy territory, they are taken to jail for a few minutes.
4. Whoever can find the opposite team's flag first and carry it back across the dividing line, without getting caught, wins!
5. If someone has found a flag and is running back to their side when tagged, they drop the flag on the ground and go to jail. The flag remains where it is dropped.

TEACHABLE MOMENT:

Say: You had to find the other team's flag. If you had just stayed on your side, you'd never would have a chance of winning the game! In the same way, we have to search after God in our relationship with him Developing a relationship with God does takes effort on our part. (*Read Deuteronomy 4:29.*)

DISCUSSION QUESTIONS:

- What was the hardest part of this game? What was the easier part of this game?
- Why does God wants us to search for him?
- What blocks our search for God or spending time with him?

SNOWMAN DECORATING

Partner Game

OVERVIEW
Kids work in pairs to decorate a snowman. Plenty of props keep the fun rolling in this game!

SCRIPTURE CONNECTION:
Psalm 139:13

SUPPLIES:
- Timer
- Lots of props
- Large field with plenty of packable snow

PREPARATION:
Gather the props

PROPS TO INCLUDE:
Scarves, hats, mittens, sticks, stones, carrots, rubber boots, buttons, spray bottles with colored water.

TIP:
Talk about how each child is the same or different. You could have everyone stand in a circle. Call out a feature, a favorite flavor of ice cream, a pet, etc. As a child hears something that applies to them they run to the center, high five each other and run back to the circle.

HOW TO PLAY:
1. Kids pair up. Show everyone the pile of props and explain that they have ten minutes to make a snowman.
2. Set the timer for ten minutes and let the kids have fun. Extend the time if everyone is still working and it isn't too cold.
3. At the end of time, take a look at all the completed snowmen. Comment on creativity, height, strength and other descriptors.

TEACHABLE MOMENT:
Say: You guys did a great job building and decorating these snowmen. Even though you all had the same task, all the snowmen (or snow ladies) look very different! That's the same way it is with people. We were all made by God, but we are all very different. Did you know that God formed each and every one of you? (*Read Psalm 139:13.*) That's amazing! God formed you in the womb. He knew you before you were born. And he loves you very much.

DISCUSSION QUESTIONS:
- What was the hardest part of making the snowman?
- Why do you think God made each of us the way we are?
- How does it make you feel to know that the same God who created everything spent special time forming you inside your mother's womb?

PIN THE NOSE ON THE SNOWMAN

OVERVIEW
You can't have a party without this classic game. In this version, a pre-built snowman is awarded a nose (or twenty!)

Team Tag

SCRIPTURE CONNECTION:
Exodus 4:11

SUPPLIES:
- Blindfold
- Bag of baby carrots
- Pre-built snowman, complete with scarf, mouth, and eyes.

PREPARATION:
Build a snowman

TIP:
Take some time before the game to research a special needs person who has done something amazing. Share that person's story and encourage them to always look for what is amazing in each person God created.

HOW TO PLAY:

1. Bring the kids to the snowman you have built and ask them if they notice anything strange about the snowman. Is anything missing? **Say:** Yes, the nose is missing! You are going to help the snowman. We're going to try to get him a nose where it belongs!
2. Select a volunteer and blindfold them. Have volunteer stand a few feet from the snowman and direct them to walk towards the snowy creation. Encourage them to stick the carrot in the snowman somewhere.
3. Play continues until everyone has a turn.

TEACHABLE MOMENT:

Say: I made this snowman before you guys got here, but I purposely left the nose out. Sometimes people are also born a little different. They could be born without functioning eyes, or with ears that don't quite work, or with some other health condition. These people are still special and important to God. (*Read Exodus 4:11.*) We don't always understand why these things happen, but it's our job to show love and compassion even if someone is not like us.

DISCUSSION QUESTIONS:

- Why do you think that God makes us all different?
- How are you different than your parents and siblings?
- How can you help someone feel important and included?

ICE HUNT

Individual Game

OVERVIEW
In this tweaked game, colored ice cubes are hidden in the snow instead of colorful eggs.

SCRIPTURE CONNECTION:
Matthew 13:44

SUPPLIES:
- Ice cube trays
- Water
- Food coloring
- Access to a freezer
- Field of snow

PREPARATION:
Prepare the ice cubes at least three to four hours ahead of time. Fill ice cube trays with water and a bit of food coloring to make colored cubes. When the ice cubes are frozen, throw them out into the field. You could walk them around, but your footprints might give away the locations.

HOW TO PLAY:

1. When the kids arrive, tell them that there is treasure hidden in field. Allow them to search for the ice cubes and bring them back to you.
2. After a few minutes, call the kids back the child who found the most ice cubes answers, or chooses a volunteer to answer, one of the Discussion Questions below..

TEACHABLE MOMENT:

Say: If you were expecting to find those colored cubes in the field. This reminds me of a parable (story) in the Bible. (*Read Matthew 13:44.*) In this story, a man finds a buried treasure in a field. He is so excited that he sells all he has and buys the field to keep the treasure. The Bible tells us that the Kingdom of God is like this buried treasure. It is so valuable and so important; it would be worth selling all we have so that we could have it. Thankfully, we don't have to sell our possessions to be a part of God's kingdom. God invites us to become a part of his family (his kingdom) by repenting of our sins and asking him to be our friend forever!

DISCUSSION QUESTIONS:

- What do you like most about being part of God's family (God's kingdom)?
- How is a buried treasure like the treasure of eternal life?
- Have you ever shared this good news with someone else?

SLED PULL

Team Race

OVERVIEW
Kids will have to muster up all their strength in this sled pulling race!

SCRIPTURE CONNECTION:
Judges 16:17

SUPPLIES:
- Sleds with rope attached to the front, one sled for each team
- Snowy play area
- Cones or rope

PREPARATION:
Use cones or rope to mark the start and finish lines.

$ TIP:
Don't have a sled? Ask the parents ahead of time if you can borrow a few. Be sure to place their name with paper tape on the underside to return the sleds.

HOW TO PLAY:
1. Kids divide into teams of four to six players. Give each team a sled. Teams line up at the start line in height order.
2. On your signal, the first player on each team will sit on the sled and the second player will pull or push them to the finish line. At the finish line, they will switch places and then race back to the start line.
3. After the first two players return, the next two players will do the same thing.
4. The first team to complete the race wins.

TEACHABLE MOMENT:
Say: That was a tough race. Now, if you had the strength of Samson, that would have been a lot easier. Samson was a special man, born to be a judge of Israel, God's special people. Samson had incredible strength, and he used this strength to defeat the Philistines. (*Read Judges 16:17.*)

DISCUSSION QUESTIONS:
- What do you think it would have been like, to have strength like Samson?
- If you could pick any superpower, what would you pick?
- What "superpowers" does God have?

ICE CUBE STRUCTURES

Team Game

OVERVIEW
In this creative activity, kids will work together to build ice cube structures that are bright and colorful.

SCRIPTURE CONNECTION:
Luke 14:28-30

SUPPLIES:
- Lots of colored ice cubes (see directions below)
- Spray bottles (one for each team of three or four)
- Timer
- Optional: Gloves, one pair for each child

PREPARATION:
Several days before your event, begin to make colored ice cubes. You can make the ice cubes in standard trays and put one drop of food coloring in each cube. When one batch is frozen, dump into a bowl and make some more! You'll want at least thirty to fifty cubes for each team.

HOW TO PLAY:
1. Kids divide into even teams. Give each team a spray bottle of water and a bowl or container full of colored ice cubes.
2. Set the timer for a few minutes. Kids work together to make a sculpture out of their ice cubes. To get the ice cubes to stick together, they will need to spray one with water and then hold another onto it for about ten seconds.
3. When the timer beeps, kids present their sculptures to the group, explaining what they did and why.
4. Declare a winner for the most creative sculpture.

TEACHABLE MOMENT:
Say: It was amazing how those ice cubes stuck together. The teams that did the best were the teams who thought of a plan before they began sculpting. It's best to think through the entire thing first before you begin the work. Do you know that the Bible advises us to do the same thing when it comes to the Christian life? (*Read Luke 14:28–33.*) Jesus told his disciples that it wouldn't always be easy to be a Christian (a follower of Jesus). They should think about what they might need to give up and "count the cost" of living life God's way.

DISCUSSION QUESTIONS:
- What are some of the costs of being part of a sports team?
- What are the benefits of being part of a sports team?
- What's some of the costs of being a Christian?
- What are the rewards of being a Christian?
- Did the ice sculpture work out exactly as you had planned?

MARSHMALLOW RACE

Team Game

OVERVIEW
Kids pick up marshmallows with straws and race to fill their team mugs.

SCRIPTURE CONNECTION:
I Chronicles 5:17

SUPPLIES:
- Mini marshmallows
- Two tables
- Straws, one per player
- Mugs, one per team
- Hot chocolate with marshmallows

PREPARATION:
Spread out some mini marshmallows on one of the tables. Place one mug per team on the second table.

TIP:
This game is designed to play inside after the kids are done playing outside, but it could easily be done outside as well.

HOW TO PLAY:

1. Kids divide into even teams and stand behind the second table. Give each kid a straw.
2. On your signal, the first player on each team will run to the marshmallow table, suck up a marshmallow with their straw and run back to their team mug to deposit it. If it falls during transit, they pick it back up using only their straw.
3. After the first marshmallow has been deposited, the second player will race. The game continues, relay-race style, until one team finishes. Whoever finishes first, wins!
4. After the race, serve hot chocolate with fresh marshmallows!

TEACHABLE MOMENT:

Say: Hot chocolate is a reward for enduring those freezing temperatures. There are many times in life that we are rewarded for hard work. The same was true in Bible times. Once, there was a King who did the right thing by tearing down idols of false gods. But he got discouraged and wasn't sure he should continue doing things God's way. (*Read 1 Chronicles 5:17.*)

DISCUSSION QUESTIONS:

- What advice was the king given?
- When was a time you felt discouraged about doing the right thing?
- How does God strengthen us?
- Has there been a time in your life when you were rewarded for hard work?

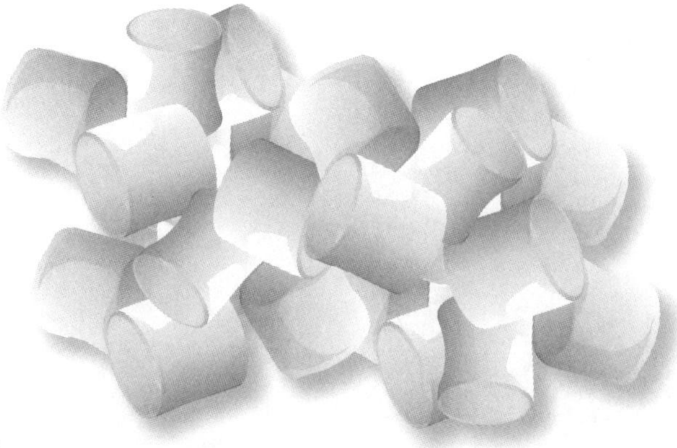

SMALL GROUP GAMES

WINDOW HOPSCOTCH

Individual Game

OVERVIEW
In this unique version of hopscotch, kids jump through a board that looks a lot like a window.

SCRIPTURE CONNECTION:
Isaiah 49:16

SUPPLIES:
- Sidewalk Chalk
- Small stone

PREPARATION:
Draw a rectangle about 3x7 feet onto the pavement and divide into twenty-one squares (each square is about 12x12 inches). Number the squares from one to twenty-one.

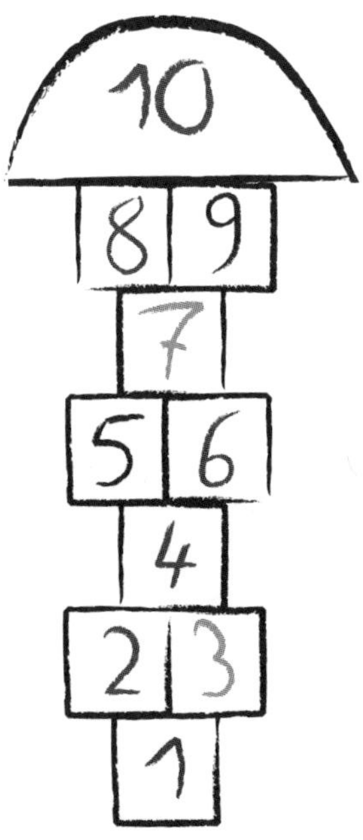

HOW TO PLAY:
1. Line kids up near the #1 square. The first player throws a stone onto any square and hops on one foot through the numbers (in order) until player retrieves their stone and hops back to the beginning of the course (still on one foot).
2. If the trip is successful, player initials the square and uses this square as a rest stop, putting both feet down. However, all other players jump over it.
3. The game continues in this way, with each player tossing a stone and hopping. If the stone lands on a square that is already initialed, the player throws again. The game ends when all the squares are initialed.
4. The player with the most initialed squares at the end of the game answers, or chooses a volunteer to answer one of the Discussion Questions below.

TEACHABLE MOMENT:
Say: We wrote our names on these squares so we could keep track of whose square was whose. If we didn't do that, we would forget where you could stop or where you needed to hop. When something is important, we write it down. There is a verse in the Bible that tells us that God writes our names in the palm of his hands. (*Read Isaiah 49:16.*)

DISCUSSION QUESTIONS:
- Writing our names on God's hand is a way of saying that God will never forget us. He wants to remember us. He loves us and wants to be a part of our lives.
- How do you think God remembers every single person in the world?
- What are other ways to remember important things?

USE YOUR NOODLE

Team Race

OVERVIEW
Kids use pool noodles to get balloons into a laundry basket.

SCRIPTURE CONNECTION:
Psalm 1:3-4

SUPPLIES:
- Pool noodle, one for each child
- Laundry baskets, one for each team
- Inflated balloons
- Timer

PREPARATION:
Place at least ten inflated balloons in the center of the room. Place a laundry basket at each of two walls opposite each other.

TIP:
This game is best played inside.

$ TIP:
If you don't have enough pool noodles, create smaller teams and take turns playing the game.

HOW TO PLAY:

1. Kids divide into two teams and give each child a pool noodle.
2. Set the timer to two to three minutes. On your signal, kids will hit a balloon out of the middle pile and towards their laundry basket.
3. The object of the game is to get as many balloons as possible into their team's basket before the timer runs out.
4. Kids may work together to hit a single balloon into the laundry basket, but they may only touch the balloon with their noodles. No hands, feet, or head.

TEACHABLE MOMENT:

Say: Those balloons were hard to keep under control! They were blowing and drifting everywhere! The Bible talks a little bit about people like this. In Psalms, David (the author) says that the wicked are like chaff blowing in the wind. Chaff is a part of the wheat plant–it is very light, just like our balloons. On the other hand, the righteous are like a tree that is planted by the water–strong, steady, and able to stay in one place. (*Read Psalm 1.*)

DISCUSSION QUESTIONS:

- What was the hardest part of this game?
- What would have happened if the balloons were weighed down with something?
- Do you think you would rather be a tree planted by the water or chaff blown about by the wind?
- Why do you think the wicked are blown around like the balloons in our game?

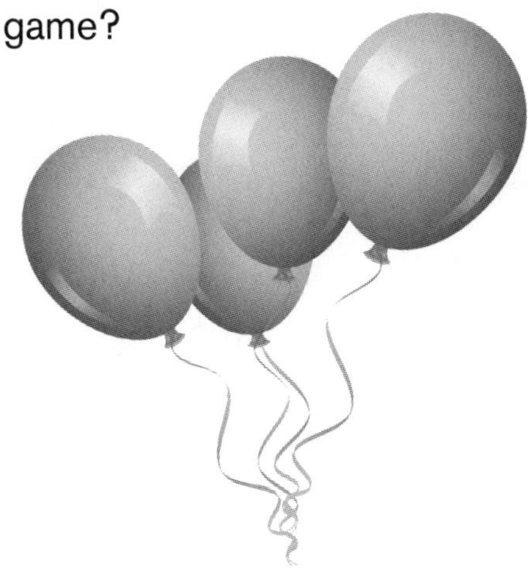

FIND YOUR SPECIES

Seek and Find Game

OVERVIEW
Kids divide into teams by type of animal and then race to find all the creatures in their category.

SCRIPTURE CONNECTION:
Genesis 1:21, 25

SUPPLIES:
- Find Your Species, Animal Cards, page 291
- Large space to hide cards in

PREPARATION:
Make one copy of the Find Your Species Animal Cards for each team or child to serve as a checklist. Make another copy to cut apart and hide throughout the room.

TIP:
You can also hide tiny plastic creatures instead of the cards. Keep an even number for each category.

HOW TO PLAY:
1. Assign each child a category of animal (mammal, bird, insect, fish, etc.). If you have more children than categories, pair them up into teams.
2. On your signal, kids will look around the room for all the creatures on their list. For example, bird kids will look for crows, ravens, blue jays, etc.
3. If they find a creature that does not fit into their category, such as a bird kid finding a frog, they should leave it where it is.
4. The first child or team to find all five creatures in their category answers one of the Discussion Questions below.
5. If you want to make it even tougher, take away the checklist and kids play without them.

TEACHABLE MOMENT:
Say: It's hard to believe there are so many different types of animals and bugs here on the earth. I wonder if it was hard for God to think of all the different animals to create? Let's take a closer look at Genesis 1 which tells about the creation of the world. (Select a few verses, such as 21 and 25 to read to the kids). God made all the creatures on the earth including humans. What an amazing God we have!

DISCUSSION QUESTIONS:
- How hard was it to find all the creatures on your list?
- What is your favorite animal? Is it on anyone's list today?
- Why do you think God created so many different types of creatures?

MONKEY IN THE MIDDLE

Individual Game

OVERVIEW
Players toss a ball around a circle, trying to keep it away from the monkey in the middle.

SCRIPTURE CONNECTION:
Hebrews 13:2

SUPPLIES:
- Playground ball

PREPARATION:
None

TIP:
This game is best played inside.

HOW TO PLAY:

1. Kids stand in a circle with one child in the middle. If you only have three kids, have the kids stand in a straight line with the person in the middle as the "monkey."
2. The object of the game is for the kids in the circle to toss the ball to one another without the monkey getting it.
3. If the monkey can snatch the ball, monkey switches place with the person who threw it, and play continues.

TEACHABLE MOMENT:

Say: This game is pretty fun–unless you are the monkey in the middle. It's tough to be that person who can never touch the ball. This game is designed to leave someone out. It's okay for a few minutes, but its not fun to play like that for long! The Bible tells us that we should provide hospitality to strangers. (*Read Hebrews 13:2.*) This means we should show kindness and help others. Often, it means using your home to make someone else feel special or included. The Bible says we might be interacting with angels when we do this!

DISCUSSION QUESTIONS:

- Have you ever felt left out in real life?
- It can be hard to include everyone all the time, but we can certainly try our best not to exclude anyone. If you notice someone feeling alone or left out, what can we do to help?
- What are ways we can show hospitality to others?

IN OR OUT

Individual Game

OVERVIEW
Players hop from square to square, trying to stay inside the box (all while blindfolded!).

SCRIPTURE CONNECTION:
Proverbs 4:26

SUPPLIES:
- Sidewalk chalk
- Blindfold
- Pavement to draw on

PREPARATION:
Draw a large rectangle on the ground. Divide it into six squares. Each square should be big enough for a child to stand in it. Number the squares from one to six.

TIP:
If you're playing this game inside, you can use painter's tape on the carpet/floor instead of the sidewalk chalk on the pavement.

HOW TO PLAY:
1. One child begins by standing in the first square and putting on blindfold. Player takes a small hop forward, trying to land squarely in the next square.
2. The rest of the children yell "In" or "Out" depending on where player has landed.
3. If player is indeed in the square, player continues trying to hop into the next square. The group calls out "In" or "Out" with each leap.
4. Players turn is over when players lands outside the square It is then the next player's turn.
5. Play continues until everyone has a chance to play. Repeat as time and interest allows.

TEACHABLE MOMENT:
Say: This game would have been pretty easy if you didn't have to wear that blindfold! You had to remember the layout of the board, but it was easy to get confused after a few jumps! The Bible tells us that we should think about the path of our feet. We need to consider where we are headed with our actions. It's easy to get off track and confused in life, just like it was in this game! (*Read Proverbs 4:26.*)

DISCUSSION QUESTIONS:
- What do you think keeps us on the right track in life?
- What do you think "blinds" us in life?
- What helps us to see clearly?
- How does reading the Bible and prayer help us in life?

BALLOON WAITER

Individual Race

OVERVIEW
Kids balance an inflated balloon on a tray. Easy does it!

SCRIPTURE CONNECTION:
Psalm 37:23-24

SUPPLIES:
- Balloons, at least one per player
- Metal or plastic trays (cookie trays, serving trays), one per player

PREPARATION:
Blow up balloons.

TIP:
This game is best played inside.

HOW TO PLAY:

1. Hand each player a balloon and a tray. Players put their balloon on top of their tray and carefully balance it.
2. Have everyone start with one foot touching a wall of the room.
3. Kids cross the room while balancing the balloon on the tray, touch the opposite wall, and return to the starting wall. If the balloon falls off the tray, the player starts again at the last wall they touched.
4. The first player to finish answers, or chooses a volunteer to answer, one of the Discussion Questions below.

TEACHABLE MOMENT:

Say: It was tricky to keep those balloons on the tray, wasn't it? Sometimes doing the right thing is kind of like this game. We try our hardest to do the right thing, but when we mess up, things come tumbling down. Thankfully, God's grace allows us to get up and keep on trying. There is a verse in the Bible that tells us that even though we might stumble, God will uphold us. We will not fall to destruction. (*Read Psalm 27:23–24.*)

DISCUSSION QUESTIONS:

- What was the hardest part of this game?
- What caused the balloon to fall off? Was going to fast a factor?
- How do you think this game relates to your life?

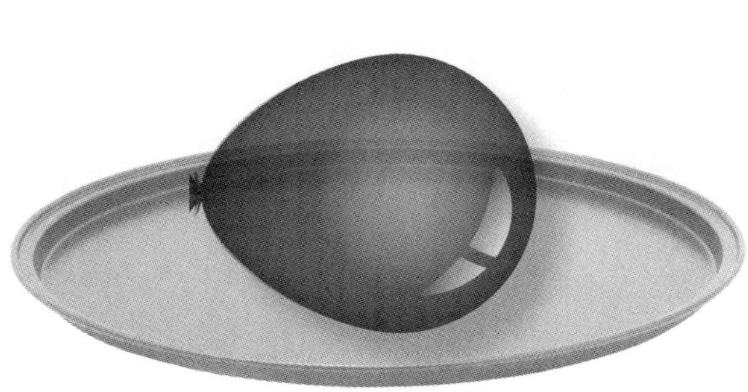

SMALL GROUP GAMES AGES: 4–12 TIME NEEDED: 10 MIN

FLYING DISC TOSS

Individual Game

OVERVIEW
Kids take turns tossing a flying disc at a target. Highest score wins!

SCRIPTURE CONNECTION:
I Samuel 17:48-49

SUPPLIES:
- Three to five flying discs
- Tall cardboard box
- Utility knife
- Permanent marker

PREPARATION:
Cut two or three slits in one side of the cardboard. Make one slit fairly small and the other slits larger. Assign points to the openings. For example, the small slit is 100 points, the larger openings are 50 or 25 points.

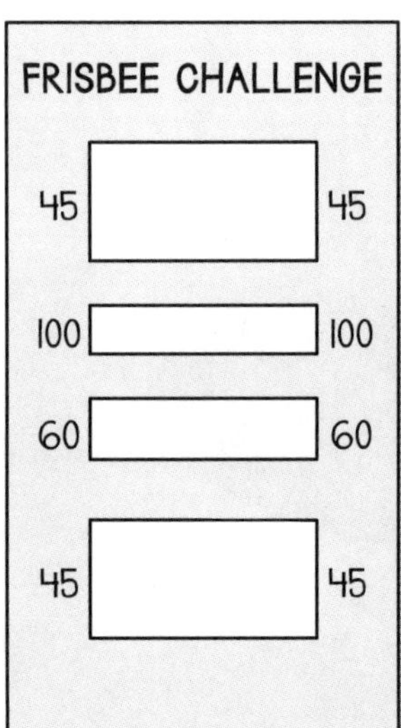

HOW TO PLAY:

1. Kids take turns tossing the flying disc towards the box. Kids stand a few feet from the cardboard box (depending on age). At each turn, they can throw three flying discs.
2. Play until everyone has had a chance to throw, keeping track of points as you go. Declare a winner!

TEACHABLE MOMENT:

Say: This game is harder than it looks, especially if you are trying to get a flying disc into the 100-point slot! Someone in the Bible had a tough task like this too. (*Read 1 Samuel 17:48–49.*) David had to hit a target as you did, but his situation was a bit different! There was a giant who challenged God's people, the Israelites. No one was brave enough to fight him, except for David. David knew, with God's help, he could defeat Goliath. He used a slingshot to throw a rock at the giant, and it hit him square in the forehead and killed him! Now that took some serious aim!

DISCUSSION QUESTIONS:

- How you think David felt about fighting Goliath?
- The Bible tells us that David brought five stones with him into battle, but he only needed one. What do you think it would have been like if David missed at first?
- Most people thought it was impossible to defeat Goliath, but we know with God, all things are possible.
- Have you ever faced a difficult situation like David?

DIGGING FOR TREASURE

Individual Race

OVERVIEW
Kids sift through rice to check things off the list.

SCRIPTURE CONNECTION:
Proverbs 2:3-5

SUPPLIES:
- Box or plastic bin filled with rice
- Small items from Rice Find Checklist, page 292
- Timer

PREPARATION:
Gather up all the items from the checklist and place them inside the bin/box filled with rice.

TIP:
Prepare two boxes or bins. Kids race against each other instead of using the timer.

HOW TO PLAY:

1. Have a child sift through the rice to find all the things on the checklist.
2. Start the timer when they begin looking and keep track of each time. Whoever can find all ten items the fastest is the winner!
3. Want to make it even harder? Make a rule that the kids find and check off the items in the same order as they are written on the checklist.

TEACHABLE MOMENT:

Say: Playing this game, you might have felt a bit like you were searching for buried treasure! Do you know that the Bible talks about buried treasure, too? In the book of Proverbs, there is a verse that says we should search for insight (wisdom) like we would search for buried treasure. (*Read Proverbs 2:3–5.*) Wisdom and understanding are very valuable—as valuable as treasure! Next time you go digging in a sandbox (or rice box!), be sure to remember how valuable wisdom and understanding are.

DISCUSSION QUESTIONS:

- Why do you think it is sometimes hard to understand the ways of God?
- Why is wisdom so valuable?
- What is one way that we can gain understanding and knowledge of God?

CRAZY COSTUMES

Individual Game

OVERVIEW

Kids dig through boxes of clothing to find something that matches the card.

SCRIPTURE CONNECTION:
Matthew 6:28-29

SUPPLIES:
- Several articles of clothing
- Boxes, one for each player
- Crazy Costume cards, page 293
- Optional: Camera

PREPARATION:
In the weeks before playing this game, ask people in church to bring their cast-off clothing. Fill each box with fifteen to twenty articles of clothing. Make a copy of the Crazy Costume Cards and cut apart the cards. Place the cards face down on the table.

HOW TO PLAY:
1. Have each player stand near a box.
2. Select one card from the pile on the table and yell out the description.
3. Children search inside their box to find something that matches that category or descriptor and put it on. The first to successfully wear the proper article of clothing wins that round.
4. Draw another card and continue the game. Kids should keep the previous article on as they search for the next article.
5. Play for five rounds, and then kids return the clothing to the boxes. Optional: Take some photos before kids return clothing to the boxes.

TEACHABLE MOMENT:

Say: Those were some pretty crazy costumes you guys. We wear clothes every day. Some days we hardly think about what to put on, but some days when we worry about what to wear. Did you know that in the Bible, people used to worry about their clothing too? (*Read Matthew 6:28–29.*) Back then people might have worried about not having enough to wear. The Bible tells us that God will take care of our needs. We are told that we should not worry about our clothing. God clothes the flowers in the fields, and he will give us what we need as well.

DISCUSSION QUESTIONS:
- Our verse mentions King Solomon. Have you ever heard of him before? What do you think kings wore in the ancient times?
- When was the last time you worried about what to wear?
- God will provide our needs, but he often uses people to provide. When you learn of this need others have, what can you do?

FOUR CORNERS CRAZY COSTUMES

Individual Race

OVERVIEW
Kids race to a box and dig through it to find something in a specific color.

SCRIPTURE CONNECTION:
Genesis 37:3-4

SUPPLIES:
- Several articles of clothing (Ask people in church bring their cast-offs!)
- Four large boxes
- List of colors (in case you're forgetful)
- Optional: Camera

PREPARATION:
Place the four boxes in the four corners of the room. Fill the boxes with various articles of clothing.

HOW TO PLAY:
1. Kids begin in the center of the room.
2. Call out a color (and cross it off your list). Kids pick a corner to run to and then try to find an article of clothing that is the appropriate color. (They cannot run to another corner if there are no appropriate colors).
3. When they find the colored clothing item, they then put it on and run back to the center of the room.
4. Wait until three kids have returned to the center and then have them repeat the words to a memory verse or tell a fact from the Bible story.
5. Have the kids return the clothing to any box of their choosing and then play again as time allows. Optional: Take some photos before kids return clothing to the boxes.

TEACHABLE MOMENT:
Say: In the Bible, we read about a boy who received a special gift from his father. Joseph was given a coat of many colors. (*Read Genesis 37:3–4.*) Most articles of clothing in ancient times were one color, so to have a coat of many colors was very unique. Joseph must have felt very loved by his father, but this special coat caused a lot of problems with his brothers. They were jealous and upset that Joseph got such an expensive gift.

DISCUSSION QUESTIONS:
- Would you like dressing in only solid colors as they did in Bible times?
- Why do you think Joseph's brothers were so jealous of the coat of many colors?
- What has made you jealous before?

DANIEL'S MENU

Individual Race

OVERVIEW
Kids will search through magazines to complete Daniel's Menu.

SCRIPTURE CONNECTION:
Daniel 1:12-13

SUPPLIES:
- Daniel's Menu on page 270
- Glue sticks
- Scissors
- Food magazines
- Grocery store ads

PREPARATION:
Make copies of the menu, one per child. Spread out the magazines and grocery store ads across the table.

HOW TO PLAY:

1. Give each child a copy of Daniel's Menu along with scissors and a glue stick.
2. On your signal, kids will look through the magazines and ads to try to find the vegetables named on the menu. They cut out pictures and glue them to their menus.
3. Whoever finishes first answers one of the Discussion Questions below or selects a volunteer to answer.

TEACHABLE MOMENT:

Say: There was some delicious looking food here, wasn't there? A long time ago, a man named Daniel was taken to Babylon. (*Read Daniel 1:12–13.*) He was to serve the king. The king wanted him to eat certain meat and wine, but Daniel didn't feel it was right. Instead, he asked for only vegetables. At first, the guard was worried. Would Daniel still be healthy with this new food? They decided to try it for ten days, and Daniel looked better than anyone else after that.

DISCUSSION QUESTIONS:

- What would it be like to use Daniel's eating plan of only vegetables?
- Why do you think Daniel looked so healthy after the ten days?
- What are your favorite foods? Which of your favorites do you think Daniel would not have eaten?

TASTE AND SEE

Partner Game

OVERVIEW
Kids race to a box and dig through it to find something in a specific color.

SCRIPTURE CONNECTION:
Psalm 34:8

SUPPLIES:
- Jelly beans
- Blindfolds, one for each pair of kids
- Note cards
- Pencils

PREPARATION:
Place jelly beans in small cups or baggies, making one per team.

HOW TO PLAY:

1. Pair kids up and give each pair a blindfold, a note card (with pencil) and a small handful of jelly beans.
2. Have one child put on a blindfold.
3. On your signal, the non-blindfolded partner will place a jelly bean in the hand of their friend. The blind-folded friend will taste the jelly bean and try to guess the color of the jelly bean.
4. If they guess correctly, they get a point (make a tally mark on the note card). If they do not guess correctly, they get no points and move onto the next jelly bean.
5. A pair wins when they guess ten beans correctly.

TEACHABLE MOMENT:

Say: That was a fun game—especially if you were already feeling hungry! It reminds me a lot of a verse in the Bible. (*Read Psalm 34:8.*)

DISCUSSION QUESTIONS:

- Why do you think this game reminded me of Psalm 34:8?
- How can we "taste and see" that the Lord is good?
- How can we hunger for a relationship with God like we hunger for food?

NUMBERS PUZZLES

Individual Game

OVERVIEW

At first, this game seems very easy, but it gets a little more challenging when the kids switch cards with each other!

SCRIPTURE CONNECTION:
Numbers 13:30

SUPPLIES:
- Numbers Puzzle, page 2
- Pencils, colored pencils, crayons
- Scissors

PREPARATION:
Copy one Number Puzzle sheet per child plus a few extra.

HOW TO PLAY:

1. Give each child one of the number puzzle sheets. Have them draw a picture in the space provided above the number. For example, on the number one rectangle, they can draw one cat. On the number two rectangle, they can draw two trees.
2. Allow everyone time to complete their drawings.
3. Kids cut out their rectangles and then cut them apart on the middle line. Have them pass their (now cut-apart) cards to the person on their right.
4. On your signal, everyone will work to reassemble the cards now in front of them.
5. The first to assemble their puzzle wins.
6. If you have extra time, have them pass the cards to the person on the right again and play again.

TEACHABLE MOMENT:

Say: In this game, we had twelve different cards to assemble. There is an important story in the Bible that talks about twelve men as well. In Numbers 13, God's people (the Israelites) are about to go into the Promised Land. Moses sends twelve men to search and explore the land. Most of the men come back scared, thinking they cannot take over the land. One man, though, is sure that God will help them. (*Read Numbers 13:30.*)

DISCUSSION QUESTIONS:

- Why do you think most of the men were so scared?
- Why was Caleb so confident?
- When had God fought for his people before?

BEAN BAG BALANCE

Individual Race

OVERVIEW
Kids balance a bean bag on their heads while following a twisty path.

SCRIPTURE CONNECTION:
Psalm 32:8

SUPPLIES:
- Yarn (playing inside)
- Chalk (playing outside)
- Bean bag (see page 284 for an easy way to make bean bags)
- Timer/Stopwatch

PREPARATION:
If playing inside, lay the yarn on the floor in a twisty and turning manner.
If playing outside, draw a squiggling line with the chalk.

HOW TO PLAY:
1. Give one child a bean bag and instruct him to walk along the chalk line or the yarn. The bean bag should be placed on his head as he walks.
2. Time each player to see how fast they can make it through the twists and turns. If the bean bag falls off, have the child stop, pick it up, and place it back on their head before they continue walking.
3. After everyone has had a chance to play, announce the fastest time as the winner!

TEACHABLE MOMENT:
Say: That game was pretty complicated, wasn't it? It would have been much easier if you didn't have to keep that bean bag on your head! But if you walked slow and steady, you eventually made it through! Life can be a lot like this game. We take it one step at a time, but sometimes sad or bad things happen, and it kind of stops us in our tracks (just like the bean bag falling off). We don't have to dwell on the sad or bad thing though. We can pick up the bean bag and keep on going! God will help direct our paths and teach us the way to go. (*Read Psalm 32:8.*)

DISCUSSION QUESTIONS:
- How will God direct our paths?
- What might cause trouble in life?
- How can we avoid these things?
- What was the best part of this game?
- What was the most frustrating part of the game?

TOOTHPICK PICK UP

Individual Game

OVERVIEW
Players try to pick up toothpicks without disturbing the rest of the pile

SCRIPTURE CONNECTION:
Joshua 7:11-12

SUPPLIES:
- Pack of toothpicks
- Small container with lid

PREPARATION:
To begin, place all the toothpicks into a small container. Shake up the container and then dump the toothpicks on the table or floor (try to keep them in a pile).

HOW TO PLAY:

1. One player tries to pick up a toothpick without disturbing any of the other toothpicks. If he can do it, he may keep that toothpick. If any other toothpicks move while he is picking up the one, he stops his turn. Play moves to the right.
2. Continue playing in this way until all the toothpicks are picked up (or set a timer). Whoever has the most toothpicks at the end of the game wins!

TEACHABLE MOMENT:

Say: It was a little tough to pick up a toothpick that wasn't touching any of the other toothpicks. This game reminds me of a story found in the book of Joshua. When the Israelites obeyed God and destroyed Jericho, there was a man named Achan who took something from that city–something God specifically told the people to destroy. (*Read Joshua 7:11–12.*) Achan thought no one would know. He thought his sin wouldn't affect anyone else, but because of Achan's action–God's people lost a big battle. Our sin always affects others more than we think it will. Because our lives are connected to other people (just like these toothpicks), our actions (right or wrong) will affect them too!

DISCUSSION QUESTIONS:

- How did the toothpicks affect one another?
- How might our wrong actions affect other people?
- Have someone else's actions affected you somehow?
- How might someone's right actions affect you?

SMALL GROUP GAMES | AGES: 4–10 | TIME NEEDED: 10 MIN

CANDY SORT

Individual Race

OVERVIEW

Quick fingers and quick thinking are needed in this sorting game!

SCRIPTURE CONNECTION:
Mathew 25:32-33

SUPPLIES:

- Candy with different colors or shapes
- Egg carton
- Timer or stopwatch
- Medium size bowl

PREPARATION:
Pour the candy into a bowl or onto the table.

HOW TO PLAY:

1. The first player puts only one color or one kind into each of the cavities of the egg carton. Time them using the stopwatch and keep track of scores.
2. Allow all kids to have a chance to sort the candy into the egg carton.
3. The fastest time wins.
4. Have some extra candy on hand for after the game.

TEACHABLE MOMENT:

Say: This was a fun game because we got to sort something delicious! Do you know things were sorted in the Bible, too? In one case, God separated different types of people, but it wasn't a fun occasion. (*Read Mathew 25:32–33.*) At the end of time, God is going to sort people into two groups: those who love him and those who don't. Those who loved him will get to live with him for eternity in heaven.

DISCUSSION QUESTIONS:

- Why do you think God sorts people?
- Why doesn't everyone get to go to heaven?
- What do you think you need to do to be a "sheep"– or someone who loves God?
- Have you ever decided to follow Jesus and serve him with your life?

SHAPES IN A SACK

Individual Game

OVERVIEW
Kids reach into a sack and try to pull out the correct shape.

SCRIPTURE CONNECTION:
Genesis 37:9

SUPPLIES:
- Cardstock cut into different shapes
- Sack, bag, or pillowcase
- Optional: Shapes in a Sack, page 296

PREPARATION:
Copy the shape template onto a few pieces of cardstock. Cut out the shapes and place them inside a small bag or pillowcase.

TIP:
If you want the game to have more of a 3-D feel, grab some toy shapes from the church nursery.

HOW TO PLAY:

1. Gather kids around the bag. Ask for a volunteer and tell them a shape. Have them reach into the bag without looking and feel the shapes inside. Their goal is to pull the correct shape out of the bag.
2. If they succeed, they get to keep the shape. If they pull out the wrong shape, they return it to the bag.
3. Select another volunteer and play again. Continue to play until there are no shapes left. Whoever has the most shapes at the end of the game, wins.

TEACHABLE MOMENT:

Say: A star is an important shape in the Bible too. (*Read Genesis 37:9.*) A star showed the wise men where to find Jesus. There were stars mentioned in the Old Testament several times as well. A young man named Joseph had a dream about stars, the sun, and the moon. He dreamed that all those things bowed down to him in his dream. His brothers did not like hearing about the dream!

DISCUSSION QUESTIONS:

- Why do you think the dream made the brothers upset?
- What did the dream mean? (*Read more in Genesis 37.*)
- How did the dream come true?

LARGE GROUP GAMES

CIRCLE UP

Team Race

OVERVIEW
Players work as a team to circle free players and capture them.

SCRIPTURE CONNECTION:
Deuteronomy 32:12

SUPPLIES:
- Large open space

PREPARATION:
None

HOW TO PLAY:
1. Divide players up into two teams.
2. One team will be the circle makers, and the other team will be the free runners.
3. The circle makers join hands, and try to capture the free runners by forming a circle around them.
4. When a free runner is surrounded and cannot escape, he is out. He sits out until the end of the round.

TEACHABLE MOMENT:
Say: In this game, you didn't want to get surrounded, it feels good to be surrounded. If we are in a new situation, it feels good to be close to someone we love and trust. The Bible tells us that we can dwell in safety because God will surround those he loves. (*Read Deuteronomy 32:12.*)

DISCUSSION QUESTIONS:
- Have you ever been in a situation where it felt good to be surrounded by someone?
- What made it feel good?
- How do you think God surrounds us?
- Can you think of examples in the Bible where God has kept someone safe?
- Can you think of examples in your life where God has kept you or someone you love safe?

PASS IT ON

Team Game

OVERVIEW
Kids race to pass small objects down the line without dropping them

SCRIPTURE CONNECTION:
James 3:5

SUPPLIES:
- Cups, one for each child
- Small but useful objects (paper clips, push pins, buttons, crayon, eraser, etc.)
- Tray
- Optional: Bucket, one for each team

PREPARATION:
For each team, place ten to twelve small objects on a tray. It should be same objects for each team, though you can repeat objects. Place the tray at the starting place. Teams line up single file behind the tray.

TIP:
Want to make it tougher? Kids pass the objects over their head or under their legs.

HOW TO PLAY:
1. Kids divide into teams of eight to ten players.
2. On your signal, the first person on each team will grab a small object, put it in their cup and then turn to dump it into the next player's cup. This continues all the way down the line until the last person receives the small object.
3. Have the last person dump it into a bucket or give them a larger container to hold all the items in.
4. Once the first small object has traveled all the way down the line, the last person will shout to the first person will start another object down the line.
5. A team wins when they have successfully passed all the objects down the line.

TEACHABLE MOMENT:
Say: These things were tough to pass down the line because they are so tiny (hold up one object for the kids to see). Even though they are small, they make a big impact. For example (hold up a paper clip), this is a little bit of metal, but it can hold papers together and help us be organized. This screw (hold up a screw or nail) is small, but it can keep a chair together or even keep walls in place! The tongue is the same way. The tongue is a small part of our body, but we can make a huge impact in the lives of others by the way we talk to them. (*Read James 3:5.*) We can brighten someone's day, or we can make them feel sad or discouraged.

DISCUSSION QUESTIONS:
- How can our words impact someone in a positive way?
- How can our words impact someone in a negative way?
- Have you ever said something that made a person feel good?
- How can we use our tongue to share God's love with others?

GRAB THAT CHEESE

Individual Race

OVERVIEW
In this action-packed game, the mice try to grab cheese while the cats try to tag the mice.

SCRIPTURE CONNECTION:
Proverbs 6:6-8

SUPPLIES:
- Large playing space
- Ping-Pong balls (or other small objects) to represent cheese
- Hula hoops
- Cones

PREPARATION:
Set up the cones in a large rectangle shape in the play area. Inside the cones is the play area. Outside the cones (lengthwise) is the safety zone. Set up hula hoops in the field. Scatter the Ping-Pong balls in the field. There should be at least four Ping-Pong balls per player.

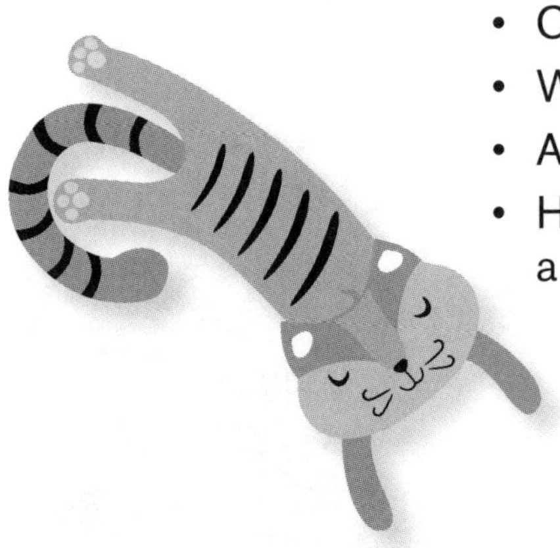

HOW TO PLAY:
1. Choose one player to be the first cat. All other players are mice and should stand in one of the safety areas.
2. The mice try to run from one side of the play area to the other, picking up cheese along the way. If they are tagged by the cat, they drop their cheese and become a cat.
3. The mice may stop for up to ten seconds in a hula hoop, which serves as a mouse hole and a safe place. Only one mouse is allowed in a mouse hole at a time.
4. A mouse can only pick up one piece of cheese each time they run across the playing field.
5. A mouse does not have to pick up cheese on his race across the playing field. He only needs to make it across without being tagged. Once a mouse has collected four pieces of cheese, mouse has successfully stored up enough food for the winter and may sit out when he pleases.
6. The game ends when all the mice are tagged or when they have stored up enough cheese. The mice with four Ping-Pong balls answer one of the Discussion Questions below.

TEACHABLE MOMENT:
Say: Normally, in games like this, you just have to make it to the other side, but in this game—you had to do some collecting too. There are plenty of animals who store up food for the winter. (*Read Proverbs 6:6–8.*) The ants are applauded for their hard work and for thinking ahead and preparing for the winter.

DISCUSSION QUESTIONS:
- Can you think of other animals that store up food for the winter?
- Why do you think there is a verse in the Bible about ants?
- Are there ways that we can work hard and prepare for the future?
- Have you ever waited until the last minute to do a chore or project for school? What happened?

GOING TO MARKET

Individual Game

OVERVIEW

Kids collect fruit cards to play a game similar to Go Fish.

SCRIPTURE CONNECTION:
Genesis 1:29

SUPPLIES:

- Going to Market Cards, page 297
- Large space to spread out and walk
- Optional: Timer

PREPARATION:

Make copies of the Going to Market Cards. You will need four copies for each player. For example, if twenty kids are playing, you will need eighty copies total. Cut the cards apart and shuffle.

HOW TO PLAY:

1. Kids line up single file. Give each player four cards.
2. The object of the game is to get four of the same fruit in your hand. Kids will wander around, ask for a fruit they need, and exchange one card at a time with another player.
3. They maintain four cards in their hands at all times. If they can't complete a trade with someone, they will have to move onto someone else.
4. Once they have four of the same fruit in their hand, they may sit down. The game continues until everyone has four of the same fruit in their hand. Optional: Set a timer for each round.

TEACHABLE MOMENT:

Say: That took some work to find four of the same kind of fruit. God gave us some amazing diversity when it comes to fruits, vegetables, and the foods we can eat. (*Read Genesis 1:29.*) God created trees to produce the same type of fruit, year after year. Whatever you plant in the ground, that's the kind of plant you will get. Can you imagine if fruit got all mixed up like this in real life? Thankfully, God created order for us in nature, and we can plant and harvest without getting all mixed up like we were in this game!

DISCUSSION QUESTIONS:

- Was it hard trying to find four of the same kind of fruit?
- What made it easy or difficult?
- Have you ever tried to grow your fruit tree?
- What would it be like if trees produced mixed up fruit like this game?

PING-PONG TOSS

Partner Game

OVERVIEW
This is similar to egg toss, but each player uses a large plastic cup to toss the ball and catch the ball.

SCRIPTURE CONNECTION:
Job 30:22

SUPPLIES:
- Large plastic cup, one for each player
- Ping-Pong balls, one for each pair of players

PREPARATION:
None

HOW TO PLAY:

1. Have children chose partners. Partners stand close to each other holding a large plastic cup.
2. Give a Ping-Pong ball to each pair and have one partner put it in their cup.
3. On your signal, the player with the ball will transfer it to their partner, using only the cup.
4. If transfer is successful, each partner will take a step backward.
5. At first, it will be easy–dump it from one cup to another. However, the further apart the partners move, the more of a challenge it will become. Kids will have to launch the ball out of the cup and catch it in a cup, without using their other hand.
6. If the ball is dropped on the ground, players sit down where they are standing.
7. The game ends when all the balls have been dropped. The pair furthest apart when they drop the ball wins the game!

TEACHABLE MOMENT:

Say: This was a little bit different version of catch, wasn't it? It wasn't so bad at first, but it quickly got pretty tough. I wonder how that Ping-Pong ball felt? This game reminds me of a story found in the Bible. There was once a man named Job who felt a lot like this Ping-Pong ball. (*Read Job 30:22.*)

DISCUSSION QUESTIONS:

- When you are sad or stressed, what do you do to cheer up?
- What are ways we can turn to God during hard times in our lives?
- What might God do to comfort us or bring us relief?

GUARD YOUR BOTTLE

Individual Game

OVERVIEW
The object is to knock over the other bottles while protecting their own.

SCRIPTURE CONNECTION:
I Peter 5:8

SUPPLIES:
- Two-liter bottle (each player)
- Area to play on
- Sidewalk chalk
- Playground balls (one for every three players)

PREPARATION:
Fill one two-liter bottle at least halfway for stability for each player.

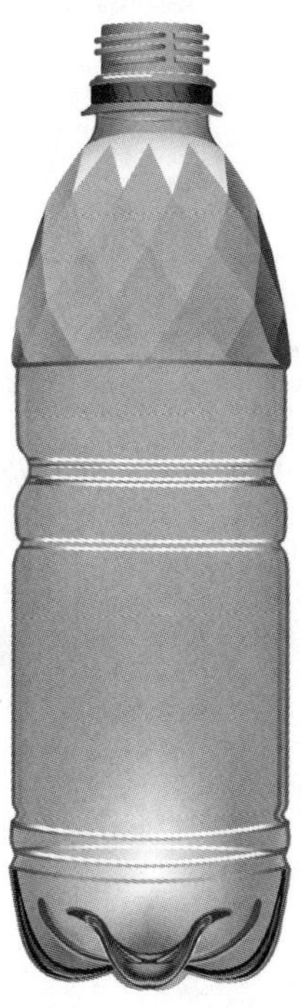

HOW TO PLAY:
1. Give each player a bottle and have them place it on the pavement.
2. Have them draw a small circle around the bottle (about the size of a toy hoop). No one can pass this circle (including the person who drew it).
3. Have everyone stand near their bottles (but on the outside of their circles) and give some players balls.
4. At your signal, players begin to kick the balls at each other's bottles. The object is to knock over all the other bottles while protecting your own. Players can only touch the balls with their feet.
5. They may move away from their bottle to retrieve a ball.
6. The game ends when only one bottle is left standing.

TEACHABLE MOMENT:

Say: There were balls flying everywhere, and you had to watch every angle to make sure something wasn't headed for your bottle! Life is kind of like that too. We're involved in a spiritual battle every day. (*Read 1 Peter 5:8.*) Your enemy, Satan, is always watching for ways to trick us into doing wrong things. The Bible tells us he prowls around like a lion, looking for someone to devour. Look out and avoid temptation. Choose friends that lead you in the right direction. We've got to be on guard to defeat Satan!

DISCUSSION QUESTIONS:
- What was the hardest part of this game?
- What are some ways that Satan tries to trick us and lead us into sin?
- What do you think of the image of Satan as a prowling lion?
- What are some ways that we can be watchful?

WHO'S GONE MISSING

Individual Game

OVERVIEW

If one of your friends suddenly went missing, you would notice, Maybe not in this mixed up, swirling game!

SCRIPTURE CONNECTION:
Matthew 10:29-31

SUPPLIES:

- Blindfold
- Somewhere a player can hide (nearby room)

PREPARATION:
None

HOW TO PLAY:

1. Everyone stands in the circle. Select one player to be "It" and stand in the center of the circle. Blindfold "It."
2. On your signal, everyone will stay in the circle and rotate around "It." As they quietly select one player to hide in a separate room (or around the corner).
3. After a minute or so, have the center person take off their blindfold and look around the circle. See if they can identify the missing person?
4. If it is too easy, kids scramble themselves and form a new circle while the center person is blindfolded.

TEACHABLE MOMENT:

Say: It seems like it would be easy to pick out the missing friend in this game, but sometimes its more work than we anticipated. Can you imagine keeping track of all the people in this town? In this state? In the world? God knows each person, and he knows what happens in their lives. The Bible tells us that God even notices when a sparrow falls to the ground, and we are much more valuable than sparrows to him. (*Read Matthew 10:29–31.*) God knows everything about us, and he loves to be in a relationship with us.

DISCUSSION QUESTIONS:

- What was the hardest part of this game?
- How do you think God to keeps track of all the people in the world?
- How does it make you feel to know God knows where you are and what you are doing?

HE'S ABOUT TO BLOW

Circle Game

OVERVIEW
A variation on Hot Potato stops when "It" counts to thirty.

SCRIPTURE CONNECTION:
Matthew 20:28

SUPPLIES:
- Blindfold
- Foam ball

PREPARATION:
None

TIP:
If you are playing with primarily younger kids, change the counting number to ten.

HOW TO PLAY:

1. Kids stand in a circle.
2. Select one child to be "It" and stand in the middle. Place a blindfold on "It."
3. Give a playground ball to a child standing in the circle. On your signal, child hands ball to the next player. Players continue to pass the ball around the circle as "It" counts to thirty silently in their head.
4. When "It" counts to 30 they shout, "Kaboom!" Whoever is holding the ball at that moment is out and sits down.
5. The rest of the players who are still standing will repeat the process. They will reach over any players to pass the ball. The game continues until there are a few players left standing in the circle who answer one of the Discussion Questions below.

TEACHABLE MOMENT:

Say: There were certainly some unexpected moments in this game! We knew the Kaboom was coming, but it was still surprising at times. In the same way, Jesus coming to Earth was a bit of a surprise for people. They knew he was coming because the prophets had told them, but they were still a bit surprised at how Jesus acted sometimes. The Jews, God's people, expected Jesus to be a great king and defeat the Romans, but Jesus was a suffering servant instead. (*Read Matthew 20:28.*)

DISCUSSION QUESTIONS:

- Were you ever surprised or startled in this game?
- What are some ways people were surprised by Jesus' actions?
- Can you think of a time when people did not like what Jesus did or said?
- How has God ever surprised you or acted in a way that you were not expecting?

WHO IS MAKING ALL THAT NOISE?

Team Game

OVERVIEW
Kids listen close and give their best guess in this animal noise game.

SCRIPTURE CONNECTION: Genesis 7:2

SUPPLIES:
- Animal sounds and player
- Small dry erase boards, one for each team
- Dry-erase markers
- Paper and pencil

PREPARATION:
Check your local library for a CD or search online for animal sounds. Have animal sounds cued up and ready to play.

$ TIP:
If you don't have enough small dry erase boards use clipboards or cardstock.

HOW TO PLAY:
1. Kids divide into evenly numbered teams. Give each team a dry-erase board and a marker.
2. Gather kids close to you and instruct them to listen well.
3. Play an animal sound for the group and have them talk as a team and decide what animal made that noise. Have them write down their answer on their dry erase board.
4. Have all the teams show you their boards at once and award points to whoever has the correct answer. (Note: If using cardstock or clipboards, have the team draw a line through there answer before the next round.)
5. Play again as time permits or consider having a cutoff score.

TEACHABLE MOMENT:
Say: Can you imagine if we played all those sounds at once? You may have heard of a man named Noah before. Noah built a large boat, according to the Lord's command and then loaded up a whole bunch of animals on it! Noah and his family were on that boat (ark) for a very long time! (*Read Genesis 7:2.*) It would have been very noisy and very smelly.

DISCUSSION QUESTIONS:
- How do you think Noah gathered up all the animals to get them onto the ark?
- What would have been the hardest part of being on that boat?
- What would have been the best part?

ALPHABET HUNT

Seek and Find

OVERVIEW
Kids work together to find all the letters of the alphabet.

SCRIPTURE CONNECTION:
Revelation 1:8

SUPPLIES:
- Alphabet cards or magnets
- Pencil, crayon, or marker (one per team)
- Large space with plenty of hiding places
- Timer

PREPARATION:
Write out each letter of the alphabet onto cardstock. Make sure they are spaced into squares. Cut each letter into its own square and hide them all over the play area. There should be at least one of each letter for every team that will be playing. Make extra copies (don't cut them) for the kids to use as a checklist.

HOW TO PLAY:

1. Divide players up into teams. In this game, players stick together and search together.
2. Set the timer for a few minutes and pass out one alphabet checklist to each team. Give them something to mark their page with (pencil, crayon, marker).
3. On your signal, start the timer and send the kids out to search for the hidden alphabet letters. The object is to find as many letters as possible. Teams cannot collect two of the same letter. If they find a letter they already have in their collection, they leave it where it is.
4. The game ends when one team finds all the letters of the alphabet or when the timer beeps. Whoever has the most letters collected when the timer ends will be declared the winner!

TEACHABLE MOMENT:

Say: All the letters of the alphabet are important. It seems like the alphabet–or at least writing–has always been around, but that's not the case. There is something (or someone) who has been around since the beginning of time. God always was and always will be. He is the Alpha and the Omega. He is the beginning and the end. We can count on God because he is beyond time. He has always existed and will always exist. (*Read Revelation 1:8.*)

DISCUSSION QUESTIONS:

- What would life be like if we didn't have any way of writing things?
- What do you think God did before he created people?
- What do you think it will be like to live for eternity?

CRAZY FISH

Individual Game

OVERVIEW
Kids try to get their tissue paper fish from one side of the room to the other.

SCRIPTURE CONNECTION:
Luke 5:4

SUPPLIES:
- Tissue paper, one piece per child
- Fish template
- Cardstock, one sheet per child
- Scissors

PREPARATION:
Draw a simple fish template. Cut a fish shape from each piece of tissue paper. Make one fish per child. You may wish to make extra templates and have kids complete this step themselves. Have each child write their name (carefully!) on their fish.

HOW TO PLAY:

1. The object of the game is for kids to be the first to get their fish across the room. Give each child a piece of cardstock and have them fold it accordion style to make a fan.
2. Kids begin on one side of a room with their fish and fan. On your signal, they will use their fan to send their fish flying.
3. Play until someone successfully gets their fish across the room. Declare a winner!

TEACHABLE MOMENT:

Say: Wow, those fish were crazy! I can't believe how they were flying all over the place. Fish are pretty unpredictable in real life too. It probably takes a while to know where fish like to swim and where you can go to catch them. In Jesus' day, some of his disciples were fishermen. One day, they had been fishing for a long, long time, but had not been able to catch anything. Jesus came along and told them where to put their nets. These were experienced fishermen! Surely, they knew the best places to look for fish. However, they trusted Jesus and did what he said. (*Read Luke 5:4–8.*) That's just amazing! Even when things don't make sense to us, we can know that God understands all things and he is in control.

DISCUSSION QUESTIONS:

- What do you think it was like for the disciples to catch all those fish?
- Do you think the fish in their lake were swimming all over the place like the fish in our game?
- Have you ever had God provide for you or someone you know in a surprising way?

BUILDING UP THE CUPS

Team Game

OVERVIEW
Creative thinking and teamwork are needed in this cup stacking game.

SCRIPTURE CONNECTION:
Genesis 11:4

SUPPLIES:
- Small paper cups
- Measuring tape
- Timer

PREPARATION:
None

HOW TO PLAY:

1. Divide players up into even teams. The object of the game is for each team to build the tallest structure possible. The structure must be stable and be able to stand on its own.
2. Give each team small paper cups and send them into different rooms. It's best if teams cannot see each other working. If you do not have enough rooms for each team to have one, try to spread them out as much as possible.
3. Set the timer for several minutes of work. When time is up, measure each of the structures. The team with the tallest structure answers the Discussion Questions below.
4. Afterwards, kids visit each other's structures to see the different building methods and designs.

TEACHABLE MOMENT:

Say: It's not easy building a super high structure, is it? There is a Bible story about building a giant tower. The book of Genesis, tells how people gathered together and wanted to build a super tall tower. They wanted to be famous because of their tower. However, God did not like their actions, and so he made them all speak different languages. After that, they gave up building the tower. (*Read Genesis 11:4.*)

DISCUSSION QUESTIONS:

- What would it be like to build the tower if everyone spoke a different language?
- Was it hard coming up with a plan for building your structure?
- What happened when the structure got too tall?
- Did anyone have to start over again?
- Why do you think the people in Genesis wanted to be famous?
- Why do you think people want to be famous today?

SIN BATTLE

Team Race

OVERVIEW
Get your swords out and get ready to whack some sin out of your play area!

SCRIPTURE CONNECTION:
Ephesians 6:10-18

SUPPLIES:
- Ping-Pong balls
- Paper towel rolls (empty), one for each player
- Cones to mark the dividing line
- Large space to play
- Timer

PREPARATION:
Set up the cones in the middle of the room to create two sides.

HOW TO PLAY:

1. The object of the game is for teams to use paper-towel tubes to hit as many of the Ping-Pong balls to the other side of the room as possible.
2. Players divide into two evenly numbered teams and stand on opposite sides of the room. Give each child a paper towel roll and scatter the Ping-Pong balls throughout the room on both sides.
3. Set timer for a few minutes and instruct the kids to hit Ping-Pong balls (the "sin") with their paper towel rolls (their "swords").
4. When time is up, everyone freezes and sits down. Count the number of Ping-Pong balls on each side. Whoever has the LEAST amount of "sin" (lowest number of Ping-Pong balls) on their side answers one of the Discussion Questions below.
5. Play continues as time and interest allows.

TEACHABLE MOMENT:

Say: Whew! That was a pretty fast-paced game! It seemed like no matter how much sin you hit away from your side; it just kept coming! Sometimes life can seem like that too—sometimes it seems like we are being tempted from every side to do something wrong! Thankfully, God gave us a weapon to fight against sin. (*Read Ephesians 6:10–18.*)

DISCUSSION QUESTIONS:

- What kind of things did God give us to protect us from sin?
- What kinds of temptations or sins do kids your age encounter every day?
- What helps you fight against sin?

BLIND BATTLESHIP

Team Game

OVERVIEW
This game is played in a similar way to the board game, but kids serve as the ships in this game.

SCRIPTURE CONNECTION:
Joshua 6:3-5, 20

SUPPLIES:
- Cones
- Large beach ball

PREPARATION:
Divide the room down the middle with cones

HOW TO PLAY:

1. Group splits in half and moves to opposite sides of the room.
2. Players pick a place to sit. Instruct them to face away from the other team.
3. Toss the beach ball in the middle of the room. Player who catches ball throws it over their shoulder towards the other team.
4. If the beach ball hits one of the other team's sitting players before touching the ground, that player is out and moves to the side.
5. Whoever is closest to the beach ball grabs it and returns the attack.
6. Play continues for several minutes. Whichever team has the most players still in the game at the end of time answers one of the Discussion Questions below.
7. Create new teams and play again as time and interest allows.

TEACHABLE MOMENT:

Say: If this were a real battle, fighting without looking wouldn't make sense, would it? Sometimes, the battle plans that God gave to his people didn't seem to make much sense either. Take, for instance, the battle of Jericho. Let's read what happened. (*Read Joshua 6:3–5, 20.*)

DISCUSSION QUESTIONS:

- What do you think God's people thought as they marched around Jericho?
- What other people in the Bible were told by God to do things that didn't seem to make sense? (Jonah was sent to the sinful city of Nineveh. Noah was told to build an ark.)
- What kinds of battles do we have today?

KEEP THE BALLOON UP

Team Race

OVERVIEW
Kids are engaged as they try to keep the balloon from touching the ground.

SCRIPTURE CONNECTION:
Matthew 10:29

SUPPLIES:
- Balloons, one for every team

PREPARATION:
Blow up all the balloons.

TIP:
To increase the challenge, tell players that the same player cannot hit the balloon twice in a row.

HOW TO PLAY:

1. The object of the game is to be the team to keep the balloon in the air the longest.
2. Kids divide into teams of five or six players. Give each team a balloon.
3. On your signal kids toss the balloon into the air. They should work together to continually hit the balloon in the air with a light tap (no holding or carrying the balloon).
4. The last team to successfully keep their balloon from touching the ground wins!

TEACHABLE MOMENT:

Say: In this game, we were working hard to keep our balloons from touching the ground. Can you think of other things that regularly fall to the ground? In the Bible, there is a verse that talks about a bird falling to the ground. (*Read Matthew 10:30–31.*) This verse reminds us that God sees all things and is ultimately in control of all things. He cares even about the little sparrows in the world. God cares about all things, especially his people!

DISCUSSION QUESTIONS:

- How many hairs do you think you have? God knows!
- Why do you think God loves people so much?
- How does God show us that he cares about us?

WHAT'S ON YOUR SPOON?

Individual Race

OVERVIEW
The kids speed walk while balancing something on a spoon.

SCRIPTURE CONNECTION:
Proverbs 21:5

SUPPLIES:
- Spoons, one per player
- Jellybeans, one per player
- Ping-Pong balls, one per player
- Optional: Cones

PREPARATION:
None

HOW TO PLAY:
1. Give each player a spoon and have them stand against one wall. Kids hold out spoon in front of them as you put one jellybean on each spoon. Optional: Set up cones if you're playing outside.
2. On your signal, kids walk quickly towards the opposite wall (or another set of cones). If their jellybean falls off, they return to the starting wall and begin again.
3. Once players reach the opposite wall, they return to the starting wall, keeping their jellybean still firmly in the spoon. If it falls out on the return trip, they will return to the opposite wall (not the starting wall) and try again.
4. Once they have successfully walked back and forth with a jellybean, players exchange their bean for a Ping-Pong ball and begin the trek again.
5. When a player has successfully walked back and forth with a bean and then a Ping-Pong ball, they win!

TEACHABLE MOMENT:
Say: Wow, this was a long and tedious race, wasn't it! It was tempting to run, but you certainly couldn't do it for long. Slow and steady was a much better way to win this race. There is a verse in the Bible that reminds us to take our time. (*Read Proverbs 21:5.*)

DISCUSSION QUESTIONS:
- How is this verse like the story of the tortoise and the hare?
- Have you ever rushed through a job just to have to go back and do it again?
- Sometimes God takes a long time to fulfill his promises or cause something to happen.
- Why do you think God moves so slowly at times?

SHARKS AND MINNOWS

Individual Race

OVERVIEW
Kids try to run across a sea of sharks without getting tagged.

SCRIPTURE CONNECTION:
Psalm 91:1-2

SUPPLIES:
None

PREPARATION:
None

HOW TO PLAY:

1. Select one volunteer to be the shark. They stand in the middle of the room. The rest of the group stand against one wall.
2. On your signal, kids attempt to run from one side of the room to the other without getting tagged by the shark.
3. If someone is tagged by a shark, they become a shark in the next round.
4. On your signal, kids play another round.
5. When only a few players remain, they answer one of the Discussion Questions below. Play additional rounds as time and interest allow.

TEACHABLE MOMENT:

Say: There wasn't a lot of strategy to this game—just get to a safe place! You knew as soon as you touched the wall, you were okay for another round. God wants to be a safe place for us as well. (*Read Psalm 91:1–2.*)

DISCUSSION QUESTIONS:

- How does this game remind you of real life?
- How do you think God is our refuge and our strength?
- Tell us about that time when a kid your age might be fearful. How could God help someone in that situation?

LITTLE ONES GAMES

GAMES FOR LITTLE ONES — AGES: 3–5 — TIME NEEDED: 10 MIN

FIND YOUR ALPHABET

Individual Game

OVERVIEW
Players work together to find the complete alphabet.

SCRIPTURE CONNECTION:
2 Timothy 3:16

SUPPLIES:
- Open playing space
- Alphabet cards
- Scissors

PREPARATION:
Write each letter of the alphabet onto cardstock. Make sure they are spaced into squares. Cut each letter into its own square and hide them throughout the play area (or use flash cards).

HOW TO PLAY:
1. When all the kids arrive, send them off in search of the alphabet. When they find a letter, they should bring it to you, and you will begin to arrange them in order.
2. Call out letters that are still needed to complete the alphabet.
3. When all the letters are found, celebrate together!

TEACHABLE MOMENT:
Say: You guys did a great job finding all those letters. Letters are very important. We can use them to write words, books, and lots of things. People wrote the Bible to tell of God's great works and to encourage and instruct us. There are many people who helped write the Bible, but everyone was inspired by God. (*Read 2 Timothy 3:16.*) They wrote down what the Holy Spirit told them to write.

DISCUSSION QUESTIONS:
- Can you think of anyone who helped write the Bible? (Moses, David, Solomon, Prophets, Disciples, Paul, etc.)
- What is your favorite book of the Bible?
- What is your favorite Bible story?

SLITHERING SNAKE

Individual Game

OVERVIEW
Children try to jump from one side of the "snake" to the other without getting bitten.

SCRIPTURE CONNECTION:
Genesis 3:1-4

SUPPLIES:
Long jump rope

PREPARATION:
Lay the rope down on the ground.

HOW TO PLAY:

1. Kids line up alongside the rope.
2. Kneel down and grab onto one end of the rope. Begin shaking it back and forth, so it looks like a slithering snake.
3. When you call, "Jump," kids try to jump from one side of the snake to the other without getting "bitten" (touched by the rope).
4. If they are bitten, players sit down at the side.
5. Play until there are only one or two players left. Play additional rounds as time and interest allow.

TEACHABLE MOMENT:

Say: The Bible mentions snakes or serpents a few times throughout Scripture. The one you are probably know the most is from the Garden of Eden. (*Read Genesis 3:1–4.*) This tricky snake did not bite Adam and Eve, but he told them lies. Adam and Eve believed the snake instead of God because of their decision, they could no longer live in the wonderful garden.

DISCUSSION QUESTIONS:

- What do you think Adam and Eve were thinking when they were talking to the tricky snake in the Garden of Eden?
- Do you think all the animals talked? What would you do if you saw a talking snake?

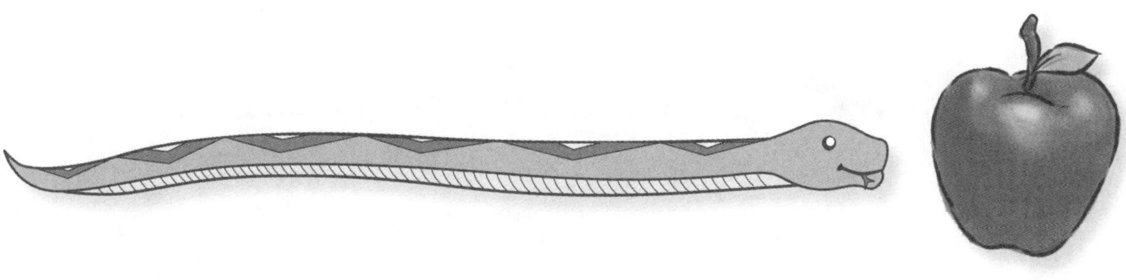

KANGAROO RACE

Individual Game

OVERVIEW
Children race from start to the finish, hopping like a kangaroo (and trying not to pop their balloon!)

SCRIPTURE CONNECTION:
Ephesians 2:10

SUPPLIES:
- Cones or rope
- Inflated balloon for each player (plus extras)

PREPARATION:
Set up cones or rope to make start and finish lines. Blow up at least one balloon per child and a few extra.

TIP:
If the balloon is too tough for the two- and three-year-olds to manage, have them just make "big hops like a kangaroo" instead.

HOW TO PLAY:

1. Hand each player a balloon and have them line up in a straight line at the start line.
2. Have the kids put the balloon between their knees and instruct them to hop like a kangaroo (at your signal!) from the start line to the finish line.
3. If a player pops their balloon on the journey, they return to the start line to get a new one.
4. If they drop their balloon on their journey, they return to the start line and start again.
5. Whoever crosses the finish line, hopping like a kangaroo, with the balloon intact first, wins!

TEACHABLE MOMENT:

Say: You guys did an amazing job hopping! All animals have a special talent or ability. God made all the animals special just like he made you and me special. God has a plan for every person, and he gave us talents too! (*Read Ephesians 2:10.*)

DISCUSSION QUESTIONS:

- What other animals can hop or jump?
- What is your favorite animal?
- Can you think of any talents or abilities that a particular animal has?
- What about you?
- Do you have any special talents or abilities?

TINY TOYS TRAY

Individual Game

OVERVIEW

Kids try to guess what toy is missing from your tray.

SCRIPTURE CONNECTION:
Isaiah 40:26

SUPPLIES:
- Tray
- Several small toys

PREPARATION:
Arrange tiny toys on a tray.

HOW TO PLAY:

1. Gather kids around the tray and look at the things on it.
2. Have everyone close their eyes or look away while you remove one toy.
3. Allow the children to look back at the tray. Have them guess which toy you just removed.
4. Keep playing in this way, until all the toys are gone.

TEACHABLE MOMENT:

Say: When we first started this game, there was a lot to keep track of! It was a little hard to remember what was missing. Can you imagine keeping track of everything on Earth? What about all the clouds in the sky? Or all the stars in the sky? Did you know there is a verse that tells us that God keeps track of all the stars in the sky? (*Read Isaiah 40:26.*) That's a lot to keep track of. God is amazing!

DISCUSSION QUESTIONS:

- Have you ever tried to count the stars at night?
- How many do you think there are?
- Why do you think God created so many stars?
- What are some other amazing things that God has created?

CUPS ON THE FLOOR

Partner Game

OVERVIEW
Kids should walk slowly and carefully as you try to navigate this cup-filled minefield.

SCRIPTURE CONNECTION:
Psalm 37:23

SUPPLIES:
- Tray
- Several small toys

PREPARATION:
Put several plastic cups (upside down) on the floor creating an obstacle course.

HOW TO PLAY:

1. Select one child to be the first player. Have them select a teammate. Blindfold the first child.
2. The object of the game is to make it through the entire playing area without stepping on or touching any of the cups. The teammate may hold the blindfolded child's hand and guide them.
3. Count how many cups the child touches.
4. After everyone has had a chance to both guide and walk, announce the scores. Whoever has the LOWEST score (touched the cups the least), wins.

TEACHABLE MOMENT:

Say: This was kind of tricky to do while blindfolded. It's a good thing you had a guide with you. God will help to guide your steps in life. (*Read Psalm 37:23.*) To be godly means to follow God's way. It's so exciting to know that God is with us every step of the way and that he cares about all the details in our lives.

DISCUSSION QUESTIONS:

- What do you think it would have been like to play this game without a guide?
- Was it hard to make it through the cups?
- How do you think God guides us in life?
- What is something you could use God's help with right now?

AGES: 2–5 | TIME NEEDED: 5 MIN

X MARKS THE SPOT

Individual Game

OVERVIEW

X marks the place where a treasure is found, but in this game, just getting to the X is the way to win!

SCRIPTURE CONNECTION:
Matthew 6:21

SUPPLIES:
- Masking tape or chalk
- Blindfolds, one for each player

PREPARATION:
Use masking tape or chalk to make an X in the center of the play area.

HOW TO PLAY:
1. Place a blindfold on each player and line them up at the start line or against one wall in the room. Show them where the X is.
2. On your signal, instruct kids to walk towards the X. They want to get as close to the X as possible and then sit down. No moving once they sit down!
3. After all the players have taken a seat, have everyone remove their blindfolds. Measure to see who is closest to the X and declare a winner.

TEACHABLE MOMENT:

Say: That was a fun game! When we see or hear about an X in a certain spot, what is usually nearby? Treasure! Yes, often X marks the spot on a treasure map. Did you know that the Bible talks about treasure too? It's not the same kind of treasure as a pirate, but it's the thing that is most important to us. (*Read Matthew 6:21.*) The Bible tells us that our treasure is where our heart is. Its the thing we think about the most and the thing that means the most to us.

DISCUSSION QUESTIONS:
- What do you think your treasure is in life?
- How does something become a treasure in our life?
- How can we make God the most important thing in our life?

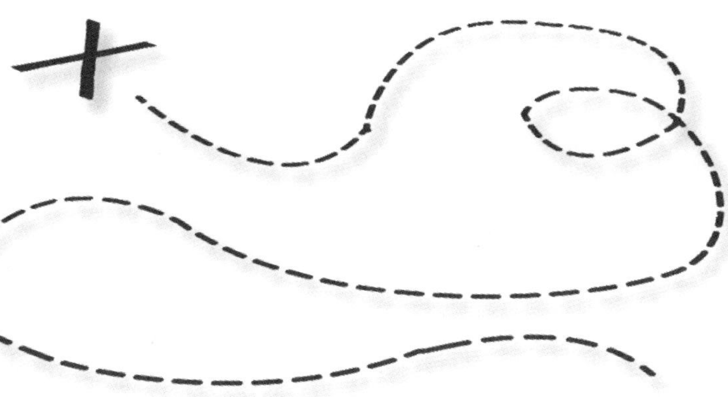

YARN CHAIR

Individual Game

OVERVIEW
In this crisscross game, kids to untangle their chair from a mass of yarn!

SCRIPTURE CONNECTION:
Hebrews 12:1

SUPPLIES:
- Chairs, one per player
- Ball of yarn, one per player
- Tape
- Optional: Empty toilet-paper roll, one for each child

PREPARATION:
Wrap a ball of yarn around each chair. Go through the legs, around the back, until the chair is one big tangled mess. Tape the end of the yarn to the chair, so it doesn't get lost!

HOW TO PLAY:
1. Assign each player a chair and show them the end of the yarn.
2. On your signal, they will begin to wind up the yarn, untangling it from the chair. Optional: Give each child an empty toilet paper roll to serve as a spool as they wind up the yarn.
3. Encourage kids to work as fast as they can.
4. The first player to complete the task wins!

TEACHABLE MOMENT:
Say: That was a lot of work! It might have seemed like we would never get those chairs untangled. It's hard to believe that one little ball of yarn could cause such a big mess! Sin is the same way. Often one sin leads to another until we are in a big mess and we don't know how to get ourselves untangled. That's why it's better to do the right thing from the beginning. (*Read Hebrews 12:1.*) Sometimes we make mistakes and do the wrong thing. It's best to say "Sorry" and make it right rather than try to cover it up. Let's keep as far away from sin as we can!

DISCUSSION QUESTIONS:
- Was it hard to untangle your chair?
- What was the hardest part?
- How is the yarn like sin?
- How can God help you with your sin?

CENTIPEDE SEARCH

Team Game

OVERVIEW
Many hands and many feet may or may not make the task easier!

SCRIPTURE CONNECTION:
John 13:4-5

SUPPLIES:
- Small objects (gold coins, pennies, plastic bugs, etc.)
- Large play area

PREPARATION:
Hide a small objects around the room.

HOW TO PLAY:
1. All the kids join hands.
2. Instruct kids to begin looking for the objects, but they continue to hold hands.
3. Tell them they are a centipede and they move all together. Only the kid at the front or very end can pick up an object with their free hand.
4. If the "centipede" breaks apart, everyone stops and immediately hook back up before they begin searching again.
5. Play until all the small objects are found.

TEACHABLE MOMENT:

Say: Have you ever thought about what it must be like to be a centipede? It's crazy to have that many feet wandering around! Did you know that the Bible talks about feet? People often would walk in bare feet or sandals, and their feet would get very dusty and dirty. Whenever they came into a house, the servants would wash their feet. Can you imagine trying to wash a centipede's feet? One day, Jesus washed his disciples' feet. (*Read John 13:4–5.*) They were very surprised! That was a job for servants, not someone important like Jesus. But Jesus told them that he wanted to be a servant to others.

DISCUSSION QUESTIONS:
- How can we serve someone?
- What is something that we can do to show others that we care?
- What is something that you can help mom or dad with?
- What is something that you can help your brother or sister with?

POM-POM SEARCH

Individual Game

OVERVIEW
Just because a kid finds the most pom-poms does not mean they are going to win!

SCRIPTURE CONNECTION:
Matthew 20:16

SUPPLIES:
- Bag of pom-pom (small fuzzy balls) in various colors
- Index card with point values written on it
- Timer

PREPARATION:
Hide the pom-poms around the room. Make a key of all the colors and assign a point value for each color (for example, yellow is 10 points, orange is 20 points, red is 30 points, etc.) Keep the point values secret!

HOW TO PLAY:
1. When kids arrive, send them out in search of the pom-pom balls. Set the timer for two minutes.
2. When the timer beeps, call all the kids back to you and reveal the point value system.
3. Add up the points based on your key and declare a winner.
4. If you want to play again, have a few kids hide the pom-poms and make up a new key to keep things surprising.

TEACHABLE MOMENT:
Say: It was surprising to learn that having the most pom-poms wasn't enough to win the game. Jesus said some pretty surprising things as well. When Jesus was here on Earth he said some things that people were not expecting! (*Read Matthew 20:16.*) Jesus didn't do the things people expected. He took extra time to care for others and to serve others. Often, we try to get the best for ourselves, but Jesus said the Christian life should be the opposite.

DISCUSSION QUESTIONS:
- What do you think the verse means when it says the first will be last and the last first? Isn't is always better to be first?
- What is something good that kids your age could do that other people might not expect?
- What are some other things that Jesus did that people did not expect?

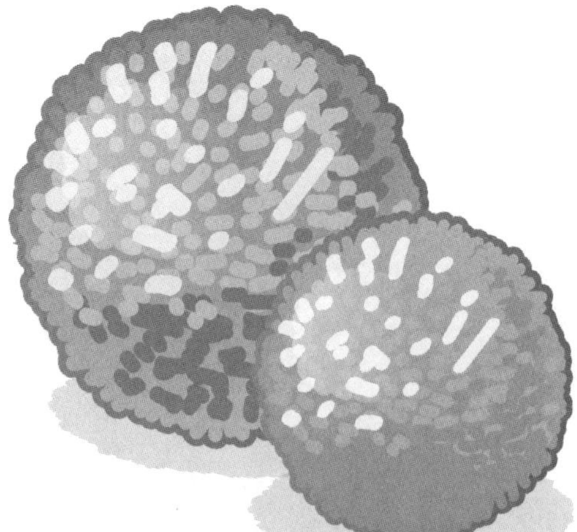

FINGERPRINT GAME

Team Game

OVERVIEW
Kids try to identify their friends by their fingerprints.

SCRIPTURE CONNECTION:
Psalm 139:14

SUPPLIES:
- Ink pad
- Note cards, one for each player
- Cleansing wipes
- Pencil or pen
- Tape
- Toys and books

PREPARATION:
As kids are playing with toys or reading books, one at a time, have children place their thumb on the ink pad and then make a thumbprint on a notecard. Hand child a cleansing wipe to clean their thumb. Label the back of the card with child's name and then tape the card to the wall, with the name covered. Complete with each child.

TIP:
This game is best played with groups of one to five players.

HOW TO PLAY:
1. When all the cards are ready, gather the kids together and point to one of the cards.
2. Say: Did you know that everyone's fingerprints are different? Let's try to guess who these thumbprints belong to."
3. Select one of the cards and have the kids look closely at the print. Have them try to guess the owner and then reveal the name on the back of the card.
4. Continue investigating in this way until all the prints and names are revealed.
5. For extra fun, follow this activity with a thumbprint themed craft (you can find fingerprint themed craft books online or at your local library).

TEACHABLE MOMENT:
Say: It's amazing that every single thumbprint is different! God made us all unique. We are all special in our ways. He is an amazing God, and he made some pretty amazing kids! (*Read Psalm 139:14.*)

DISCUSSION QUESTIONS:
- What are some ways that God made the kids in this room the same?
- What are some ways that we are different?
- Do you think it is good that people are different than each other?
- Have you ever looked closely at your fingerprints?
- What else is special or unique about you?

BABY DETECTIVE

Individual Game

OVERVIEW
Kids are challenged to remember a whole pile of baby supplies.

SCRIPTURE CONNECTION:
Genesis 21:1-3

SUPPLIES:
- Assortment of baby supplies
- Tray
- Blanket or cloth to cover up supplies

PREPARATION:
Lay your baby supplies out on the tray so that each item can be easily seen.

TRAY ITEMS:
Baby bottle, rubber duck, rattle, baby spoon, baby food, bib, washcloth, binky, sippy cup, diaper

HOW TO PLAY:

1. Gather kids around tray and have them look carefully at the objects for thirty seconds.
2. After 30 seconds, cover up the tray with the blanket. Carefully put your hand underneath and remove one object (you might want to have the kids cover up their eyes during this part).
3. Remove the blanket and have the kids guess what object you removed. When they guess correctly, place the item back on the tray.
4. Play again as time allows.

TEACHABLE MOMENT:

Say: Babies sure need a lot of stuff, don't they? Sometimes it seems like too many things! There was a couple in the Bible who wanted a baby, but it seemed like it might never happen. They were getting older and older and still did not have a baby. One day, God promised this couple, Abraham and Sarah, that they would have a baby. It was hard to believe, but they trusted God. (*Read Genesis 21:1–3.*)

DISCUSSION QUESTIONS:

- What kind of things do you think Abraham and Sarah had to do to care for their baby?
- What is the hardest part about caring for babies?
- What is the best thing about babies?

GOING ON A BEAR HUNT

Seek and Find Game

OVERVIEW
Little ones travel over a variety of (pretend) terrains to find a bear.

SCRIPTURE CONNECTION:
Luke 15:4

SUPPLIES:
- Colored fabric or cardstock, green, brown, blue, dark green, white,

PREPARATION:
If desired, set up colored fabric around the room to represent the different areas kids will traverse in this game.

HOW TO PLAY:

1. Kids line up behind you. Let them know you're going to be searching for a bear.
2. Walk through the room chanting "We're going on a bear hunt!" (There are demonstrations of this song online if you want to check them out first).
3. During your trek, you should walk through tall wavy grass (green fabric), sticky, gooey mud (brown fabric), a deep cold river (blue fabric), a big dark forest (dark green fabric), and a swirling snowstorm (white fabric).
4. At the end of your journey, you will look inside a cave together, pretend to spot a bear and run as fast as you can back through all the areas you just traversed.
5. Kids will be delighted by the anticipation as well as the hurry back home.

TEACHABLE MOMENT:

Say: Even though we were looking for a bear, I wasn't sure I wanted to find one! There is a story in the Bible about a shepherd who was looking for a sheep. (*Read Luke 15:4.*) He wanted to find the sheep, so he searched high and low. When he found the sheep, he brought the sheep home to safety. God loves us so much–just like that shepherd loved his sheep. He doesn't want us to get lost and will come looking for us if we wander away.

DISCUSSION QUESTIONS:

- What was your favorite part of the bear hunt?
- Have you ever lost something that was very important to you?
- Why do you think you are very important to God?

NAME A WORD

Individual Game

OVERVIEW

Kids will stretch their brains in this game as they try to think of three words that begin with a particular letter.

SCRIPTURE CONNECTION:
Psalm 119

SUPPLIES:

- Bible with marker at Psalm 119
- Alphabet letters (magnets or another type of 3-D letter)
- Bucket

PREPARATION:

Put all the letters in the bucket.

HOW TO PLAY:

1. Select one child to start the game. They should select a letter and then say three words that begin with that letter. If they get stuck, allow the other kids to work together to help them.
2. Choose someone else to pick a letter.
3. Continue playing in this way as time and interest allow.

TEACHABLE MOMENT:

Say: There are a lot of letters in the alphabet and a lot of words that start with those letters! At first, it might be hard to think of words, but before long, we've got all kinds of words flowing out! The book of Psalms in the Bible is made up of poems and songs. In one particular psalm, the author used every letter in the Hebrew alphabet to begin. (*Show Bible open to Psalm 119.*) They were playing a game kind of like us!

DISCUSSION QUESTIONS:

- Poems sound like nursery rhymes. What is your favorite one?
- What are your favorite songs or poems about?
- Can you think of rhyming words?
  (Use a few of the words the kids came up with and rhyme them.)

SOCK TOSS

Circle Game

OVERVIEW

This sock toss game is milder than other versions since all the kids remain seated as they throw.

SCRIPTURE CONNECTION:
Psalm 64:3

SUPPLIES:
- Balled-up socks, at least one for each child

PREPARATION:
None.

HOW TO PLAY:

1. Select one person to be the first volunteer. They should stand up, and the rest of the group should form a circle around them. The rest of the kids should be sitting.
2. On your signal, kids can throw sock balls at the volunteer. The goal is to hit the volunteer's hands with a sock ball. If a child succeeds in this task, they can switch places with the volunteer and become the new target.
3. Continue playing until kids lose interest.

TEACHABLE MOMENT:

Say: In this game, we were working hard to hit the volunteer's hands with our socks. It was a fun game, and no one got hurt. However, in life, we can sometimes throw things at others that will hurt them—things like unkind words. The Bible tells us that unkind (or cruel) words can feel like deadly arrows. (*Read Psalm 64:3.*)

DISCUSSION QUESTIONS:

- How do unkind words make people feel?
- Why do you think we say mean things to each other sometimes?
- How can we prevent ourselves from saying mean things?

WHERE IS THE COIN?

Team Game

OVERVIEW
Preschoolers try to intently follow the coin as cups move back and forth in this game.

SCRIPTURE CONNECTION:
Psalm 139:3-4

SUPPLIES:
- 3 cups
- Coin or small ball

PREPARATION:
None

HOW TO PLAY:

1. Gather the kids around you. Show them the coin/ball and then place the coin/ball under one of the cups.
2. Move the cups around on the table, switch places and swirl them around. Encourage kids to keep watching the cup with the coin/ball under it.
3. After a few seconds, stop the cups and arrange them in a straight line. Ask the kids to guess what cup the coin/ball is under. Lift the cup to see if they are right or not.

TEACHABLE MOMENT:

Say: This seems like an easy game at first, but if you lose sight of the special cup even for a second, it's hard to figure out where that coin is! With all the people in the world, you might think that God could lose track of a single person easily. But that's not the case! God knows each one of us, and he knows where we are at all times. (*Read Psalm 139:3–4.*) God knows when we get up, when we leave the house, and even all the things we say!

DISCUSSION QUESTIONS:

- How does it make you feel to know that God knows all those things about you?
- How does it make you feel to know that God could never lose track of you?
- How can we feel God's love every day?

HOT AND COLD

Seek and Find Game

OVERVIEW
Kids get hotter or colder depending on how close they are to a missing coin.

SCRIPTURE CONNECTION:
Luke 15:8-10

SUPPLIES:
- Coin or small object

PREPARATION:
Hide the coin somewhere in the room before the kids arrive or when the kids are focused on something else.

HOW TO PLAY:

1. Tell the kids that your coin is missing! Ask them if they will help you find it.
2. As they begin to look, give them clues about how close they are to the coin. The closer they are, the "hotter" they are. You can name specific kids (i.e., Callie is freezing, but Marco is hot, hot, hot!) to help kids get an idea of where to look.
3. Whoever finds the coin first wins.
4. If the kids are old enough, you might let a volunteer hide the coin for the next round.

TEACHABLE MOMENT:

Say: You guys were really good about finding my lost coin! This game reminds me a lot about a parable that Jesus told his followers. (*Read Luke 15:8–10.*) We were just like that coin the woman was looking for. Isn't it great to know that God cares about us so much that he won't let us stay lost?

DISCUSSION QUESTIONS:

- Why do you think God loves us so much?
- What do you think it means to be lost?

WHAT TIME IS IT, MR. FOX?

Team Game

OVERVIEW
This easy to follow game is great for when you want kids to be active without getting too crazy!

SCRIPTURE CONNECTION:
Matthew 24:36

SUPPLIES:
None

PREPARATION:
None

HOW TO PLAY:

1. One child is chosen to be Mr. Fox. He should stand ten feet away from the other players with his back to them.
2. The other players stand against a wall, facing Mr. Fox's back. As a group, they call out, "What's the time, Mr. Fox?"
3. Mr. Fox calls out a time between 1:00 and 12:00. The other players take the selected number of steps towards Mr. Fox. For example, "Three o'clock," would mean the players take three steps towards Mr. Fox.
4. Continue playing in this way. Players should get closer and closer to Mr. Fox.
5. When Mr. Fox is ready, he changes his response. Instead of saying a time, he will yell, "Dinner time!" At this cue, all of the players turn around and race back to the starting wall with Mr. Fox chasing after them to try and catch his dinner. The player who is caught becomes the next Mr. Fox, and the game continues.

TEACHABLE MOMENT:

Say: That was a fun game. We never knew when it was going to be Mr. Fox's dinner time. There is another big event that could happen at any moment–Jesus coming back! (*Read Matthew 24:36.*)

DISCUSSION QUESTIONS:

- Did you know that Jesus is going to return to Earth someday?
- Jesus will take all his followers back with him to heaven.
- Why do you think no one knows the hour or day when Jesus will come back?

QUIET GAMES

WAIT A MINUTE

Card Games

OVERVIEW
Kids have to bluff their way through this game to get rid of all their cards.

SCRIPTURE CONNECTION:
Acts 5:1-11

SUPPLIES:
- Deck of cards, one for every six to ten players

PREPARATION:
None

HOW TO PLAY:

1. Kids divide into groups of six to ten players and give each group a deck of cards.
2. Kids divide cards among all the players (until there are no cards left).
3. Ask if anyone has an ace. If so, they should place it face down on the table. If not, ask if anyone has a two or a three until you get someone with the specified card. This person is the first to play.
4. Play now passes to the right. The next player lays down the next card in order (a two or 3, etc.). If they do not have the card, they lay down any card in their hand and bluff, saying "I am laying down a two" or whatever is the correct card in the order. But are they telling the truth? It's up to the rest of the players to decide.
5. If a player thinks that another player is bluffing, player says, "You're bluffing!" If the bluffer is caught, bluffer takes up all the discarded cards. If the accuser is wrong, accuser takes up the discarded cards.
6. Play continues until someone gets rid of all their cards or as time and interest allow.

TEACHABLE MOMENT:

Say: In this game, you had to be good at lying to win. That's not really how we want to live life though. When we lie to others, we can ruin a good relationship and cause people not to trust us anymore. (*Read Acts 5:1–11.*)

DISCUSSION QUESTIONS:

- Why do you think Ananias and Sapphira lied about the money?
- Why does the Bible tell us not to lie?
- What can you do to make up for telling a lie?

CARD TOSS

Card Game

OVERVIEW
Children race against the clock to toss cards into a bucket.

SCRIPTURE CONNECTION:
Ephesians 4:14

SUPPLIES:
- Two decks of cards, with different backs
- Wastebasket, bucket
- Timer

PREPARATION:
None

TIP:
Tossing cards into a bucket or hat is a long-forgotten skill. The kids may need to practice a bit before the game begins.

HOW TO PLAY:

1. Kids sit in a circle around the basket, a few feet away.
2. Divide the kids up into teams, by having them count off by twos.
3. Give each of the players, on Team #1, a handful of cards from one of the decks.
4. Give each of the players, on Team #2, a handful of cards from the other deck.
5. Set the timer for one minute and give the kids a signal to begin.
6. Players toss cards into the bucket until the timer beeps.
7. Sort cards into two piles, according to the pictures on the back of the cards. Count cards. Team with the most points answers one of the Discussion Questions below.

TEACHABLE MOMENT:

Say: Can you imagine if we were playing this game outside with the wind blowing? The cards were already pretty unpredictable without adding wind! The Bible talks about being blown about by wind or tossed about every which way. (*Read Ephesians 4:14.*) In this verse, Paul is encouraging his readers to continue to grow in the faith. We grow in the faith when we spend time reading the Bible, praying, attending church, and encouraging one another. When we grow in our faith, it is easier for us to recognize what is right, instead of being tossed around like the cards in our game!

DISCUSSION QUESTIONS:

- Do you ever find it hard to know who is telling the truth?
- How does reading the Bible help us to know the truth?
- What was the hardest part of this game?
- What is the hardest part of growing in your Christian faith?

PENNY TOSS

Individual Game

OVERVIEW
In this tabletop game, kids toss pennies into an empty egg carton to score points.

SCRIPTURE CONNECTION:
Luke 21:1-4

SUPPLIES:
- Two egg cartons
- Pennies
- Marker
- Timer
- Optional: Calculator

PREPARATION:
Remove lid from egg cartons and write scores inside each cup. Tape the egg cartons to the table to keep them stable. To reduce the noise, you could play with egg cartons on the carpet.

TIP:
Want to take this game up a notch? Search online for "how to make a penny catapult."

HOW TO PLAY:

1. Kids divide into groups of six to ten players. Ask one child to sit at each end of a table and place an empty egg carton about a foot in front of each child.
2. Give each player a pile of pennies (about twenty to thirty each) and set the timer for one minute.
3. On your signal, allow kids to begin tossing pennies into the egg carton. At the end of the minute, count up the scores according to where the pennies landed in the carton (calculator might be needed!).
4. Declare a winner, gather up the scattered pennies, and play again as time allows.

TEACHABLE MOMENT:
Say: Those pennies were flying in this game! What if you only had a few coins or dollars to live on? There was a woman in the Bible who was in this situation. The Bible tells us in Luke 21 that a widow only had two mites. (*Read Luke 21:1–4.*) We don't know exactly how much this was, but it was very little. What she did with two mites is very surprising. She chose to give them to God. In faith, she knew that God would provide for her, even when it didn't make sense.

DISCUSSION QUESTIONS:

- Why do you think that woman gave her two mites?
- What can you give to God if you don't have money?
- Is there anything in your life that you won't give up? Why do you think that is?

SANDMAN

Circle Game

OVERVIEW

Children are sitting ducks in this "go to sleep" game, unless the awake children can solve the mystery quick!

SCRIPTURE CONNECTION:
James 1:19

SUPPLIES:
- Small pieces of paper
- Pencil

PREPARATION:
Gather enough small pieces of paper for each player. On one piece, make an X (this will be the Sandman). All the other pieces should be blank.

TIP:
This game plays best with eight or more players.

HOW TO PLAY:

1. Have all the kids sit in a circle facing each other.
2. Pass out the papers and have kids keep their assignments secret.
3. When the game begins, kids will glance at one another, trying to determine who is the Sandman. The Sandman also looks around. When Sandman makes eye contact with someone, Sandman winks (or blinks) in order to put the other player to sleep. When a player gets winked (or blinked) at, player immediately falls over asleep.
4. When someone falls asleep, the rest of the players can make a guess at who the sandman is. A player says, "I think the Sandman is_______". If player agrees with them, the accused shows their paper.
5. If the accusers have guessed incorrectly, they also fall asleep until the Sandman is found.
6. Continue play until the Sandman has put everyone to sleep or is discovered.

TEACHABLE MOMENT:

Say: In this game, you had to be very sure to make an accusation. You didn't want to fall asleep for the rest of the round for no reason! In the same way, the Bible advises us to take our time before we leap into action. It tells us to be slow to speak and slow to get angry. (*Read James 1:19.*)

DISCUSSION QUESTIONS:

- Why do you think the Bible tells us to be slow to speak?
- Why do you think the Bible tells us to be slow to become angry?
- What is the hardest part of controlling your anger?

POM-POM SORT

Team Game

OVERVIEW
Kids sort colored fuzzy balls into color-coordinated containers

SCRIPTURE CONNECTION:
Ecclesiastes 3:1

SUPPLIES:
- Assorted colors of pom-poms
- Toilet paper or paper towel tubes
- Paint or construction paper in the same colors as the pom-poms
- Tape, scissors, stapler
- Optional: Chopsticks or clothespins

PREPARATION:
Paint the tubes to match the pom-poms or cover them in colored construction paper. If you have a large group, you will want to make a set for every two or three kids.

TIP:
If you don't want to prepare the toilet paper tubes, grab some small colored containers that match the colors of the pom-pom balls.

HOW TO PLAY:
1. Pair the kids up or put them in groups of three.
2. Distribute a set of tubes and a handful (or two) of pom-poms to each group of kids.
3. Allow the kids to place the pom-poms in the tubes of the same color.
4. When they are finished, check to make sure they sorted them correctly.
5. If the kids are up for more of a challenge, have them try throwing the pom-poms into the correctly colored tube. Optional: Children pick up pom-poms with chopsticks or clothespins.

TEACHABLE MOMENT:
Say: Just like there was a proper place to put each of these colors, the Bible tells us that there are a proper time and place for everything. (*Read Ecclesiastes 3:1.*)

DISCUSSION QUESTIONS:
- Was it hard to sort the pom-poms into the correct colored tubes?
- What do you think of the verse Ecclesiastes 3:1?
- What do you do when you have to wait for something?
- Do you think it is sometimes hard to wait for God's timing?

QUIET ANIMAL

Circle Game

OVERVIEW
Whoever is the quietest in this game gets to hold the stuffed animal next.

SCRIPTURE CONNECTION:
I Chronicles 22:9

SUPPLIES:
- One small stuffed animal

PREPARATION:
None

HOW TO PLAY:
1. Gather the kids up and have them sit in a circle.
2. Tell the kids that you are looking for the child who is being the quietest in the group.
3. When you have found a very quiet child, hand them the stuffed animal.
4. They will then look for the next quietest child in the group. They will then pass on the stuffed animal (with no talking, laughing, or sound) to another child.
5. This continues with the stuffed animal being passed on from child to child based on whoever is being quietest at the moment.
6. If a child laughs or talks, they scoot out from the circle a bit. They are not eligible to catch the stuffed animal until the next round.

TEACHABLE MOMENT:

Say: We're not usually quite so silent! In the Bible times, people often valued times of peace and quiet. During the time of kings in Israel, there were often wars and battles among the people. David was a king who loved God. When David had a son, God made a special promise to David. (*Read 1 Chronicles 22:9.*) Solomon did have peace and quiet during his reign. He was a very wise man and all the people must have appreciated the time of peace.

DISCUSSION QUESTIONS:
- Are there times when you enjoy peace and quiet?
- When do you like to be quiet?
- When do you like to be loud?
- What kind of a king was Solomon?
- Why did God grant him peace?

ROCK, PAPER, SCISSORS

Partner Game

OVERVIEW
This game will keep kids occupied for a few minutes without a lot of noise!

SCRIPTURE CONNECTION:
I Samuel 2:2

SUPPLIES:
None

PREPARATION:
None

HOW TO PLAY:

1. Pair kids up into twos.
2. Kids hold their hands in a fist and count together to three.
3. When the count is up, they will form their hand into one of these three shapes: rock (fist), paper, (flat hand), or scissors (index and middle fingers snipping like scissors).
4. Winner gets one point per round and is determined like this:
    - Rock beats scissors (smashes them)
    - Paper beats rock (covers it up)
    - Scissors beat paper (cuts it up)
5. If both players put out the same tool, it is a tie, and no one wins.
6. Play until the time is up or until one player scores five points.

TEACHABLE MOMENT:

Say: Many of you have played this game before. It's quick and easy and a whole lot of fun. Did you know that the Bible talks about rocks too? In fact, the word "rock" is mentioned in the Bible almost 150 times! (*Read 1 Samuel 2:2.*)

DISCUSSION QUESTIONS:

- How is God like a rock?
- What does Deuteronomy 32:4 say about God being like a rock?
- Can you think of other times that a rock is mentioned in the Bible?

HEADS UP, SEVEN UP

Individual Game

OVERVIEW
Kids sit with their heads down on the table, hoping to get picked. Then the guessing begins!

SCRIPTURE CONNECTION:
I Samuel 16:6-7,10-13

SUPPLIES:
- Table
- Chairs

PREPARATION:
None

TIP:
The game is best with twenty or more players

HOW TO PLAY:

1. Kids sit around the table. Select seven to be the first tappers. If you have a smaller group, select fewer kids.
2. Tappers stand at the front of the room. Everyone else puts their head down on the table, covers their eyes and puts one thumb up.
3. Tappers walk around the room and touch someone's thumb. That person puts their thumb down.
4. When all the tappers have made their selection, they go back to the front of the room. **Say:** "Heads up, seven up."
5. Players who had their thumbs touched stand up.
6. One by one, they guess who touched their thumb. If a child guesses correctly, they change places with their tapper.
7. Play continues as time and interest allow.

TEACHABLE MOMENT:

Say: It was hard to guess who picked you wasn't it? Sometimes a tapper would give it away by smiling, but that wasn't always the case! In the same way, we can't always tell what's going on in a person's heart by how they look on the outside. A long time ago, a man named Samuel was sent to pick a new king of Israel. He went to a certain house that had lots of sons. When he saw the oldest son, the boy was strong and handsome. Samuel thought that he would be a great king, but God told him no. (*Read 1 Samuel 16:6–7.*) God chose the youngest son David, because David loved God. God cares much more about our heart and our actions than the way we look.

DISCUSSION QUESTIONS:

- Why was it hard to know who to pick?
- Why did Samuel have hard time picking the next king if God didn't help him?
- Why do you think God cares about our hearts?
- What's one way we can learn to love God more?

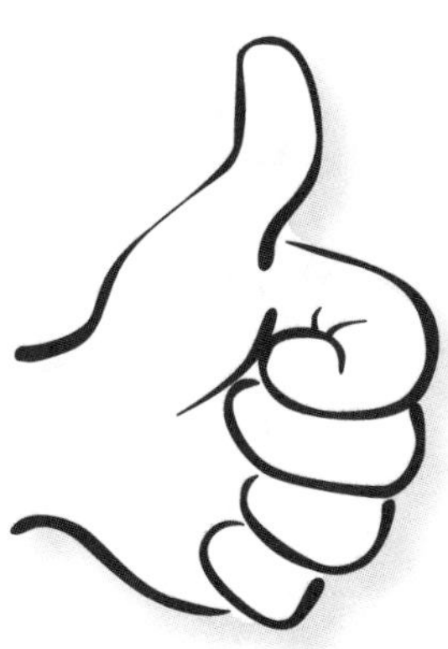

PUT THE PEOPLE IN ORDER

Team Race

OVERVIEW
Kids work to put Bible People Cards in alphabetical order.

SCRIPTURE CONNECTION:
Various

SUPPLIES:
- Bible People Cards, page 298

PREPARATION:
Copy one set of Bible People Cards for each group. Cut the cards apart and mix up each set. Do not mix them with other sets. Each group needs a set.

TIP:
If kids want to play with the cards after the alphabetical order challenge is complete, have them join with another group and play a round or two of Concentration.

HOW TO PLAY:
1. Kids divide into teams of four to five players.
2. Give each group a set of Bible People cards.
3. On your signal, kids will work together to put the cards into alphabetical order.
4. The first team to finish organizing the cards wins!

TEACHABLE MOMENT:

Say: There were lots of people who lived during the time that the Bible was written. These are only a few of the people, but everyone played a part in God's story. You are a part of God's story too! Just like God had a special plan for each of these people on the cards, God has a special plan for your life too. Our job is to glorify God and show people how great he is. Sometimes we can do that by sharing our talents, and sometimes we can do that by just sharing the good news of what Jesus did so that we can become members of God's family.

DISCUSSION QUESTIONS:
- Who is your favorite person on these cards?
- Is there anyone you have never heard of?
- How does it make you feel to know that God has a special plan for your life?
- What kind of talents can you use to glorify God?

ARMOR OF GOD ASSEMBLY

Team Game

OVERVIEW

Kids will roll a number cube to assemble a complete Armor of God.

SCRIPTURE CONNECTION: Ephesians 6:10-18

SUPPLIES:
- Armor of God, page 299
- Number cube
- Construction paper
- Crayons
- Scissors
- Glue

PREPARATION:
Copy the Armor of God page for each child. Create a copy of the Roll Guide below on a board or poster. Optional: Make a number cube using instructions on page 308

ROLL GUIDE:
- Helmet
- Breastplate
- Belt
- Sword
- Shield
- Shoes

HOW TO PLAY:

1. Pass out the construction paper and have everyone draw a person figure on their paper.
2. Pass out the Armor of God page and have everyone cut out the various pieces.
3. Kids divide into groups of three or four. Give each group a number cube.
4. Start with the youngest player in the group, have them roll the number cube. (Checking the roll guide) Have them glue the matching piece of armor to the paper.
5. Play passes to the person on the right. They will roll the number cube and glue on the appropriate piece as well. If you roll a number you already have, your turn is over, and the next person plays.
6. Continue playing until someone gets a complete set of armor.

TEACHABLE MOMENT:

Say: It took a long time to gather up all the armor we needed in this game, didn't it? Thankfully, God doesn't make us roll a number cube to get the spiritual armor! He gives it freely. (*Read Ephesians 6:10–18.*)

DISCUSSION QUESTIONS:

- What is your favorite piece of armor? Why?
- How can we remember to "put on our armor" each day?
- What might happen if we don't bother to equip ourselves with the armor of God?

SILENT BALL

Circle Game

OVERVIEW
This game is a super quiet version of catch.

SCRIPTURE CONNECTION:
Luke 1:20

SUPPLIES:
- Small foam ball or stuffed animal

PREPARATION:
None

HOW TO PLAY:

1. Kids stand in a circle. Give the ball to one child. Instruct child to toss the ball to another, but remain completely silent. Children continue tossing ball.
2. If someone talks, they sit down.
3. If someone drops the ball, they sit down.
4. If someone throws away from other children, they sit down.
5. Last kid to remains standing, wins!

TEACHABLE MOMENT:

Say: This is a game that you probably have played before—but the quiet thing was something new! It was hard to stay quiet in a game that is normally pretty loud. Imagine if we had to go all day like that! That is exactly what happened to a man named Zachariah. (*Read Luke 1:20.*) An angel gave Zachariah a message, but the man did not believe the angel. Because of this, Zachariah had to remain silent for a long time!

DISCUSSION QUESTIONS:

- What was the message from the angel?
- Why do you think Zachariah did not believe him?
- What do you think it was like to be silent for so long?
- How long do you think you could remain silent?

THERE SHE BLOWS!

Individual Race

OVERVIEW
Contestants will be busy trying to blow a Ping-Pong ball off the table with a straw.

SCRIPTURE CONNECTION:
Ecclesiastes 11:5

SUPPLIES:
- Ping-Pong ball
- Painters tape
- Straw
- Rectangle table

PREPARATION:
Place the tape across the middle of a table, dividing it in half lengthwise.

HOW TO PLAY:
1. Select two players and have them stand on each end of the table.
2. Give each player a straw and place the Ping-Pong ball in the center of the table (on the tape).
3. On your signal, players will blow with their straws to try and get the Ping-Pong ball to fall off the table on the opposing player's side.
4. Players cannot move from the end of the table.
5. Whoever can successfully blow the ball off the table first, wins!

TEACHABLE MOMENT:
Say: Are you out of breath? It was hard to keep that ping pong ball under control. Just like the wind, it was hard to predict what blowing on the ball would do. Have you ever been outside and tried to predict what the wind is going to do? It's impossible! Just as we cannot understand the path of the wind, we cannot understand all the ways of God. He's just too great for us. (*Read Ecclesiastes 11:5.*)

DISCUSSION QUESTIONS:
- Why is it sometimes hard to understand what God is doing?
- Have you ever watched wind swirling leaves or snow?
- What is it like?

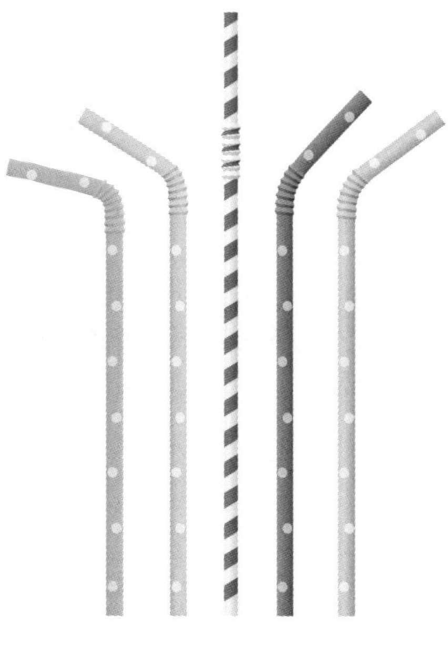

QUIET GAMES | AGES: 5–12 | TIME NEEDED: 15 MIN

MARBLE RUN

Team Race

OVERVIEW
Kids work together to get a marble from one side of the room to the other.

SCRIPTURE CONNECTION:
Psalm 127:1

SUPPLIES:
- Toilet paper tubes, twenty to thirty for each team
- paper towel tubes
- Masking tape, one roll for each team plus extras
- Scissors
- Marbles, one for each team

PREPARATION:
None

TIP:
Ask family and friends to donate their old cardboard tubes. Soon your classroom will be overflowing with them!

HOW TO PLAY:

1. The object of this game is to get the marble from one side of the room to the other using the cardboard tubes.
2. Divide the kids up into teams of four players each.
3. Divide the tubes up evenly among all the teams. Each team should have at least twenty to thirty tubes. Give each team a roll of masking tape and a marble.
4. Teams tape tubes together so that the marble can travel along the tube the entire way. Once the team places the marble on the tube run, they cannot touch it again, so they will need to use gravity to help move it along.
5. If you do not have enough tubes to successfully make it across the room, have each team try to build the longest run possible with the tubes they do have.
6. After ten to fifteen minutes, stop the teams and test the marble runs. Whoever can complete the task, wins!

TEACHABLE MOMENT:

Say: You worked hard as a team to complete the marble run. How was building a marble run like building a house? Building a house takes a lot of planning. The Bible tells us that unless the Lord is with us when we build a house, we will be working for nothing. In the same way, unless God watches over a city, the city will never be safe, no matter how many guards there are. (*Read Psalm 127:1.*) This verse reminds us that we need to trust in God for all things, and remember that all good things come from God's blessing.

DISCUSSION QUESTIONS:

- How do you think God might help keep a city safe?
- How might God help build a house?
- How might he destroy a house?
- What was the hardest part of this game?
- What was the best part of this game?

AGES: 5–10 TIME NEEDED: 5 MIN

BUILD A WORD

Individual Race

OVERVIEW
Kids use letter tiles to build words in this game.

SCRIPTURE CONNECTION:
2 Timothy 3:16

SUPPLIES:
- Letter tiles
- Build a Word, page 277

PREPARATION:
Make one copy of the word sheet. Fill in the squares to make words from a recent lesson, memory verse, or Bible-related words. The words cannot be more than five letters long. Then make copies for the kids in your group. If you have a large group, make a few different sheets, so they will not all be trying to grab the same letters.

HOW TO PLAY:
1. Give a sheet to each child and scatter the letter tiles across the table.
2. On your signal, kids will attempt to fill in their sheet by placing the correct letter tile over each space. The first one to finish all the words wins.

TEACHABLE MOMENT:
Say: These words are all things we can find in the Bible. The Bible is filled with all kinds of words, historical accounts, lessons, proverbs, and parables. Everything in the Bible is useful, and everything comes from God. (*Read 2 Timothy 3:16.*)

DISCUSSION QUESTIONS:
- What is your favorite Bible verse or favorite Bible story?
- What Bible verse have you memorized?
- Why should we read and memorize the Bible?
- What is one verse you can work on learning this week?
- Which Bible stories have taught you something you didn't know before? What did you learn?

Q-TIP MAZE

Partner Game

OVERVIEW
This fun game is a way for kids to stretch their thinking skills as they build a maze for a toy to walk through.

SCRIPTURE CONNECTION:
Psalm 119:176

SUPPLIES:
- Ear swabs (one pack per two players)
- Small person figure toy (one per child)
- Timer

PREPARATION:
None

TIP:
Ask family and friends to donate their old cardboard tubes. Soon your classroom will be overflowing with them!

HOW TO PLAY:
1. Kids divide into teams of two and give each team a pack of ear swabs.
2. Set the timer for ten minutes. Each group creates a maze using the ear swabs (it works best if they work directly on the carpet).
3. If all the groups finish early, you don't have to wait for the timer.
4. When the timer beeps, give each team a small person figure. Teams select a maze (other than their own) and walk their figure through the maze.
5. If you wish, you can time how fast each person can make it through the various mazes.
6. Declare winners based on fastest times.

TEACHABLE MOMENT:
Say: This was a fun game! Not only were you able to make a maze, but you could also explore everyone else's maze too. It was pretty easy to make it through these mazes because we could see from the top, but if these were actual walls, it would be tougher! Sometimes we might feel a little lost in life as well. We might head down a path thinking it's the right way to go, when suddenly, you've run into a dead end. Often, when we forget to read God's word and choose not to obey his commandments, we end up getting lost. (*Read Psalm 119:176.*)

DISCUSSION QUESTIONS:
- Why do you think sheep get lost?
- What are some ways we act like sheep?
- Why did David compare himself to a lost sheep?
- When do you feel like life is a bit of a maze?

POM-POM TOSS

Individual Game

OVERVIEW
Kids toss colored pom-poms through the air to get points!

SCRIPTURE CONNECTION:
Genesis 9:13

SUPPLIES:
- Colored pom-poms
- Small bowls
- Timer

PREPARATION:
Line up five small bowls on the table.

HOW TO PLAY:

1. Depending on child's age, give a child five to ten pom-poms.
2. Set the timer for one minute. Child tosses pom-pom balls into the bowls. They will get a point for every ball that successfully lands in a bowl. If they can get a pom-pom into every one of the five bowls, they will get a bonus point.
3. At the end of one minute, count up child's points and let another child play.
4. Repeat with other children until everyone has a turn.

TEACHABLE MOMENT:

Say: I loved seeing all those colors flying through the air. It reminded me a lot of a rainbow. Can you think of a time when a rainbow was very important in the Bible? (*Read Genesis 9:13.*)

DISCUSSION QUESTIONS:

- Why did God put a rainbow in the sky?
- Have you ever seen a rainbow?
- What do rainbows make you think of?

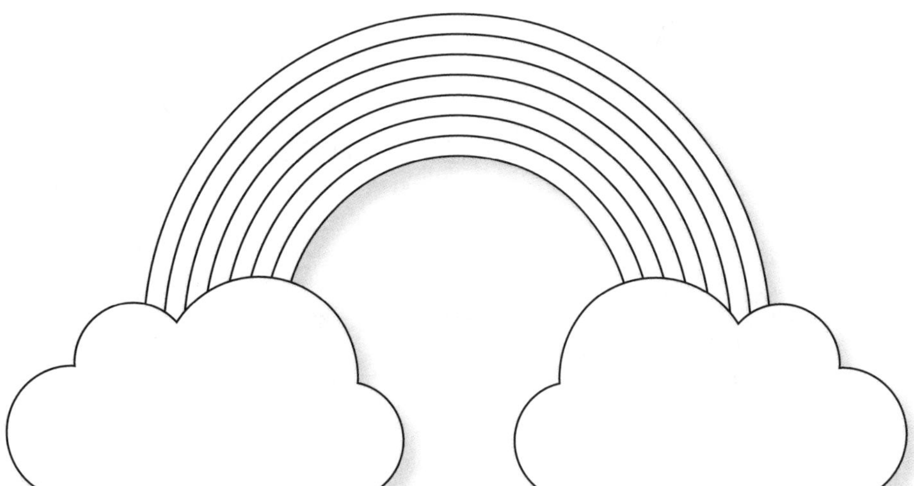

STORY STONES

Individual Game

OVERVIEW
Kids draw pictures on rocks and make up a story with the different pieces!

SCRIPTURE CONNECTION:
Psalm 107:2

SUPPLIES:
- Smooth stones, one per player
- Markers

PREPARATION:
None

TIP:
Take children outside to find their own stones.

HOW TO PLAY:

1. Give each player a smooth stone and a few markers.
2. Have them draw a picture on their stone.
3. When everyone has drawn a picture, have them all sit in a circle (bring their stone with them).
4. Begin a story by giving a setting and a main character (i.e., Once upon a time there was a boy who lived in a big city)
5. Play passes to your right, and that child shows their stone. They add to the story by using the picture on their stone. Once they have added a sentence, play passes to the right.
6. Continue in this way until everyone has contributed to the story.
7. If you would like to play again, have kids switch rocks with someone and play again.

TEACHABLE MOMENT:

Say: That was a pretty crazy story we made up! Sometimes it's hard to make up a story on the spot like that, isn't it? It's easier to talk about something you've recently experience like a trip you took or something fun that you did. God is glorified is when we explain our experiences with him. If God has helped you through something, be sure to tell your friends. (*Read Psalm 107:2.*) God wants us to share our story and tell others about how he impacts our lives.

DISCUSSION QUESTIONS:

- What is a way that God has impacted your life?
- Can you think of a story you've heard about how God has helped someone else?
- How has God saved us?
- What Bible story do you like to tell?

QUICK, NO PREP GAMES

GRAB IT!

Circle Game

OVERVIEW

Stand in a circle and listen close. If your name is called, you've got to grab the scarf before it touches the ground!

SCRIPTURE CONNECTION:
Matthew 10:29

SUPPLIES:
- Scarf
- bandana, or a light piece of fabric

PREPARATION:
None

HOW TO PLAY:

1. Have all the kids stand in a circle. One player stands in the middle holding the scarf or handkerchief.
2. The middle person throws the fabric in the air and calls the name of one of their friends.
3. That player then reaches out and catches the fabric before it touches the ground. If they succeed, they get to stand in the middle and call out the next name.
4. If the game seems too easy for the group, have everyone take one step backward.
5. If the player does not catch it before it hits the ground, the original thrower will get another turn.

TEACHABLE MOMENT:

Say: You had to be paying attention to play this game! Can you imagine paying this close attention to everything in the world all at once? That's how God operates–he pays close attention to everything that is happening in the world and your life. The Bible tells us that not even a sparrow will fall to the ground without God noticing. (*Read Matthew 10:29.*)

DISCUSSION QUESTIONS:

- Why do you think that you are important to God?
- How does God pay attention to everything all the time?
- If you were God, what would you like to watch?
- Why do you think God wants to be involved in our lives?

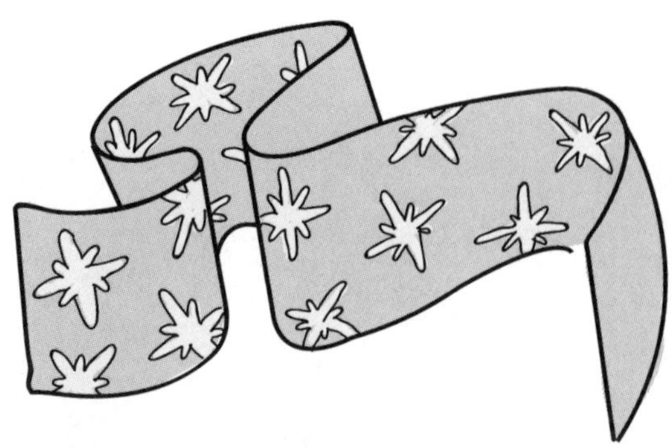

LAUGH ATTACK

Circle Game

OVERVIEW
Laugh at a falling bandana and at a moment's notice, completely stop.

SCRIPTURE CONNECTION:
Proverbs 17:22

SUPPLIES:
- Scarf
- bandana, or a light piece of fabric

PREPARATION:
None

HOW TO PLAY:
1. Kids stand in a circle. Have one person stand in the middle and toss the scarf or handkerchief into the air.
2. Once it is in the air, everyone laughs until the handkerchief touches the ground.
3. As soon as it touches the ground, everyone immediately stop laughing and maintain complete silence.
4. Whoever breaks the silence first loses that round.
5. Play again as time permits.

TEACHABLE MOMENT:
Say: I don't know if I've laughed that much in a long time. Did you know that the Bible tells us that a joyful heart (or laughter) is good medicine? (*Read Proverbs 17:22.*) I guess you guys got a good dose of laughing medicine today!

DISCUSSION QUESTIONS:
- Why do you think that laughing or having a joyful heart is good medicine?
- What are things that often make us laugh?
- What are things that often make us sad?
- What are ways that we can cheer someone else up when they are down?

FIRST NAME GAME

Individual Game

OVERVIEW
Kids make new words out of the names in their class

SCRIPTURE CONNECTION:
Proverbs 22:1

SUPPLIES:
- Paper and pencils
- Whiteboard and dry-erase markers
- Table and chairs
- Optional: Timer

PREPARATION:
None

HOW TO PLAY:

1. Kids sit around a table. Distribute paper and pencils to everyone. In large letters, use dry-erase markers to write the name of one of the children on the whiteboard.
2. On your signal, kids write down as many words as they can create from the letters on the board. Allow them to write for one minute.
3. After a minute is up, check the words. Child who has the most words answers, or chooses a volunteer to answer, one of the Discussion Questions below.
4. Pick another name and continue playing as time permits.

TEACHABLE MOMENT:

Say: Names are very important. They were important in Bible times, and they are important today. Often, God would give someone a very specific name to tell others more about their purpose or the circumstances in which they were born. For example, Abram meant "multitude" because of the many descendants he would have. The name Elijah means "my God is Yahweh (the one true God)." (*Read Proverbs 22:1.*)

DISCUSSION QUESTIONS:

- Our parents often choose our names before we are born. How can we create a "good name" for ourselves?
- What does our reputation have to do with a good name?
- People in the Bible often changed their names when their life significantly changed. What do you think it would be like if we did that now?
- Can you think of a time that people change their names?

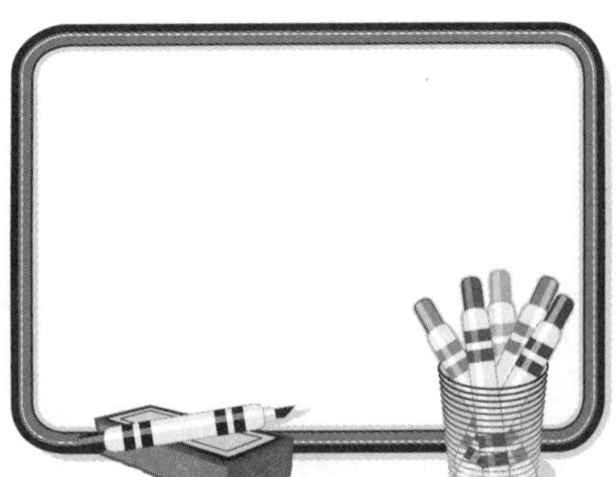

I SPY

Individual Game

OVERVIEW
Kids try to discover a described object.

SCRIPTURE CONNECTION:
Deuteronomy 1:22

SUPPLIES:
None

PREPARATION:
None

HOW TO PLAY:

1. Begin by looking around the room and mentally selecting an object and saying, "I spy with my little eye, something __________," filling in an appropriate descriptor. For example, if you decide on the door, say, "I spy with my little eye, something brown."
2. Kids take turns by looking around the room and guessing anything that matches the description.
3. When someone guesses successfully, it is then their turn to silently select something and giving the clue.
4. Play again as time permits.

TEACHABLE MOMENT:

Say: Whenever we hear the word "spy," it sounds like something dangerous and mysterious. This game wasn't too dangerous, but it was fun trying to solve the mystery! Did you know that there were spies in the Bible? Before God's people went into battle, they would send spies into the land to see how strong their enemies were. (*Read Deuteronomy 1:22.)*

DISCUSSION QUESTIONS:

- What do you think it was like to be a spy in Bible times?
- How do you think spies are able to sneak around?
- What purpose do spies usually have?

CRAFT STICK PUZZLE

Individual Game

OVERVIEW
Kids will make their own puzzles and then work to reassemble it.

SCRIPTURE CONNECTION:
Ecclesiastes 3:11

SUPPLIES:
- Craft sticks, five to ten for each child
- Markers
- Optional: Scotch tape

PREPARATION:
None

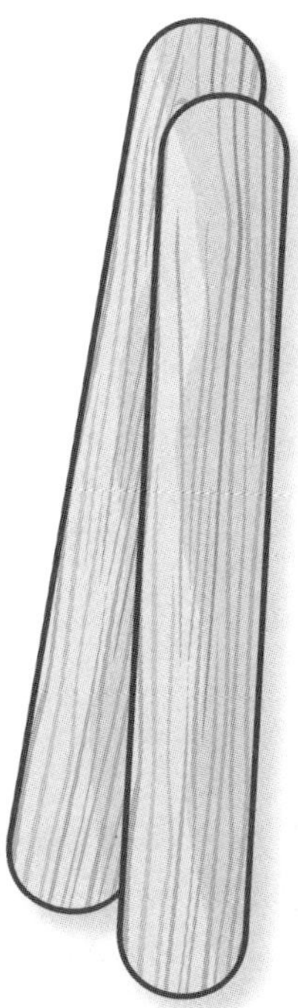

HOW TO PLAY:
1. Begin by passing out five to ten craft sticks to each child.
2. Optional: Have them tape the craft sticks together with tape.
3. Flip over the craft sticks (non-tape side) and have them draw a picture with the markers across all the sticks.
4. When everyone is done with their pictures, they remove the tape, and scramble up their sticks.
5. On your signal, they will work to reassemble their picture (now a puzzle). The first to complete the task wins.
6. If you have extra time and want the game to continue, have everyone pass their sticks to the person on the right. On your mark, have them reassemble the picture puzzle.
7. Continue playing in this way, passing the sticks to the right and racing to reassemble as time permits.

TEACHABLE MOMENT:

Say: At first, it was easy for you to put the picture back together because you knew just what it was, but it became difficult when you had to assemble someone else's picture.

God can see the complete picture. He's slowly assembling the pieces of our lives to make a beautiful things, but we don't always understand what he's up to. (*Read Ecclesiastes 3:11.*)

DISCUSSION QUESTIONS:
- Why is it hard to wait for God to make everything beautiful in his time?
- If we were created for eternity, why do you think God put us here on Earth?
- What do you think it would be like to be able to see all of time at once?
- Why do you think it's so hard for us to see God's plan sometimes?

CRAFT STICK SHAPES

Individual Game

OVERVIEW
Kids create shapes out of craft sticks.

SCRIPTURE CONNECTION:
Job 10:8

SUPPLIES:
- Craft sticks
- Optional: Timer

BASIC SHAPES TO CALL:
Square, triangle, pentagon, octagon, hexagon. More complex shapes to call: house, tree, rectangle, heart, star, bridge, fish.

PREPARATION:
None

HOW TO PLAY:

1. Give each child a pile of craft sticks (ten each should be good).
2. Call out a shape and have children form that shape with their popsicle sticks.
3. Kids race to see who can make the shape first. Optional: Set the timer for thirty seconds. Everyone tries to make the shape in the allotted time.

TEACHABLE MOMENT:

Say: Some of these shapes were pretty easy to make and some were more complex! Can you imagine trying to create a human body? That's exactly what God did. He made humans, animals, trees, and everything in creation. It is simply amazing. In the book of Job, we read that God's hands shaped and made Job. (*Read Job 10:8.*) The same is true for each of us–God made each person here. What an amazing God we have.

DISCUSSION QUESTIONS:

- What is the most complicated thing you have ever built?
- What do you think it would be like creating human beings?
- Why do you think God wanted to make humans?
- Why did God make trees, flowers, and animals?

UPSET THE FRUIT BASKET

Circle Game

OVERVIEW
In this classic game of switching seats, kids get to know each other and get some exercise too!

SCRIPTURE CONNECTION:
Psalm 139:1-6

SUPPLIES:
- Chairs, one less than the number of kids

PREPARATION:
Place chairs in a circle.

HOW TO PLAY:

1. Choose a child to be "It." "It" stands in the middle of the circle of chairs. Remaining kids sit in the chairs.
2. "It" calls out a description (anyone who is wearing red, anyone who has a dog, anyone who has ever been to New York). Kids who fit that description get up and switch to an empty seat.
3. "It" tries to steal a newly available seat, leaving a new child to be "It." The new "It" calls out another description and the game continues.
4. Continue playing this way as time permits.

TEACHABLE MOMENT:

Say: Sometimes it was easy to come up with a description and know just who was going to move–like when you picked a color of clothing. Other times, it was kind of a guess to see if anyone would move (like when you mentioned a type of pet). I bet this game would be a lot different if we knew every single little about each other? Did you know that God knows every single little thing about you? Let's read Psalm 139:1–6 together.

DISCUSSION QUESTIONS:

- How does it feel to know that God knows everything about you?
- What do you think we can hide from God?
- Can you think of anyone in the Bible that tried to hide something from God?
- Why do you think God made us all so different?

FOUR CORNERS

Individual Game

OVERVIEW
Kids run to a corner in the hopes that their corner will not get eliminated.

SCRIPTURE CONNECTION:
Revelation 7:1

SUPPLIES:
- Marker
- Four sheets of paper

PREPARATION:
Number the papers from one to four and post in the corners of the room.

HOW TO PLAY:

1. Select one child to stand in the middle of the room and be "It." "It" closes their eyes while the rest of the kids run to one of the corners of the room.
2. When all the kids have picked a corner, "It" calls out a number from one to four. All the players in the called-out corner are out sit off to the side until the end of the round.
3. This process is repeated until there are only a few kids left. These kids answer one of the Discussion Questions below.
4. Pick a new "It." Continue play as time and interest allow.

TEACHABLE MOMENT:

Say: This was a fun game! It was hard to predict which corner would be safe and which corner would not. Did you know that the Bible mentions the four corners too? (*Read Revelation 7:1.*) It doesn't sound like this verse is talking about a game, does it? This verse is talking about some of the things that will happen when God carries out his plan for us and the earth. It's a little confusing to understand how things will happen, but we know that God will be in control.

DISCUSSION QUESTIONS:

- How did you feel when you picked the wrong corner and were out?
- What do you think it would be like if the angels sent the wind flying?

FREEZE DANCE

Individual Race

OVERVIEW
Kids dance their hearts out until the music stops, and they freeze!

SCRIPTURE CONNECTION:
Psalm 149:3

SUPPLIES:
- Children's worship CD and player

PREPARATION:
None

HOW TO PLAY:

1. Kids spread out in the room, at least arms-length away from each other.
2. Begin by playing an upbeat song and encouraging kids to dance along with the music.
3. Stop the music suddenly and tell the kids to freeze!
4. No one moves (not even slightly!) after the music stops or else they are out.
5. If they are out, have them sit to the side till the round is over.
6. Continue until only one or two kids are left. Remaining player(s) answer one of the Discussion Questions below or choose a volunteer to answer.

TEACHABLE MOMENT:

Say: We often dance when we feel happy or excited. Dancing often goes with a celebration of some kind. It's good to move our bodies, and it's a great way to praise the Lord! Did you know that people often danced and sang as a way of worshiping the Lord? (*Read Psalm 149:3.*)

DISCUSSION QUESTIONS:

- What in the Bible did God's people celebrate?
- Do you think they danced during those times?
- Why do you think it's so natural to dance when we hear music?

HOT POTATO

Circle Game

OVERVIEW
Kids toss an object from player to player in the hopes that they will not be holding it when the music stops.

SCRIPTURE CONNECTION:
Exodus 19:12

SUPPLIES:
- Children's worship CD and player
- Small ball

PREPARATION:
None

HOW TO PLAY:
1. Kids sit in a circle.
2. Hand one child the ball and start to play the music.
3. Children pass the ball around the circle as the music is played.
4. Stop the music suddenly. Whoever is holding the ball when the music stops is out and sits outside the circle.
5. Continue playing until only one player is left. This player answers, or chooses a volunteer to answer, one of the Discussion Questions below.

TEACHABLE MOMENT:
Say: In this game, you didn't want to be touching the ball/potato when the music stopped. If you were holding it, you were out. This wasn't much fun, but it wasn't a very serious consequence either. In the Bible, there were times when God commanded his people not to touch something or even go near it. The consequences in those situations were much more serious. *Read Exodus 19:12.*

DISCUSSION QUESTIONS:
- Why do you think the punishment was so severe?
- Why didn't God want the people to touch the mountain?
- Can you think of other examples in the Bible when God told people not to touch something?
- Why do grown-ups tell kids not to touch some things?

SILENT SPEED BALL

Individual Race

OVERVIEW
This toss and catch game begins by requiring absolute silence.

SCRIPTURE CONNECTION:
Luke 6:31

SUPPLIES:
- Small ball

PREPARATION:
None

HOW TO PLAY:

1. In this game, there is no talking—make sure to let kids know that rule first.
2. Kids spread out around the room. Once they pick a spot, they cannot move from it.
3. Toss the ball to one child. Child tosses the ball to someone else who tosses the ball to someone else.
4. The ball continues being tossed from person to person all around the room. Players cannot toss the ball back to the person who tossed it to them.
5. Players can get out by talking, not catching the ball or by tossing the ball away from other players.
6. Play until there are only one or two kids left. These kids answer one of the Discussion Questions below.
7. Kids pick new spots in the room and play continues as time and interest allow.

TEACHABLE MOMENT:

Say: In this game, it was tempting to toss the ball poorly so that the other person would get out, but that's not a good way to play. In fact, that's not a good way to live life either. Sometimes we're tempted to blame other people when something goes wrong, or we purposely don't help so that we can win, but that's not God's design on how to live life. (*Read Luke 6:31.*)

DISCUSSION QUESTIONS:

- Have you ever heard this verse before?
- It's often called the "Golden Rule." Why do you think that is?
- Why is it sometimes hard to live by the Golden Rule?
- Why do you think God wants to think about others?

ELBOW TAG

Tag

OVERVIEW
Tag gets a little more complicated as kids have to link elbows and unhook as they are tagged.

SCRIPTURE CONNECTION:
Ecclesiastes 4:9-10

SUPPLIES:
None

PREPARATION:
None

HOW TO PLAY:

1. Have everyone pick a partner and link arms. Select one pair to split up. One child in the pair will be "It," and the other child will be chased.
2. The child being chased runs to a linked pair and links up with them. When this happens, the person on the opposite end breaks off and get chased.
3. If the new runner gets tagged, they are "It." The game continues as time and interest allow.
4. To make things a little more complicated, start the game with two or three runners.

TEACHABLE MOMENT:

Say: This was an interesting game–there was a lot of movement, but there was only one or two people who was in danger of being tagged (and turned into "It") at any given time. Did you know the Bible talks about teaming up in twos as well? (*Read Ecclesiastes 4:9–10.*)

DISCUSSION QUESTIONS:

- When is it good to be with a friend instead of all alone?
- In this game, what was it like to be kicked out of your pair, and sent running?
- Was it hard to find a new pair to link up with?
- What is one way that you can encourage your friends (or help them up when they are down)?
- What is one way that we can encourage people who might not have a lot of friends?

HEADS OR TAILS

Individual Race

OVERVIEW
Kids will guess how the coin will land. Guess correctly, and you stay in the game.

SCRIPTURE CONNECTION:
Matthew 17:26-27, Matthew 18:27-29, Mark 12:41-44, or Luke 15:8

SUPPLIES:
- Coin

PREPARATION:
None

HOW TO PLAY:

1. Kids stand around a table. Tell them you are going to flip a coin and they need to guess how the coin will land—heads or tails.
2. To show they are guessing "Heads," kids put their hands on their head. To show they are guessing "Tails," they should put their hands where a tail would be.
3. Flip the coin. Kids do motion to show their guess. Whoever has guessed correctly remains standing. Whoever has not guessed correctly sits down.
4. Continue playing in this way until you have a few players left. These players answer one of the Discussion Questions below.

TEACHABLE MOMENT:

Say: The Bible not only talks about coins, but it also talks about money and how we should use it too. Everything we have is a blessing from God, and we should use it in a way that would make him pleased.

DISCUSSION QUESTIONS:

- Have you heard any of those stories or parables before?
- Which one is your favorite?
- Why does God want us to be careful with our money?
- How could you please God with your money? What could you do with it?

HAPPY HOPPY

Individual Game

OVERVIEW

This is a great way to introduce a new song or to get the wiggles out!

SCRIPTURE CONNECTION:
Ecclesiastes 3:4

SUPPLIES:
- Children's worship CD and player

PREPARATION:
None

HOW TO PLAY:

1. Kids stand up and spread apart from each other. Children pick a leg to stand on and hold the other leg behind their back with their hand.
2. Start the music and instruct the kids to hop on one foot to the rhythm.
3. If a child stops hopping, they are out. If they attempt to switch legs, they are out.
4. The last child to keep hopping to the music wins!

TEACHABLE MOMENT:

Say: At first, this seems like a pretty easy game, but after a few minutes of hopping, it's not quite so easy anymore! It's fun to dance and move to music, especially when we are praising the Lord. After a while though, it's time to stop and take a rest. We can't be hoppy happy all the time! (*Read Ecclesiastes 3:4.*)

DISCUSSION QUESTIONS:

- What does this verse mean?
- What was something that recently made you laugh?
- When do we usually dance?
- Do you think it is true that there is a time for everything?

TABLE, BABY, BACKPACK

Partner Game

OVERVIEW
Kids think quickly and move even quicker as they get into pre-determined positions with a teammate.

SCRIPTURE CONNECTION:
Ephesians 4:16

SUPPLIES:
None

PREPARATION:
None

HOW TO PLAY:

1. Kids divide into two teams of partners.
2. Call out one of the following words: "table," "baby," or "backpack."
3. For the table, one partner gets on all fours like a table, and the other partner sits on their back.
4. For a baby, one partner holds cradles the other like a baby.
5. For a backpack, one partner hops on the other's back piggyback-style.
6. Continue calling out the positions in random order. If a pair messes up, they are out.
7. When there are only two pairs left, whoever gets into position last is out. The remaining pair answers one of the Discussion Questions below.

TEACHABLE MOMENT:

Say: In this game, you had to quickly decide who was going to do what, and get into the correct position. There was no time for arguing or change the plan. Life usually works best when we all work together to do our part. God told us that the church is supposed to work this way too—everyone working together to help the body of Christ work properly. (*Read Ephesians 4:16.*)

DISCUSSION QUESTIONS:

- How have you seen people working together to do their part?
- Why might people not work together well?
- Have you ever had trouble with someone when you were working on a project together?
- How can we resolve difficulties when trying to work with others?

SHARKS, FISH, AND SEAWEED

Individual Game

OVERVIEW

This game gets a new twist as children who are caught by the shark become seaweed and help the remaining fish get across the ocean.

SCRIPTURE CONNECTION:
Psalm 148:7

SUPPLIES:

- Large play area

PREPARATION:
None

HOW TO PLAY:

1. Kids line up on one side of the room against a wall. They are the minnows. Select one child to be the shark and have him stand in the middle of the room.
2. On your signal, kids should "swim" from the wall to the opposite wall, trying not to get tagged by the shark.
3. If they are tagged by the shark, they should immediately stop where they are. They are now seaweed. On the next round, a fish can stop and "hide" in the seaweed by touching the stationary child. A shark cannot tag a minnow when he is hiding in the seaweed.
4. Continue playing in this way until there are only one or two minnows left. Declare a winner!

TEACHABLE MOMENT:

Say: This was a fun game. Isn't it amazing to think of all the incredible creatures that are in the ocean? In fact, there are over 400 species of sharks alone! And everything in the sea works together, just the way God created it too. Have you ever thought about the sea creatures praising the Lord? (*Read Psalm 148:7.*)

DISCUSSION QUESTIONS:

- How might a sea creature praise the Lord?
- Why do you think God wants his creation to praise him?
- What is one way we can praise the Lord?

COW, CHICKEN, PIG

Individual Game

OVERVIEW
Kids will select an animal to be and hope that the animal is not eliminated from the game!

SCRIPTURE CONNECTION:
Genesis 1:25

SUPPLIES:
- Optional: Three scraps of paper
- Optional: Pencil or pen

PREPARATION:
Optional: On separate scraps of paper, write the words "Chicken," "Cow," and "Pig."

HOW TO PLAY:

1. Kids line up in a straight line. Show children how to make the following animal faces.
2. For the chicken, kids will put a hand in the middle of their forehead like a rooster's comb.
3. For the cow, kids will make horns behind their head with their pinkies.
4. For the pig, they will use a finger to raise their nose up to look like a pig's snout.
5. On your signal, children make the animal face of their choice. Randomly call out one of the animal names. Whoever is making that face sits down. Optional: Instead of randomly choosing an animal, select a scrap of paper and read the written animal name.
6. Continue playing in this way until only one child remains.

TEACHABLE MOMENT:
Say: God made so many amazing animals. These three are animals on a farm, but there are lots of other habitats where they live as well. (*Read Genesis 1:25.*)

DISCUSSION QUESTIONS:
- What is your favorite animal?
- What is the funniest animal you've ever seen?
- What wild animal have you seen in person (like at a zoo)?
- Why do you think God created so many different animals?

LESSON REVIEW GAMES

DELIVER MAIL

Individual Game

OVERVIEW
Kids have to quickly deliver mail, reviewing recently learned about people and places.

SUPPLIES:
- Name tags
- Envelopes
- Markers
- Stopwatch
- Paper and pencil

PREPARATION:
Label name tags with people or places you have learned about from recent lessons. For example, Adam, Eve, Garden of Eden, Noah, Babel, Joseph, etc. Make one name tag for every child plus a few extras. Label the envelopes to match the name tags. Put all the envelopes in a pile. Select one child to be the "mail carrier." Hand them the envelopes.

HOW TO PLAY:
1. Give everyone a name tag. Players put on name tags and scatter around the room.
2. Start stopwatch. The mail carrier "delivers" the mail to the matching people/places as quickly as they can. Envelopes labeled "Adam" are delivered to child wearing "Adam" name tag. Envelope labeled "Garden of Eden" is delivered to child wearing "Garden of Eden name tag. Keep track of the time.
3. Once they have completed the delivery, select another volunteer and repeat the process (they will have to switch name tags).
4. Keep track of scores and after everyone has had a chance to deliver mail, reveal the fastest time.
5. If you have extra time, hold up the envelopes one by one and have volunteers tell you something about each person or place.

Variation:
Say: If you want to have two or three mail carriers delivering the mail at once (and played as a race), write the names of cities and places onto a piece of paper (instead of the envelopes). Copy the paper in two or three different colors of cardstock. Hand a complete stack (one color) to each mail carrier. Have them race to deliver the mail. The colors help to make sure the mail is delivered correctly (you can tell who delivered in case of an incorrect delivery).

FAMOUS PAIR

Partner Game

OVERVIEW
Kids find their match by saying a key phrase from that person's life.

SUPPLIES:

- Paper
- Pen
- Famous Pairs Template, page 301
- Optional: Bible People Review Sheets, pages 302-303.

PREPARATION:

List all the key people you've recently learned about. Think about a key phrase they said. Write down the name and phrase on the template. Use the Bible People Review Sheets. You will need one Bible person for every two players. Make as many copies as the template (after it is filled in) as you need. Make sure there is one card for every player.

HOW TO PLAY:

1. Give each player a card and tell them to keep it hidden and their person's name a secret.
2. On your signal, kids wander around the play area saying their key phrase while listening for the kid saying the same phrase.
3. When a player finds their match, the children sit down together.
4. Game ends when everyone has found their pair/group and has sat down.
5. Review all the names together and talk about the key phrases.

WHERE CAN YOU FIND IT?

Individual Game

OVERVIEW

In this paper and pencil game, kids match a story with the book of the Bible where it is found.

SUPPLIES:

- Bible Story Matching Sheet, page 304

PREPARATION:

Photocopy Bible Story Matching Sheet, making one for each child.

HOW TO PLAY:

1. Kids work at their own pace to match up the Bible stories with the book of the Bible in which they can be found.
2. When everyone is finished, check their answers. The answer key is on page 305.
3. Award ten points for every correct answer. Child with the highest score tells a sentence about any one of the Bible stories listed, or chooses a volunteer to tell a sentence.

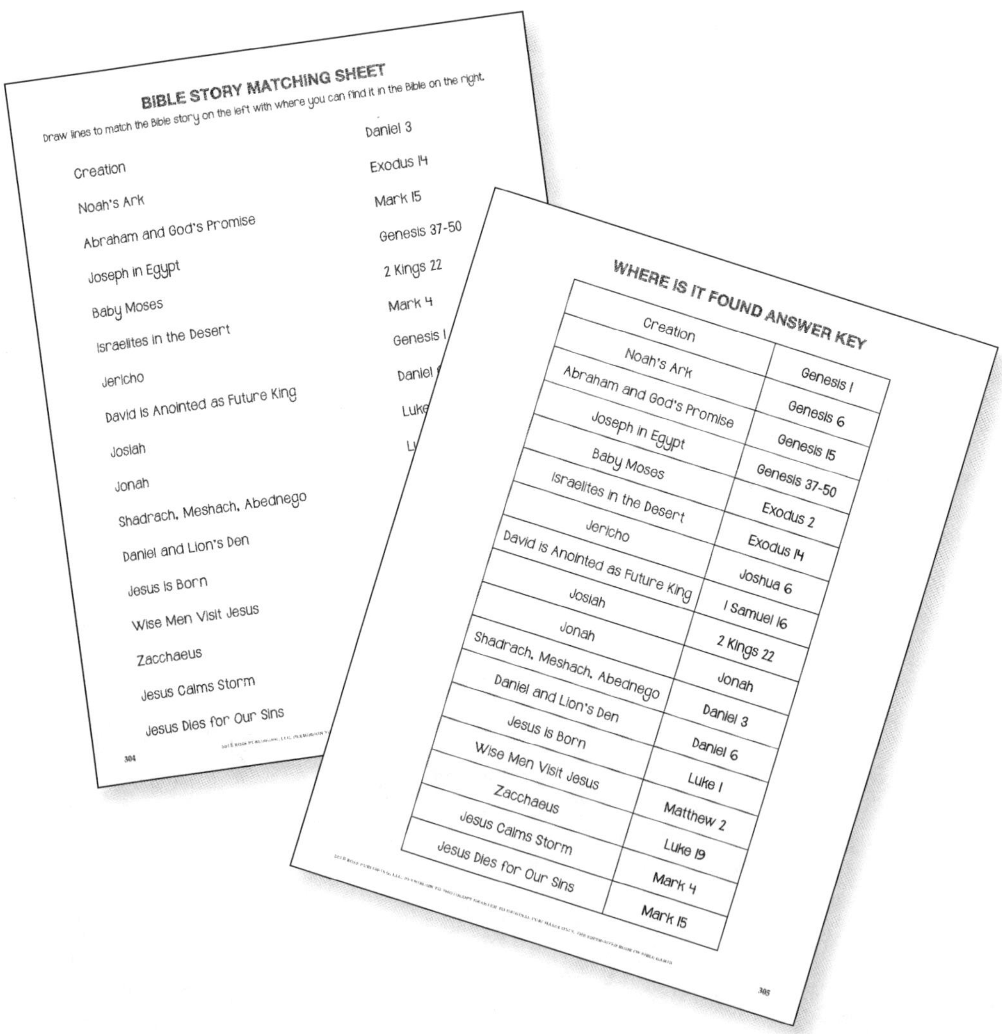

BIBLE STORY MATCHING SHEET

Draw lines to match the Bible story on the left with where you can find it in the Bible on the right.

Creation	Daniel 3
Noah's Ark	Exodus 14
Abraham and God's Promise	Mark 15
Joseph in Egypt	Genesis 37-50
Baby Moses	2 Kings 22
Israelites in the Desert	Mark 4
Jericho	Genesis 1
David is Anointed as Future King	Daniel
Josiah	Luke
Jonah	
Shadrach, Meshach, Abednego	
Daniel and Lion's Den	
Jesus is Born	
Wise Men Visit Jesus	
Zacchaeus	
Jesus Calms Storm	
Jesus Dies for Our Sins	

304

WHERE IS IT FOUND ANSWER KEY

Creation	Genesis 1
Noah's Ark	Genesis 6
Abraham and God's Promise	Genesis 15
Joseph in Egypt	Genesis 37-50
Baby Moses	Exodus 2
Israelites in the Desert	Exodus 14
Jericho	Joshua 6
David is Anointed as Future King	1 Samuel 16
Josiah	2 Kings 22
Jonah	Jonah
Shadrach, Meshach, Abednego	Daniel 3
Daniel and Lion's Den	Daniel 6
Jesus is Born	Luke 1
Wise Men Visit Jesus	Matthew 2
Zacchaeus	Luke 19
Jesus Calms Storm	Mark 4
Jesus Dies for Our Sins	Mark 15

305

DRAWING REVIEW

Team Race

OVERVIEW
Teams try to guess what their teammate is drawing before time runs out!

SUPPLIES:
- Whiteboard
- Dry-erase markers
- Eraser or wet wipes
- Clues, written on small pieces of paper
- Something to put the clues in (box, bag, etc.)
- Timer

PREPARATION:
Look back through your recent lessons (usually every twelve weeks is a good time to review) and pick out key places, people, events, or items. Write these things down on pieces of paper and place them inside a box.

HOW TO PLAY:
1. Kids divide into two teams. For extra fun, members pick team names.
2. Select a volunteer, and have them pick a clue. They should draw that things/person/place on the whiteboard for their team.
3. Their team will shout out guesses as the volunteer draws. The team has one minute to guess correctly. If they do not guess, the team does not score any points.
4. After the first team finishes drawing, play passes to the second team who repeats the process.
5. Continue playing as time and interest allow.

PIN THE . . .

Individual Game

OVERVIEW
Adapt Pin the Tail on the Donkey to any Bible story!

SUPPLIES:
- Poster board
- Markers
- Small lesson-themed pieces (see below)
- Masking tape
- Blindfold

PREPARATION:
Draw a poster from a recent lesson, but leave out a key feature. (See ideas at right.) Make small pictures of the missing feature and put a masking-tape loop on the back.

HOW TO PLAY:
1. Give each child the small pictures of missing features.
2. Blindfold a child who then tries to attach the feature in the right place on the poster.
3. Repeat until each child has a turn.

Ideas to Get You Started:
- Pin the fruit on the tree (Adam and Eve)
- Pin the animals in the ark (Noah)
- Pin the coat on Joseph (Joseph's coat of many colors)
- Pin baby in the basket (Moses)
- Pin the wheat in the basket (Ruth)
- Pin Daniel in the Den (Daniel and the Lion's Den)
- Pin the crown on the Queen (Esther)
- Pin the Wise men on the Camels (Wise men visit Jesus)
- Pin the stone on the tomb (Jesus rises from the dead)

BIBLE STORY DOMINOES

Individual Game

OVERVIEW

Instead of dots on each end of the domino, kids will be matching up people, places, and things from their recent lessons.

SUPPLIES:

- Note cards
- Markers
- Domino Cards template on page 282

PREPARATION:

Prepare the Domino cards ahead of time by looking through your recent lessons (usually every twelve weeks is a good time to review). Pick out key places, people, events, or items. On the Domino template, write out the review words you have chosen. Make sure there are two of each word so that children can match them up while playing the domino game.

HOW TO PLAY:

1. When the kids arrive, divide the domino cards up evenly among all the kids. Each child should have between five to ten cards.
2. Have a volunteer place one of their cards on the table. The next player (to the right) should try to match up one of her cards to the card on the table. If she cannot, play continues to the right.
3. The game continues in this way, with play passing to the right, and players trying to match up their cards to what is already on the table.
4. The first player to get rid of all their domino cards wins.
5. After the game is complete, look at the cards and talk with the kids about the people, places, and things that are mentioned.

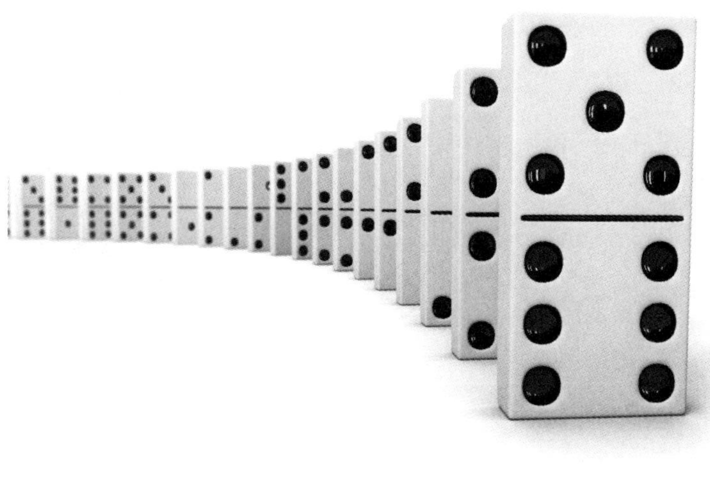

PICTURE MEMORY

Individual Game

OVERVIEW
Kids play Concentration with pictures of their own memories!

SUPPLIES:
- Camera
- Printer

PREPARATION:
At the beginning of a new unit, take pictures each week. You might take a picture of the object lesson, craft, a key Bible verse, or a lesson-related game the kids played. Print two copies of each picture.

HOW TO PLAY:
1. Place the pictures face down on the table. Kids play a game of Concentration with pictures.
2. Whenever a match is made, have a volunteer tell more about the picture (what the lesson was about, etc.).

PICTURE PERFECT PUZZLE

Individual Game

OVERVIEW
Kids make puzzles from their own pictures!

SUPPLIES:

- Camera
- Printer
- Laminating machine
- Laminating sheets
- Resealable plastic bags

PREPARATION:
Take pictures each week. You might take a picture of the object lesson, craft, a key Bible verse, or a lesson-related game. If your curriculum already has visual aids (skip this step). Print to 8x10 size. Laminate pictures (or print on foam board) and then cut them into five to twenty pieces depending on the age of your group. Then, place it inside a zippered bag. Make one puzzle for each kid in your group.

HOW TO PLAY:

1. When the kids arrive, give each child a puzzle and have them work at their own pace. Once the puzzles are complete, have kids look at each other's pictures and talk about what that particular lesson was about.
2. If time allows, kids swap puzzles with each other and play again.

RUNNING TRUE OR FALSE

Individual Game

OVERVIEW

In this running-themed game, kids decide if a statement is true or false by running to the appropriate wall.

SUPPLIES:

- Large area
- Marker
- Two sheets of paper

PREPARATION:

Use marker to print, "True" and "False," one word on each sheet of paper. Ahead of time, prepare statements by looking through your recent lessons and picking out key ideas, specific lesson phrases, or events that occurred. Many times, lessons will have review questions at the end, use these for inspiration. Tape the True and False signs to opposite walls.

HOW TO PLAY:

1. Have all the kids stand in the middle of the room.
2. Read one of your prepared statements.
3. The kids decide if the statement is true or false, and run to the wall that is labeled appropriately.
4. When everyone has picked a wall, reveal the answer. Have the children tell you what needs to be fixed to make the false statement true.
5. Have everyone return to the center and read another statement.
6. Continue this way until you have read all your prepared statements or as time allows.

LESSON REVIEW BINGO

Individual Game

OVERVIEW
Kids help make their own Bingo cards, adding to the unpredictability of the game!

SUPPLIES:
- Whiteboard
- Bingo template page 283
- Pens or markers
- Coins, beads, small glass gems, or other marker

PREPARATION:
Look through your recent lessons for key words, places, people, or books of the Bible. Make a master list of these words. Write the master list on the whiteboard. Make one copy per child of the bingo template, (plus a few extra).

HOW TO PLAY:
1. Give each child a Bingo template. Players look at the master list on the whiteboard and put one word in each box. Encourage the kids to hop around the squares as they put the words on the cards. That way everyone doesn't have an identical card.
2. Begin the game by reading one of the words from your master list. Make a check mark next to work on the board to keep track of what you've read.
3. If kids have that word on their paper, they cover their word with a coin, bead, small glass gem, or other marker.
4. Continue calling out words as kids cover them. When a player gets five in a row, player calls out, "Bingo!"
5. After each round, kids switch cards and play again.

FISH RACE

Team Race

OVERVIEW

As kids review the lessons, they move their fish forward on its path. First to finish wins!

SUPPLIES:

- Poster Board
- Markers
- Sticky tack

PREPARATION:

Look through the recent lessons for review questions (often found at the end of each chapter). Prepare the poster board by drawing wavy lines across the board horizontally. Each line should have the same number of wave peaks. Draw and cut out a simple fish template in different colors for each team.

HOW TO PLAY:

1. Kids divide into two teams. Give each team a fish.
2. Teams place their fish at the beginning of the wavy line.
3. Ask one team a review question. If they get the question correct, they move their fish to the next wave peak.
4. Continue asking questions to each team as they move their fish each time they get a question correct.

GAME SHOW

Team Game

OVERVIEW
Kids earn points by answering questions about past lessons.

SUPPLIES:
- Note cards

PREPARATION:
Find questions related to your past lessons and write them on the cards. Assign each card a point value, write this on the back of the card. Usually, there is 100, 200, 300, 400, and 500 within each category. You should have about twenty-five questions, five for each category. Categories can include people, places, events, Bible verses, miracles, etc. Write the categories on a sheet of paper and post on a wall. Under each category, make a column of the question cards score side out, hiding the questions.

TIP:
You can find game templates online.

HOW TO PLAY:
1. Kids divide into two teams.
2. Have the first player on one of the teams choose a card. Player gets a chance to answer on their own, or ask to the team for help.
3. If team cannot answer after one minute, or if they answer incorrectly, the opposing team gets a turn to answer.
4. Team answering the question correctly gets the points indicated on the card.
5. Play until all the cards are selected and answered or as time and interest allow.

MONEY MAKING REVIEW

Individual Game

OVERVIEW
Kids wager fake money as they answer each question.

SUPPLIES:
- Pretend money
- Review questions

PREPARATION:
Prepare review questions from previous lessons. Make three times more than the number of players you will have.

HOW TO PLAY:

1. Give each child the same amount of money to begin the game ($10 in ones is a good place to start).
2. Select one player to go first. They wager some of their money before you ask a question. They will set the money they are wagering in front of them.
3. Ask the first player a question. If they get that question correct, they receive double their wager back. If they do not answer correctly, they lose their money.
4. Select another player and repeat this process. If the original player cannot answer correctly, any other player can answer and receive a one dollar bonus for answering.
5. Each child should have at least two or three questions asked of them directly.
6. At the end of the game, kids count their money.

PASS THE CHICKEN

Circle Game

OVERVIEW

Kids answer questions before the "chicken" makes it around the circle.

SUPPLIES:

- Rubber or stuffed-toy chicken
- Review questions

PREPARATION:

Look through the recent lessons for review questions (often found at the end of each chapter).

HOW TO PLAY:

1. Kids sit in a circle. Give one child the chicken.
2. Ask the child a review question as they pass the chicken to the right. The child must answer the question correctly before the chicken makes it all the way around the circle.
3. If child cannot answer the question, they sit the middle of the circle. Child remains "in the pot" until another player misses a question and takes their place.
4. If child does answer correctly, the chicken is give to the next player and game begins again.

PING-PONG DUNK

Team Game

OVERVIEW

Kids earn points for answering review questions correctly and have a chance to earn bonus points for tossing a Ping-Pong ball.

SUPPLIES:

- Ping-Pong ball
- Small bucket
- Review questions
- Score board

PREPARATION:

Set buckets up for each team. Prepare lines with paper tape on the ground. Create different standing lines for different ages.

HOW TO PLAY:

1. Kids divide into two teams. Have them name their teams for a little extra fun.
2. Begin by asking one team a review question. They may work together to answer the question. If they answer correctly, one player can come up to the front and toss a Ping-Pong ball into a bucket.
3. If they answer a question correctly, they get 100 points. If they are also able to toss the ball into the bucket, they get a bonus 100 points.
4. If a team does not answer a question correctly, they cannot attempt to toss the Ping-Pong ball.
5. Continue alternating between teams, asking questions and allowing an opportunity for bonus points when appropriate.
6. When you are out of questions (or if time is nearly up), tally up the score. Team with the most points tells a sentence about one of the Bible stories reviewed.

REVIEW BASEBALL

Team Race

OVERVIEW
Kids advance through the bases as they answer questions correctly.

SUPPLIES:
- Four sheets of construction paper
- Review questions

PREPARATION:
Set out construction-paper sheets like bases on a baseball diamond, (1st, 2nd, 3rd, and home plate).
Write out review questions from the previous lessons.

HOW TO PLAY:
1. Kids divide into two teams. Flip a coin to see which team will be "up to bat" first.
2. Have the first team line up to "bat." Ask the first player a review question. If they answer correctly, they may advance to first base.
3. Ask the second player a review question. If they answer correctly, they may advance to first base, forcing the first player to advance to second base.
4. If a player answers incorrectly, they go to the end of the line and that team has one "out."
5. When a team has three outs, the teams switch places.
6. If you want to involve the other team, you can have them read the review questions to the players who are at bat.
7. Play for ten minutes (or whatever time limit you have set) and then tally up the points. Team with the most points tells a sentence about one of the Bible stories reviewed.

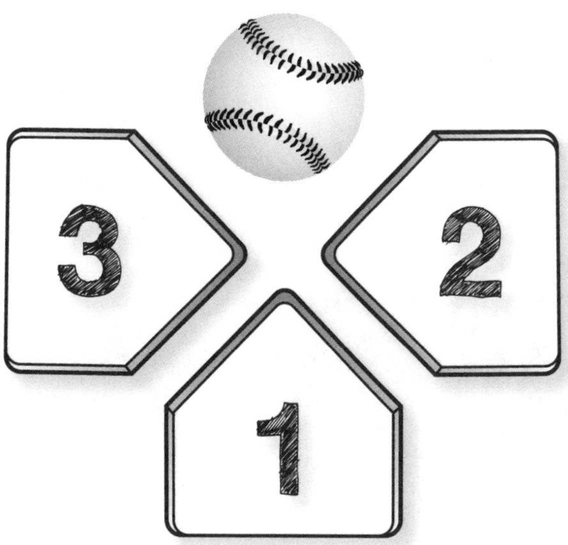

FISHING FOR POINTS

Team Game

OVERVIEW
Kids fish for points as they answer review questions.

SUPPLIES:
- Paper clips
- Toy Fishing pole with magnet on the end
- Score board
- Review questions
- Optional: Inflatable wading pool

PREPARATION:
Draw and cut out several paper fish and write various point values on each fish (100 to 1,000 by 100s is a good range to work with). Place a paper clip on the fish's "mouth" and then lay the fish point-side down in a baby pool or on the ground. Print out review questions from recent lessons.

$ TIP:
Can't find a magnetic fishing pole? You can make your own by gluing twine to a small dowel rod (or ruler) and then gluing a magnet to the other end of the string.

HOW TO PLAY:
1. Divide the kids up into two teams. Select a volunteer from the first team to answer a question. If they answer correctly, they can go "fishing." They will use the rod to grab a fish and they are then awarded the number of points on the fish.
2. Select a volunteer from the opposite team and repeat the process.
3. Continue in this way until everyone has had a chance to answer at least one review question. You can continue playing until you run out of questions or until your designated time is up.
4. When time is up, tally up the points. Team with the most points tells a sentence about one of the Bible stories reviewed.

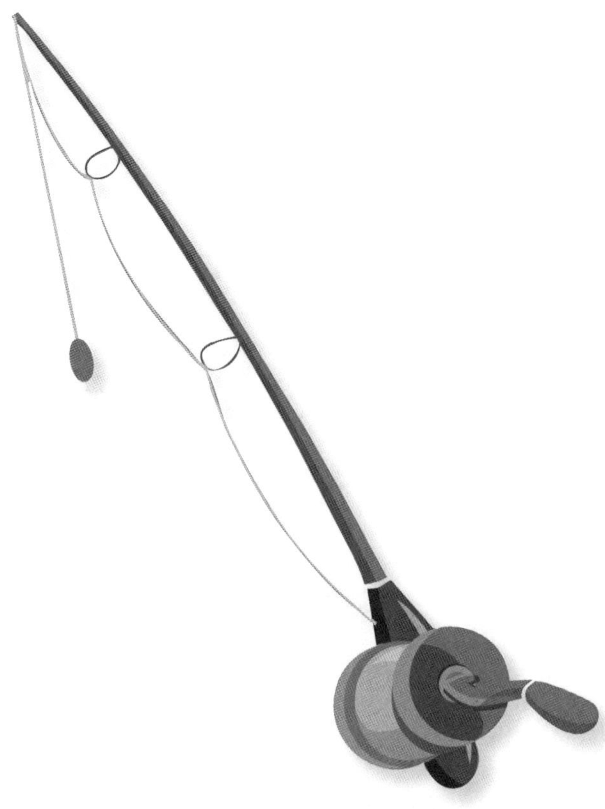

FISHING FOR QUESTIONS

Team Race

OVERVIEW
Kids will fish for questions as they play together to review a recent lesson.

SUPPLIES:
- Paper clips
- Fishing pole with magnet on the end
- Score board
- Optional: Inflatable wading pool

PREPARATION:
Make several paper fish and on them, write review questions. Each fish is worth 100 points. Place a paper clip on the fish's "mouth" and then lay the fish writing side down on the ground. Optional: Place prepared fish in an inflatable wading pool.

$ TIP:
See tip on page 242 for making your own magnetic fishing pole.

HOW TO PLAY:
1. Divide the kids up into two teams. Select a volunteer from the first team to go "fishing". They will use the rod to grab a fish and then attempt to answer the question. If they get the question correct, they earn the appropriate amount of points for their team.
2. Select a volunteer from the opposite team and repeat the process.
3. Continue in this way until everyone has had a chance to answer at least one review question. You can continue playing until you run out of questions or until your designated time is up.
4. When time is up, tally up the points. Team with the most points tells a sentence about one of the Bible stories reviewed.

WHITEBOARD REVIEW

Team Game

OVERVIEW

Kids all answer the review questions on their own personal whiteboard.

SUPPLIES:

- Small whiteboards
- Dry-erase markers, one for each player
- Score board
- Review questions

PREPARATION:

Write out review questions from previous lessons.

$ TIP:

If you don't have a small dry erase boards, use clipboards and paper, or cardstock for extra sturdiness. Be sure the kids draw a line through their answer after each round to avoid confusion.

HOW TO PLAY:

1. Give each child a whiteboard and a dry-erase marker.
2. Kids divide into two evenly numbered teams.
3. Ask a review question. Players to write the correct answer on their board.
4. When it seems like everyone is done writing (or after several seconds), kids turn all their boards to face you at once.
5. Count the correct answers for each team and award points accordingly.
6. Continue playing until you have used all your questions. Tally up the team points. Team with the most points tells a sentence about one of the Bible stories reviewed.

REVIEW FOOTBALL

Team Race

OVERVIEW
Kids advance their football players towards a goal when they answer a question correctly.

SUPPLIES:
- Small picture of a football player
- Poster of football field
- Review questions
- Sticky tack
- Timer

PREPARATION:
Print up a small picture of a football player and the grid of a football field.

HOW TO PLAY:

1. Set timer for ten minutes. Kids divide into two teams. Give each team a football figure.
2. Both figures should start on the fifty-yard line, facing opposite directions.
3. Ask the first team a review question (you can pose it to an individual or allow them to answer as a team). If they answer correctly, they can advance their football figure ten yards towards their goal. If they answer incorrectly, the opposite team has a chance to steal their yardage (by answering correctly).
4. Both teams will advance towards their assigned end zones as questions are answered. However, as soon as one team scores by making it into the end zone, the field resets and both figures begin again in the middle.
5. Play until the timer beeps. Whoever has the most points at the end of this time team tells a sentence about one of the Bible stories reviewed.

CRAZY SCORE

Team Game

OVERVIEW

Crazy scores are awarded for each correctly answered question. The game could go either way at any moment!

SUPPLIES:

- Note cards
- Review questions
- Calculator

PREPARATION:

Make note cards with various crazy scores written on them (i.e., 15, 34, 47, 58, 643, etc.) Arrange the note cards, point side down on the floor or table. Write out review questions from previous lessons.

HOW TO PLAY:

1. Divide the kids up into two teams.
2. Ask a player on Team #1 a review question. If they answer correctly, they can choose a note card. They will hold the card for the remainder of the game (or you might want to designate a leader to do this for each team).
3. Repeat this process with a player from Team #2.
4. Continue playing in this way until you are out of review questions or until the time is up. At the end of the game, all the scorecards are added up. Team with the most points tells a sentence about one of the Bible stories reviewed.

BUCKET TOSS

Team Race

OVERVIEW
Kids choose where to stand and toss a ball to get bonus points.

SUPPLIES:
- Large bucket or trash can
- Foam softball
- Painters tape or masking tape
- Review questions
- Scoreboard
- Markers

PREPARATION:
Set up the bucket in the front of the room. Put the tape down on the floor for throwing lines. The first line should be two feet from the bucket (worth 100 points), the second line should be four feet (worth 200 points), and the third line should be 6 feet from the bucket (worth 500 points).

HOW TO PLAY:
1. Divide the kids up into two teams.
2. Begin by asking a player on Team #1 a review question. If they answer correctly, they get 100 points. They also have the option of earning bonus points. They choose where to stand to throw the ball into the bucket. If they can make the toss, they get the appropriate number of points added to their score (based on where they were standing).
3. Play then passes to the other team. Repeat this same process with Team #2.
4. Continue playing until you are out of questions or until time is up. Then tally up the points! Team with the most points tells a sentence about one of the Bible stories reviewed.

SINK OR SWIM

Team Game

OVERVIEW
Kids choose to sink a player on the opposing team or rescue one of their own.

SUPPLIES:
- Review questions

PREPARATION:
None

HOW TO PLAY:

1. Kids divide into two teams. Kids line up across the room (side to side) as a team. The teams will face each other.
2. Ask a player on Team #1 a review question. If they answer correctly, they may choose to "sink" a player on the opposite team. When they do this, the sunk player sits down. He cannot answer any review questions.
3. Next, you will ask a player on Team #2 a review question. If they answer correctly, they may choose to sink a player on the opposite team or rescue one of their players that are currently sunk.
4. A player who is sunk can't answer review questions. If one team can sink all the players on the other team, they win. Each team must carefully balance offense and defense.
5. If one team is not able to sink the other team, the game is over when you run out of review questions or when your designated time is up. Whoever has the most players still "swimming" at the end of the game tells a sentence about one of the Bible stories reviewed.

LEAP FROG

Team Race

OVERVIEW

Kids earn points for each correct answer. However, points can "leap frog" to the opposite team at any moment!

SUPPLIES:

- Plastic frogs big enough to write a score on the bottom
- Paper and pen or pencil

PREPARATION:

Write point values on the bottom of each frog. On a few frogs, print "Leap Frog." Print review questions from previous lessons.

$ TIP:

Can't find any plastic frogs? Just write the scores on note cards with frog stickers on the back.

HOW TO PLAY:

1. Kids divide into teams of four or five players.
2. Ask a team a review question. If they answer the question correctly, one player picks up a frog and the team is awarded whatever point value is on the bottom of that frog.
3. If a player picks up a frog with "Leap Frog" on the bottom, they can steal all the points from any other team.
4. Continue asking players from each team questions until you are out of questions or until time is up.
5. The team with the most points at the end of the game tells a sentence about one of the Bible stories reviewed.

AROUND THE WORLD

Individual Game

OVERVIEW

Kids travel from friend to friend, competing to answer the question first.

SUPPLIES:

- Review questions

PREPARATION:

Write out review questions from previous lessons.

TIP:

Kids should be close in age to compete against each other.

HOW TO PLAY:

1. Kids choose a place to sit on the floor. Ideally, they should be in rows.
2. Select one child to start the game. They will stand next to another child in the first row.
3. You, as the leader, will ask a review question. Whoever is the first to answer the question is the winner of that round. If the two kids answer simultaneously, it is a tie, and the leader will ask another question.
4. The winner will advance to the next child in the row, and the process will be repeated.
5. The goal is to move as many seats as possible before losing. When a player loses, they will take the place/seat of the person who beat them.
6. The game continues until one student makes it "around the world" and gets all the way back to his seat. Often, though, the game simply ends when the time is up, and the person who traveled the farthest tells a sentence about one of the Bible stories reviewed.

CONNECT FOUR

Team Race

OVERVIEW
Kids work as a team answer four questions correctly to score!

SUPPLIES:
- Post-It Notes in a different color for each team
- Whiteboard
- Marker
- Review questions

PREPARATION:
Draw a giant grid on the whiteboard (about thirty-five squares big enough for a Post-It Note to fit inside). Write out review questions from previous lessons.

HOW TO PLAY:
1. Kids divide into teams.
2. Ask the first team a question. If they get the question correct, they may place a Post-It Note anywhere in the grid.
3. The next team then as an opportunity to answer a question and also place a Post-It Note.
4. The game continues this way. When a team successfully gets four sticky notes in a row on the board, they tell a sentence about one of the Bible stories reviewed.

SUPER GIANT MEMORY GAME

Individual Game

OVERVIEW

In this oversized memory game, kids get a chance to move around and improve their memory!

SUPPLIES:

- Review questions
- Construction paper or quarter sheets of poster board

PREPARATION:

Write review questions and answers on the paper (the question should be on one piece and the answer should be on another). You may also wish to number the cards as pairs, so it is easy to know when you've gotten a "match."
Lay all the papers face down on the ground, so the writing is hidden.

TIP:

To change this for little ones, print pictures from the lessons instead of questions.

HOW TO PLAY:

1. Give kids two cards to flip over. If the question and answer go together, the child can keep the cards. If not, they will flip them back over and play passes to the next player.
2. Continue the game this way, with kids taking turns flipping over two cards each and trying to get a match.
3. The game is over when there are no cards left. Whoever has the most matches at the end of the game wins!

BIBLE CHARADES

Team Race

OVERVIEW

Kids will compete to guess what the contestant is drawing to earn points for their team.

SUPPLIES:

- Index cards
- Whiteboard
- Markers
- Eraser
- Timer

PREPARATION:

Write clues on the cards from previous lessons.

TIP:

Look back through your lesson book for people, places, and things that were major factors in each lesson. For example, if you recently taught on Genesis 3, include Adam & Eve, the tree of knowledge, the serpent, and the angel with a flaming sword on the index cards.

HOW TO PLAY:

1. Kids divide into two teams (have them pick team names for some extra fun!)
2. Pick one player from the first team and give them a clue card. Have them draw the picture on the whiteboard while their team tries to guess what they are drawing. If the team can guess correctly within a minute, they are awarded 100 points.
3. Pick a player from the other team and repeat the process.
4. The first team with 1,000 points wins.

MEMORY VERSE REVIEW GAMES

WORD WIPE-OUT

Individual Game

OVERVIEW
Words are slowly erased one by one as kids memorize a verse.

SUPPLIES:
- Dry erase board
- Markers
- Eraser
- Bible

PREPARATION:
Write the verse on a dry erase board.

HOW TO PLAY:
1. Say the verse all together as a group.
2. Allow a child to erase one word.
3. Say the verse again as a group.
4. Repeat this process until all the words are erased, and kids can say the verse without any help.

GUESS THE LETTER

Team Race

OVERVIEW

Played much like *Wheel of Fortune*, this game is great for any age. Just guess a letter!

SUPPLIES:

- Dry erase board
- Markers
- Eraser
- Bible

PREPARATION:

Write the verse on the board, using a blank line for every letter. Write the alphabet on the bottom so you can cross out letters as kids guess them.

HOW TO PLAY:

1. Break the group up into two teams (girls vs. boys is always fun.) Teams pick team names.
2. Allow the first team to guess a letter (cross it off the list). Fill in any appropriate blanks and award 100 points for each correct letter.
3. Play until all the letters are guessed. Team with the most points at the end of the game recites the verse.

PASS THE BALL

Circle Game

OVERVIEW
A simple ball keeps this game rolling as kids say one word of the verse and then pass the ball along.

SUPPLIES:
- Foam ball
- Optional: Stopwatch

PREPARATION:
None

HOW TO PLAY:
1. Kids stand in a circle, all facing in towards the middle.
2. Say the verse all together as a group.
3. Toss the ball to one child and have them say the first word of the verse.
4. They will then toss the ball to another player, who will say the second word of the verse (be prepared to help if they get stuck).
5. Process continues until the entire verse–including reference is said.
6. Optional: Time each round and encourage children to beat their last time.

MEMORY VERSE GAMES | AGES: 6–12 | TIME NEEDED: 8 MIN

WHAT A PUZZLE

Team Race

OVERVIEW
Kids complete to assemble a larger than life puzzle.

SUPPLIES:

- Large pieces of poster board, one for every four players
- Broad tip markers
- Scissors
- Optional: Gallon-sized resealable bags

PREPARATION:

Write the memory verse on each of the poster boards with broad markers. Cut up the poster board into ten to fifteen puzzle pieces.

Optional: Place the pieces from each poster board puzzle into a separate resealable bag so that they don't get mixed up or lost.

HOW TO PLAY:

1. Kids divide into two teams
2. Give each team a set of pieces.
3. On your signal, teams work together to assemble the verse puzzle.
4. First team to finish wins.

BEAN BAG TOSS

Partner Race

OVERVIEW
Toss bean bags back and forth as they say the verse in this quick and easy game.

SUPPLIES:
- Bean bags, one for each pair of children

PREPARATION:
Optional: Make bean bags. Instructions for a simple way to make bean bags are on page 308

HOW TO PLAY:
1. Kids divide into pairs and stand about five feet away from their partner. Give each pair a bean bag to toss.
2. Say the verse as a group a few times before you start.
3. The first player begins by tossing the bean bag to their partner while saying the first word of the verse.
4. The second player tosses the bean bag back while saying the second word in the verse.
5. This continues with the pairs tossing bean bag back and forth as they say the next word in the verse.
6. Encourage the teams to get into a good rhythm of saying the verse instead of trying to go fast.

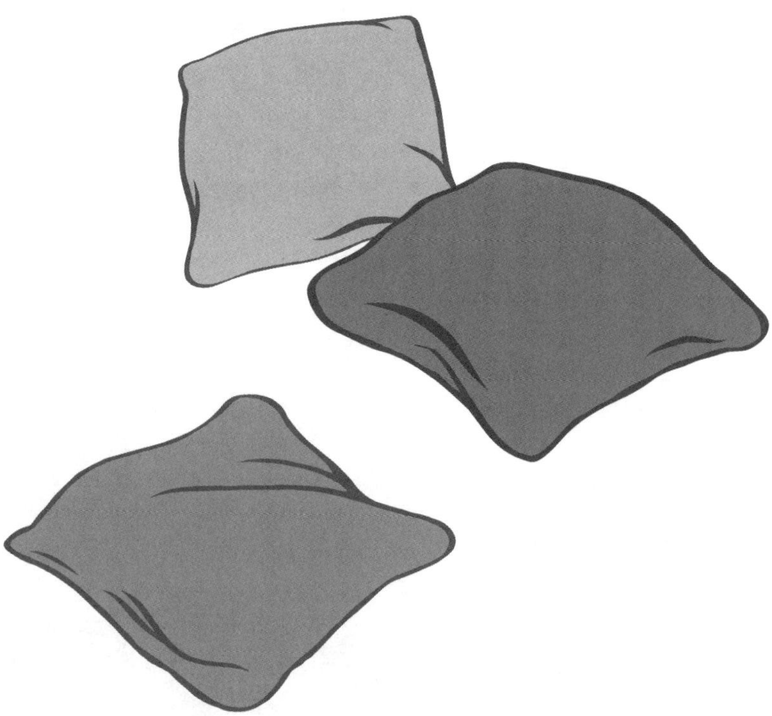

ERASE THIS WORD

Team Race

OVERVIEW

In this high energy twist on Word Wipe Out, kids run to erase words that match their card.

SUPPLIES:

- Note cards,
- Bowl
- Whiteboard
- Dry-erase markers
- Eraser
- Stool for shorter kids

PREPARATION:

Write one word of the verse on each note cards and put them in the bowl.
Write the complete verse on the whiteboard.

HOW TO PLAY:

1. Divide the kids up into two teams.
2. On your signal, one player from each team will take a word from the bowl, run to the board, erase that particular word, and then run back to their team. They should keep the card they took.
3. The game continues until all the words in the verse are erased. Count the number of cards each team has collected. Whichever team has the most cards recites the verse..

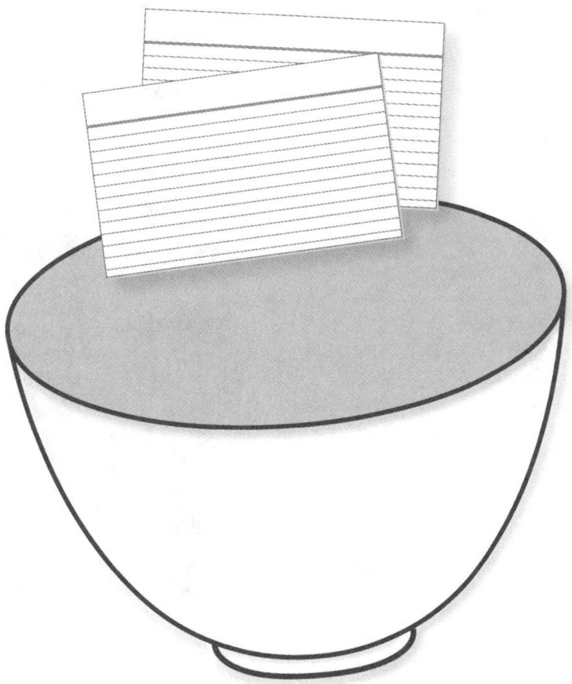

MUSICAL VERSE CHAIRS

Circle Game

OVERVIEW
This memory verse version of musical chairs helps kids learn the verse one word at a time.

SUPPLIES:
- Chairs
- Memory verse,
- Note cards
- Tape
- Music player
- Poster board

PREPARATION:
Memory verse written on a sheet of poster board (large letters).
Write memory verse on note cards (one word per card).
Set the chairs up in a circle, with seats facing out. Tape one note card to the back (or bottom) of each chair.

HOW TO PLAY:
1. Play the music. Kids walk around the circle of chairs.
2. When the music stops, everyone looks on the back (or bottom) of their chair to see if they have the first word of the verse. If so, they take it off and tape it to the poster board.
3. Begin playing the music again, stopping after about ten to twenty seconds. This time, kids look for the second word of the verse. Whoever is sitting in the chair with that word removes it from the chair and tapes it to the poster board over the existing word.
4. The game continues in this manner until all the words are transferred to the poster board.

WALK A VERSE

Individual Game

OVERVIEW

Kids walk on construction paper, saying the words of the verse along the way.

SUPPLIES:

- Construction Paper
- Painters Tape
- Markers

PREPARATION:

Write one or two words on each piece of construction paper. Using the painter's tape, attach the paper to the floor, in order. The papers should be about 1 foot apart from each other.

HOW TO PLAY:

1. Kids walk along the path, saying the word as they step on each paper.
2. If they seem to get the hang of it, cover a few words with blank construction paper and continue the walking process.
3. You can time the kids to see who can make it through the verse walk the fastest.

VERSE HOPSCOTCH

Individual Game

OVERVIEW
Hop on the words to memorize the verse

SUPPLIES:
- Sidewalk chalk
- Parking lot or sidewalk

PREPARATION:
Make a standard hopscotch board with ten spaces.

HOW TO PLAY:
1. Divide the verse up that a few words go into each space. Save the reference for space number ten.
2. Have the kids play hopscotch, saying the verse as they hop from square to square.

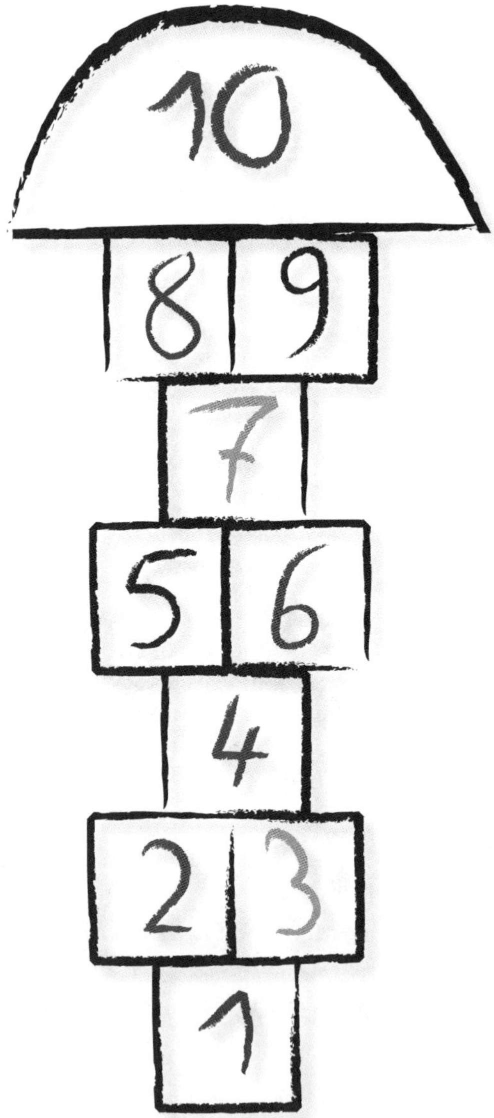

VERSE JUMP

Individual Game

OVERVIEW

This game has kids hopping from word to word in order to complete the memory verse.

SUPPLIES:

- Sidewalk chalk
- Parking lot or sidewalk

PREPARATION:

Draw several large circles on the pavement, fairly close to one another. The circles should be large enough for a child to stand inside of it. Write a word or few words from the memory verse in each circle. Make sure that a child can jump from circle to circle in verse order.

HOW TO PLAY:

1. Children stand next to the first word of the verse.
2. Children jump from circle to circle, going in verses order until they reach the end.
3. Have them say the verse out loud as they jump.
4. If you want to heat up the game a bit, time the kids to see who can get through the jumping the fastest.

PASS THE (VERSE) PARCEL

Circle Game

OVERVIEW
Kids unwrap the layers of wrapping to find the words of the verse

SUPPLIES:

- Memory verse,
- Note cards
- Several boxes in graduated sizes
- Wrapping paper or tissue paper
- Children's worship CD and player

PREPARATION:
Write one word of the verse on each note card. Put one note card in each of the boxes. Wrap the smallest box (with the note card inside) and then put it in the next biggest box. Wrap that box (with another note card inside) and then nest it inside the next biggest. Continue this process until all the note cards are wrapped up inside of boxes. Optional: Wrap the note cards without putting them in boxes.

HOW TO PLAY:

1. Kids sit in a circle.
2. Hand the super-wrapped package to one of the kids who begins passing it around the circle. Play the music.
3. After about ten to twenty seconds, stop the music. Whoever is holding the package unwraps one layer. They will hang onto the card until all the boxes are unwrapped. Have them show the others the cards.
4. Continue playing until all the cards are revealed. The kids reassemble cards in the correct order. Bonus points if anyone can guess the verse before all the cards are revealed.

BLAST THAT VERSE!

Team Race

OVERVIEW

This water-blasting game will be sure to leave an impression on the kids as they work to squirt cups off the table.

SUPPLIES:

- Table
- Plastic cups
- Water guns
- Masking tape or chalk
- Permanent marker

PREPARATION:

Begin by writing one word of the verse on each of the cups. Mark the shooting line with masking tape or chalk. Set the cups up on the table in a straight line. Repeat for the other team.

HOW TO PLAY:

1. Kids divide into two teams that line up next to the shooting line.
2. Give the first player on each team a squirt gun and tell them to aim for the verse.
3. When you say "Go" or "Blast that verse" (whichever you prefer), players shoot at the cups, trying to knock them off the back of the table. Make sure they remain behind the shooting line that you drew on the ground.
4. When a player successfully knocks one cup off the table, player passes the gun to the next player in line.
5. When all the cups are blasted off the table, the team recites the verse.
6. If some kids are having trouble with their aim, players pass the water gun down the line every ten seconds instead of every time they knock down a cup.

BALLOON POP VERSE

Individual Game

OVERVIEW

Kids grab a balloon and race to find the words needed to complete the verse!

SUPPLIES:

- Balloons, one for each word of the verse
- Small slips of paper
- Timer

PREPARATION:

Write one word of the verse on each slip of paper. Roll it up and slip it inside a deflated balloon. Blow up the balloon and tie it off, so the word is inside of the balloon. Scatter the balloons around the room.

TIP:

If you want to play this as a race between two teams, gather up balloons in two different colors. Assign one color to each team and put the complete verse inside each set of balloons.

HOW TO PLAY:

1. On your signal, kids run to a balloon and pop it. (Sitting on it works well!)
2. Kids bring the paper back to a centralized place and unscramble the words to the verse.
3. See if they get all this done in two minutes or less!

CHINESE FOOD VERSE

Team Race

OVERVIEW

This game requires some serious fine motor skills as kids pick lup bottle caps with the words of the verse written on them.

SUPPLIES:

- Bowls, one for each team)
- Rice
- Chopsticks, one pair for each team
- Bottle caps, one for each team
- Permanent marker

PREPARATION:

Write the memory verse on the bottle caps with the permanent marker. One cap for each word of the memory verse. One set for every team. Place the bottle caps in a bowl and then fill with rice.

TIP:

If you think chopsticks are going to be too challenging for your kids, use tongs.

HOW TO PLAY:

1. Divide the kids up into teams that sit in a straight line on the floor.
2. Hand the first player on each team the bowl and chopsticks. Their goal is to get one bottle cap out of the bowl with the chopsticks. Then they hand the bowl and chopsticks to the next player on the team.
3. The next player also tries to grab a bottle cap with the chopsticks and then passes the bowl.
4. This continues until all the bottle caps are retrieved from the bowl. A few players may need to take additional turns.
5. After all the bottle caps are rescued from the rice, the team work together to put the words in correct verse order. Don't forget about the reference!
6. The first team to assemble the complete verse wins.

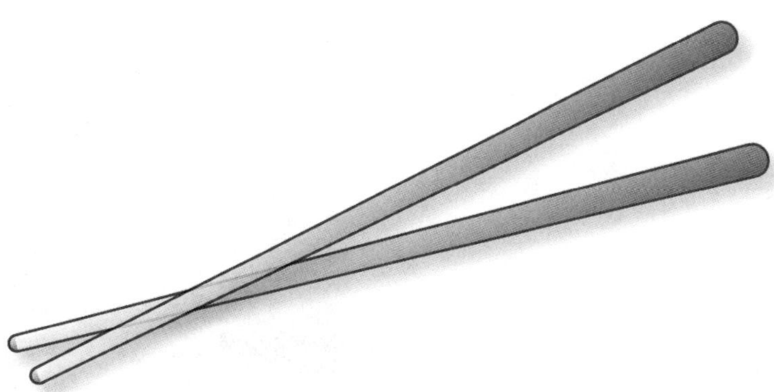

WRITE IT DOWN

Team Race

OVERVIEW
Kids race to the board to fill in the verse one word at a time.

SUPPLIES:
- Bibles (if kids need to look up the verse)
- Cones or rope
- Poster board for each team.
- Markers (place them on the floor beneath the poster board)

PREPARATION:
Use cones or rope to mark start line Tape posters on the wall at kids' eye level.

TIP:
Players should be able to read and write fairly quickly to play this game.

HOW TO PLAY:
1. Kids divide into teams of five to eight players.
2. Line each team up behind the start line and directly across from their poster board.
3. On your signal, the first player on each team runs to the poster board, writes the first word of the verse with the provided markers and returns to their team.
4. The second player runs to the poster board, writes the second word of the verse on the poster board and then returns to their team.
5. This continues until the entire verse (including the reference) is written on the poster board. The first team to complete the task wins.

Bonus:
- Take a picture of poster boards and make copies to send home with the kids to continue practicing the verse.

HIDDEN VERSE

Individual Race

OVERVIEW
This game makes finding all the words of the verse a real adventure

SUPPLIES:
- Large craft sticks
- Markers
- Large play area
- Timer

PREPARATION:
Write one word of the verse on each of the craft sticks. Hide the craft sticks in the play area.

HOW TO PLAY:
1. On your signal, kids scramble to find all the craft sticks and bring them back to you (the leader).
2. As they bring them to you, assemble them in verse order so you can tell how many are still missing.
3. Time the kids as they complete task to see how fast they can find all the craft sticks.

HIDE A WORD

Individual Race

OVERVIEW
Words are hidden all over the room, and kids have to work together to complete a memory verse poster.

SUPPLIES:
- Poster board
- Note cards
- Sticky tack or glue sticks
- Large space to hide note cards

PREPARATION:
Prepare note cards with the memory verse on them. There should be one word per card. Prepare a memory verse poster by placing all the note cards on the poster in order and then tracing around them. Remove the cards and write the word that should go in that space. The idea is for kids to find a note card and glue/sticky tack it to the appropriate space on the poster. Hide the note cards throughout the room.

HOW TO PLAY:
1. When the kids arrive, send them out to find the note cards.
2. Kids bring the cards they find to you to place on the poster board in the correct order. If you have older kids, they can do this step themselves.
3. The game ends when all the words are found and placed in the appropriate box on the poster.

ILLUSTRATE A VERSE

Individual Game

OVERVIEW

Kids are given a past memory verse and asked to illustrate it. Other kids guess the verse based on the drawing.

SUPPLIES:

- Paper
- Crayons, markers, or colored pencils
- List of ten recent memory verses

PREPARATION:

Type out ten of your recent memory verses. Make at least two copies. Cut up one of the sheets and hand out one verse to each child (if you have more than ten kids, you'll need to make additional copies). Hang up one paper on the wall where everyone can see it (for later).

HOW TO PLAY:

1. Give kids five to ten minutes to illustrate their verse. Encourage them not to put words on the page.
2. When everyone is finished, ask someone to show everyone their illustrated verse. Encourage kids to look at the list of verses hanging on the wall and try to guess what verse that child has illustrated. Allow three guesses and then reveal the answer.
3. Continue in this way until everyone has had a chance to show their illustrated verse.

WRONG WORD

Individual Game

OVERVIEW
Kids try to guess the word that is wrong on the verse.

SUPPLIES:

- List of ten recent memory verses, written correctly
- Same ten memory verses, with one word incorrect
- Bibles

PREPARATION:

Type out ten of your recent memory verses. Print out the list for your reference, and then make changes to each of the verses. Replace one of the main words with a different word. Make the font very large so that there is only one verse per page. (Of course, you could also write these out by hand).

HOW TO PLAY:

1. Show the kids one verse at a time and see if they can guess the wrong word. Check your original list if you need.
2. If they cannot guess the wrong word, have them use their Bibles to look up the verse and try again.
3. Play until you have reviewed all ten of the verses.

Examples of Incorrect Verse Words:

- Genesis 1:1—In the beginning, God created the planets and the earth.
- Deuteronomy 6:4—Americans, listen to me. The LORD is our God. The LORD is the one and only God.

WHERE'S IT FROM?

Individual Race

OVERVIEW

Kids match past memory verses with their Scripture references

SUPPLIES:

- List of ten recent memory verses, with references
- Bibles
- Timer

PREPARATION:

Type or write out ten of your recent memory verses with references. Arrange the verse so that the reference and the verse can easily be cut apart. Print out the list and then cut apart the verse from the reference. Scramble up the pieces.

HOW TO PLAY:

1. Explain that you are going to match up the verse with its proper reference. Do the activity once as a group. Kids use Bibles if needed.
2. After the group has completed the activity once, ask for a volunteer. Volunteer completes the activity on their own while you time them. Keep track of fast times.
3. Continue playing in this way until everyone has a chance to complete the activity on their own. Whoever has the quickest time recites the verse.

REPRODUCIBLE PAGES

MATCH ANIMAL CARDS

ELEPHANT	TIGER	FROG

BEAR	**CAT**	**DOG**

SNAKE	**OWL**	**FISH**

MONKEY	**WHALE**	**COW**

Directions:
Make at least two copies of the cards above. Cut apart and pass out so that each child has a match.

CHECKLIST OF COLORS

☐	**RED**
☐	**YELLOW**
☐	**ORANGE**
☐	**PURPLE**
☐	**BLUE**
☐	**GREEN**
☐	**BROWN**

Directions:
Check off the colors as you go and go to your leaders when you have found all the colors.

CHECKLIST OF THINGS TO PACK

SHIRT

SHAMPOO

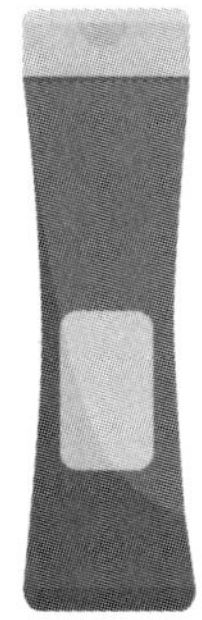

PANTS

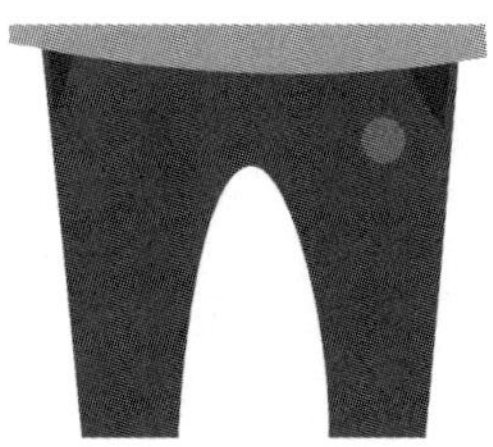

TOOTHBRUSH

COMB

SOCKS

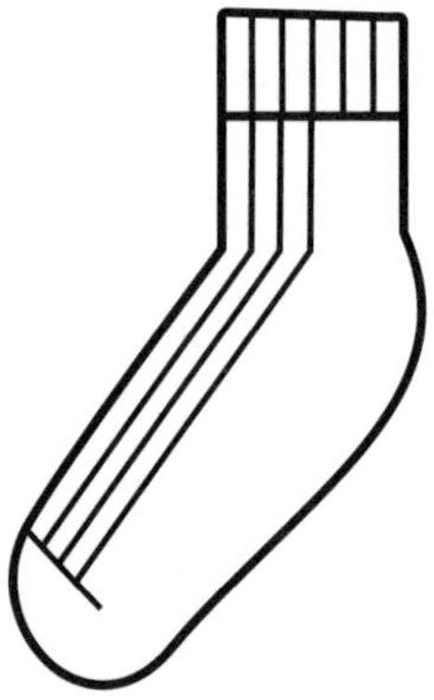

JESUS IS BORN QUESTIONS

SONGS (Fill in the blank):

- 100: O Little Town of ____________________(Bethlehem)
- 200: O Come, O Come __________________ (Emmanuel)
- 300: O Come, All Ye ____________________(Faithful)
- 400: Hark, the Herald ___________________(Angels Sign)
- 500: God Rest Ye Merry _________________(Gentlemen)

TRADITIONS

- 100: Name a Christmas decoration
- 200: Why do we give gifts? (Because the wise men did)
- 300: What is the time/month leading up to Christmas called? (Advent)
- 400: What were the first Christmas tree lights? (Candles)
- 500: Name the eight original reindeer (Dasher, Dancer, Prancer, Vixen, Comet, Cupid, Donner, Blitzen)

EVENTS

- 100: We were in the field tending the sheep when something exciting happened. What was it?
- 200: After being warned in a dream about King Herod's evil plan, what did Joseph do? (Egypt)
- 300: T or F: Prophets were telling about the birth of Jesus more than 400 years before it happened. (True)
- 400: After the angel Gabriel visited Mary, she sang a song. Where can we find her song? (Luke 1) Bonus: Find it in the Bible.
- 500: Why did Mary and Joseph have to travel to Bethlehem (to be counted for the census). Bonus: Bethlehem was called the city of __________ (David).

CHARACTERS (4-5 Year olds only)

- 100: I am Jesus' mother
- 200: We traveled from afar, following a star
- 300: I didn't have any room for Jesus (inn keeper)
- 400: I am Mary's cousin–the one she visited after she was pregnant (Elizabeth)
- 500: I tried to kill all the baby boys when I found out about King Jesus. (King Herod)

PLACES

- 100: Where was Jesus born? (Bethlehem)
- 200: Where was Mary when the angel came to visit? (Her house)
- Bonus: What was his name? (Gabriel)
- 300: Where was Joseph when the angel came to visit? (In his bed, sleeping)
- 400: Where did the first Christmas tree show up? (Germany)
- 500: Where did the wise men stop in order to ask about the new baby king? (Jerusalem)

ARMOR OF GOD CARDS

TRUTH

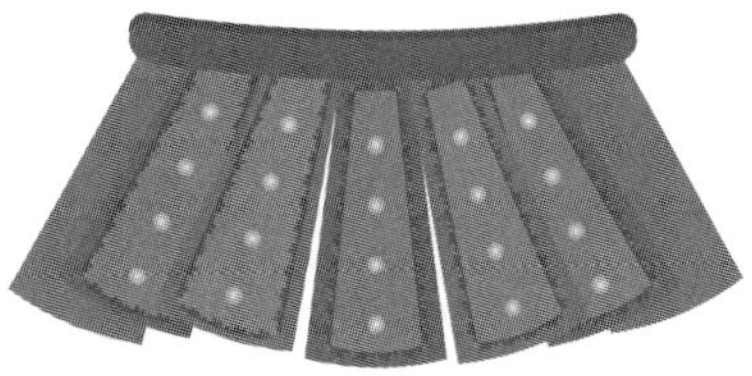

RIGHTEOUSNESS

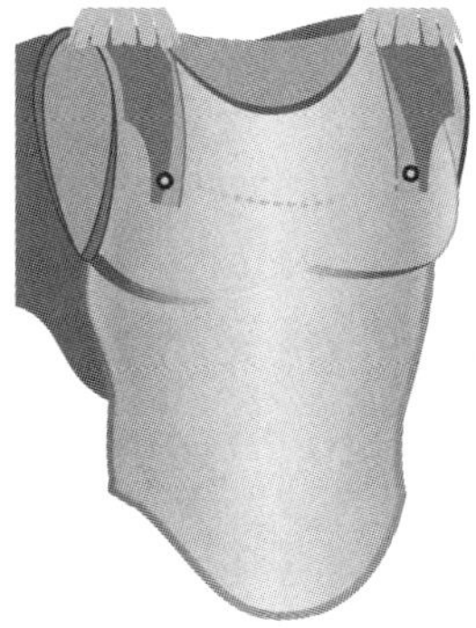

GOODNESS

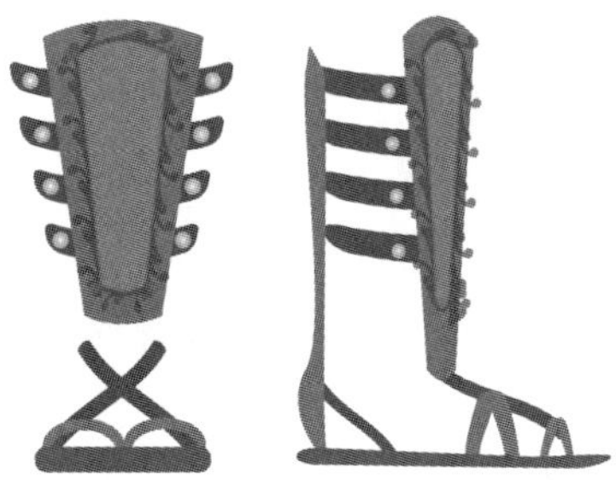

FAITH

SALVATION

SWORD OF THE WORD

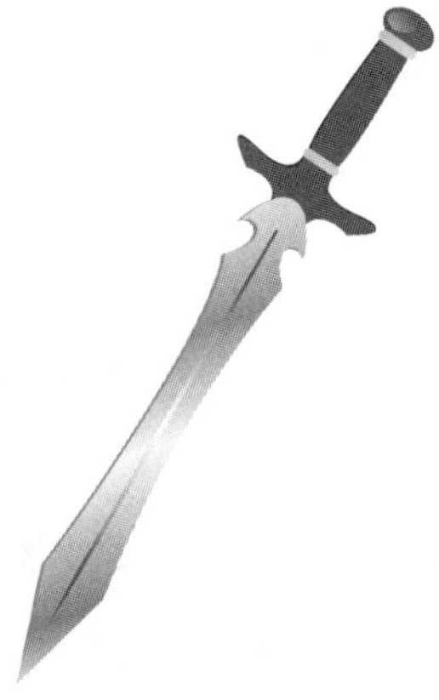

SHAKE THE BOX ANSWER KEY

BOX #1 IS	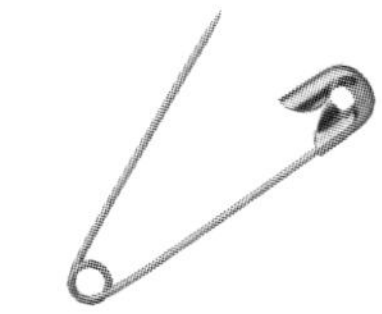	OR	
BOX #2 IS		OR	
BOX #3 IS	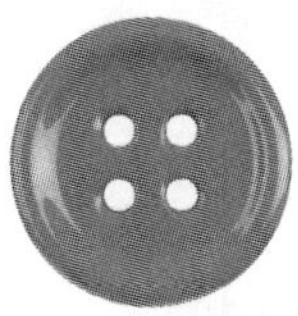	OR	
BOX #4 IS	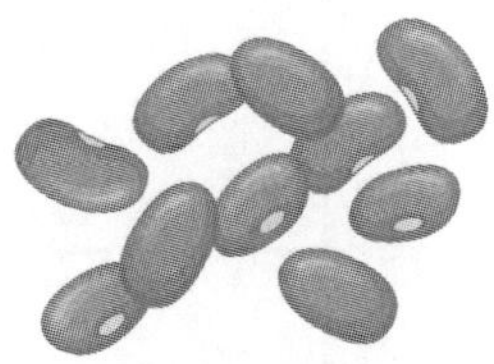	OR	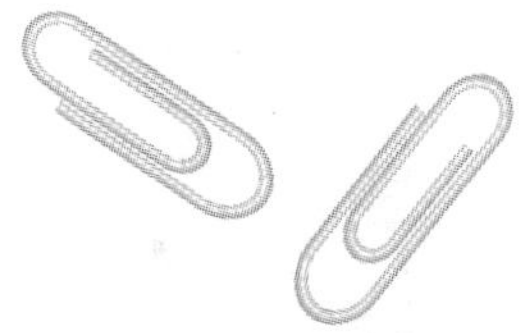
BOX #5 IS		OR	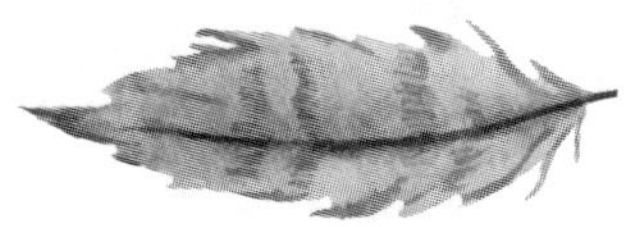
BOX #6 IS		OR	
BOX #7 IS		OR	
BOX #8 IS		OR	

WHO AM I? CARDS

ABEL	CAIN
SAMSON	NOAH
ABRAHAM	GIDEON
DAVID	SARAH
ESAU	JOSEPH
MOSES	PHARAOH

NAME BINGO

DO YOU HAVE A DOG?	HAVE YOU EVER BROKEN A BONE?	HAVE YOU EVER RODE IN A PLANE?
DO YOU HAVE A CAT?	HAVE YOU EVER RODE IN A BOAT?	DO YOU HAVE MORE THAN THREE PETS?
DO YOU HAVE A BROTHER?	DO YOU HAVE A SISTER?	HAVE YOU EVER LOST A TOOTH?
HAVE YOU EVER TRAVELED OUTSIDE OF THIS STATE?	WHAT IS YOUR FAVORITE SPORT?	WHAT IS YOUR FAVORITE DESSERT?

FRUIT OF THE SPIRIT CARDS

LOVE 	JOY 
PEACE 	PATIENCE 
KINDNESS 	GOODNESS 
FAITHFULNESS 	GENTLENESS 
SELF-CONTROL 	

SCAVENGER HUNT LIST

☐ TREE 

☐ BUTTERFLY 

☐ FEATHER 

☐ CLOUD 

☐ SEEDS 

☐ BUGS 

☐ LEAF 

☐ BIRD 

☐ CATERPILLAR 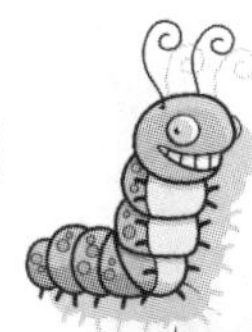

☐ WATER 

☐ STONE 

☐ WEB 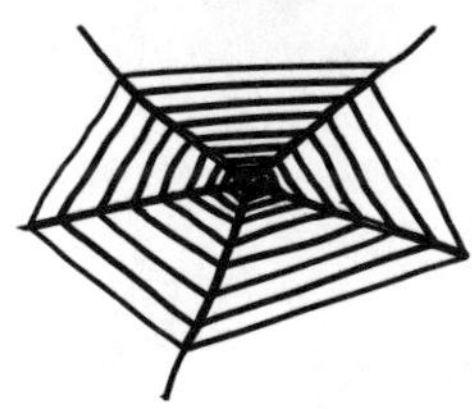

HUMAN BOARD GAME

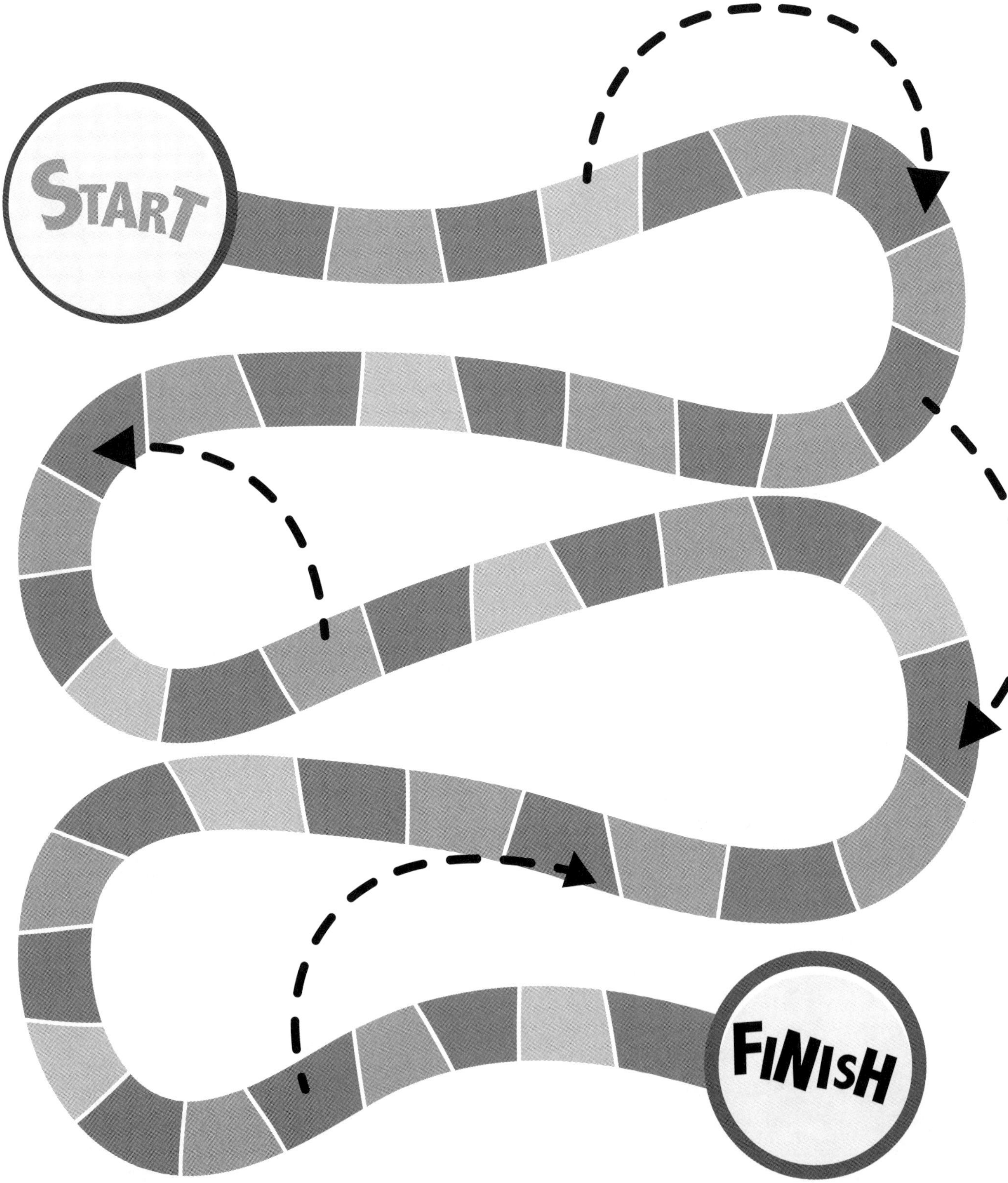

LAWN TWIST CARDS

LEFT HAND RED	LEFT HAND GREEN	LEFT HAND BLUE	LEFT HAND YELLOW
RIGHT HAND RED	RIGHT HAND GREEN	RIGHT HAND BLUE	RIGHT HAND YELLOW
LEFT FOOT RED	LEFT FOOT GREEN	LEFT FOOT BLUE	LEFT FOOT YELLOW
RIGHT FOOT RED	RIGHT FOOT GREEN	RIGHT FOOT BLUE	RIGHT FOOT YELLOW

WATER BALLOON OBSTACLE COURSE IDEAS

- Crawl under a table.
- Jump over a string tied between two chairs.
- Crawl through a toy hoop (and adult will have to hold).
- Run around cones (weaving in and out).
- Do a certain activity–jump up and down three times, spin in 5 circles, roll back and forth.
- Walk on a rope "tight rope" style.
- Open an umbrella and run with it.
- Lay a ladder on the ground and have kids jump in between the rungs.
- Jump over buckets.
- Crawl through a fabric tunnel.
- Put stakes in the ground, tie strings between the stakes and have kids either crawl under strings or step over (add a jingle bell to one of the strings to make sure no one is hitting it!).
- Jump from brick to brick (or stone to stone) (or tile to tile).
- Climb into a pillow case (or potato sack) and hop from one place to another.
- Put a board across a blue tarp and have kids "walk across the lake".
- Throw plastic bugs on a sheet and have kids run across it without stepping on any bugs.
- Put two old pillows on the ground (or two carpet squares or two cardboard squares) and have kids get from one cone to another by only stepping on the pillows (they will have to move one in front of the other as they progress along the path).
- Sit down in a tub of freezing water.
- Climb up a set of steps and jump off the side (or climb onto a stool and jump).
- Gather plastic eggs in rainbow order and put them in a bucket.
- Toss a ball into a baby pool or plastic bin/tub (or you could use beanbags for this).
- Pick up a kettle ball or weighted ball and carry it a short distance.
- Put on a oversized coat, run a short distance, and then take it off again.

FIND YOUR SPECIES ANIMAL CARDS

FISH	BIRDS	WILD ANIMALS	FARM ANIMALS

RICE FIND CHECKLIST

________ Marshmallow

________ Piece of candy

________ Jingle bell

________ Eraser

________ Stamp

________ Small animal figure

________ Bead

________ Earring

________ Paper clip

________ Flower shaped button

________ Regular shaped button

________ Lego piece

________ Golf tee

________ Puzzle piece

________ Small person figure

Directions:
Find the items above in the rice. Check off each one as you find it.

CRAZY COSTUME CARDS

COAT	PANTS	SHIRT
SOMETHING THAT IS RED	SOMETHING THAT HAS BUTTONS	SOMETHING THAT HAS A ZIPPER
SOMETHING SOFT	HAT	SOCKS
SCARF	SOMETHING TO KEEP YOU WARM	SOMETHING FANCY
SOMETHING CASUAL (EVERYDAY WEAR)	SOMETHING WITH BLUE ON IT	SOMETHING WITH STRIPES ON IT
SOMETHING RELATED TO SPORTS	SOMETHING WITH YELLOW IN IT	SOMETHING WITH WORDS/ LETTERS ON IT
SOMETHING WITH GRAY ON IT	SKIRT	BELT

DANIEL'S MENU

LETTUCE OR SALAD	ONIONS
CORN	BREAD
PEPPERS	TOMATO

Directions:

For ten days, Daniel and his friends only ate vegetables and water. Find images of the listed vegetables and glue them to the menu above.

NUMBERS PUZZLE

______ 1	______ 2	______ 3	______ 4
______ 5	______ 6	______ 7	______ 8
______ 9	______ 10	______ 11	______ 12

SHAPES IN A SACK

GOING TO MARKET CARDS

BIBLE PEOPLE CARDS

AARON	BOAZ	CALEB	DANIEL	ELIJAH
FELIX	GOLIATH	HANNAH	ISAIAH	JEREMIAH
KING DAVID	LAZARUS	MALACHI	NAAMAN	OTHNIEL
PAUL	QUEEN ESTHER	REBEKAH	SAMSON	THOMAS
UZZIAH	VASHTI	WOMAN AT WELL	YOUNG RICH RULER	ZACHARIAH

THE WHOLE ARMOR OF GOD
EPHESIANS 6:10-20
HELMET OF SALVATION
SWORD OF THE WORD
SHIELD OF FAITH
BELT OF TRUTH
BREASTPLATE OF RIGHTEOUSNESS
SHOES OF GOODNEWS

BUILD A WORD

FAMOUS PAIRS TEMPLATE

Hello! My name is: ________________ You can read my story in: ________________ Something I once said is: ________________
Hello! My name is: ________________ You can read my story in: ________________ Something I once said is: ________________
Hello! My name is: ________________ You can read my story in: ________________ Something I once said is: ________________
Hello! My name is: ________________ You can read my story in: ________________ Something I once said is: ________________
Hello! My name is: ________________ You can read my story in: ________________ Something I once said is: ________________

BIBLE PEOPLE REVIEW SHEET

Hello! My name is: Adam You can read my story in: Genesis Something I said: The woman you put in the garden with me! She gave me the fruit.
Hello! My name is: Boaz You can read my story in: Ruth Something I said: Don't go and glean in another field and don't go away from here. Stay here with the women who work for me.
Hello! My name is: Caleb You can read my story in: Numbers Something I said: We should go up and take possession of the land, for we can certainly do it.
Hello! My name is: Daniel You can read my story in: Daniel Something I said: God will help me interpret your dream, O King.
Hello! My name is: Elizabeth You can read my story in: Luke Something I said: Blessed are you among women, and blessed is the child you will bear! But why am I so favored, that the mother of my Lord should come to me?
Hello! My name is: Goliath You can read my story in: I Samuel Something I said: Why do you come out and line up for battle? Choose a man and have him come down to me.

BIBLE PEOPLE REVIEW SHEET

Hello! My name is: Josiah You can read my story in: 2 Kings Something I said: Gather men together and repair the temple of the Lord.
Hello! My name is: Lazarus You can read my story in: John 11 Something I said: Thank you, Jesus, for raising me from the dead!* * We don't actually know if he said this, but it's likely!
Hello! My name is: Naaman You can read my story in: 2 Kings 5 Something I said: I thought that he would surely come out to me and stand and call on the name of the LORD his God, wave his hand over the spot and cure me of my leprosy.
Hello! My name is: Queen Esther You can read my story in: Esther Something I said: When this is done, I will go to the king, even though it is against the law. And if I perish, I perish.
Hello! My name is: Samson You can read my story in: Judges Something I said: No razor has ever been used on my head... If my head were shaved, my strength would leave me, and I would become as weak as any other man.
Hello! My name is: Zacchaeus You can read my story in: Luke 19 Something I said: Here and now I give half of my possessions to the poor; and if I have cheated anybody out of anything, I will pay back four times the amount.

BIBLE STORY MATCHING SHEET

Draw lines to match the Bible story on the left with where you can find it in the Bible on the right.

Creation	Daniel 3
Noah's Ark	Exodus 14
Abraham and God's Promise	Mark 15
Joseph in Egypt	Genesis 37-50
Baby Moses	2 Kings 22
Israelites in the Desert	Mark 4
Jericho	Genesis 1
David is Anointed as Future King	Daniel 6
Josiah	Luke 19
Jonah	Luke 1
Shadrach, Meshach, Abednego	Matthew 2
Daniel and Lion's Den	Jonah
Jesus is Born	Joshua 6
Wise Men Visit Jesus	Exodus 2
Zacchaeus	Genesis 15
Jesus Calms Storm	1 Samuel 16
Jesus Dies for Our Sins	Genesis 6

WHERE IS IT FOUND ANSWER KEY

Creation	Genesis 1
Noah's Ark	Genesis 6
Abraham and God's Promise	Genesis 15
Joseph in Egypt	Genesis 37-50
Baby Moses	Exodus 2
Israelites in the Desert	Exodus 14
Jericho	Joshua 6
David is Anointed as Future King	1 Samuel 16
Josiah	2 Kings 22
Jonah	Jonah
Shadrach, Meshach, Abednego	Daniel 3
Daniel and Lion's Den	Daniel 6
Jesus is Born	Luke 1
Wise Men Visit Jesus	Matthew 2
Zacchaeus	Luke 19
Jesus Calms Storm	Mark 4
Jesus Dies for Our Sins	Mark 15

DOMINO CARD TEMPLATE

BINGO TEMPLATE

		FREE SPACE		

SIMPLE WAY TO MAKE BEAN BAGS

Step One:
Using very sharp scissors, cut 4 inch squares from felt.

Step Two:
Put two squares together and either sew around the outside edge (hand stitching or by machine) or glue together with a hot glue gun. Leave a small one- to two-inch opening in the middle of one of the side.

Step Three:
Fill the (now-sealed) squares with dried corn, dried beans, or rice until it is about of the way full.

Step Four:
Hold the opening closed and stitch or glue together to finish sealing off the bag.

Tip:
You can use other material besides felt, such as cotton, flannel or fleece, but the edges may fray after use. You can minimize fraying by cutting the square with pinking shears.

SIMPLE WAY TO MAKE A NUMBER CUBE

Step One:
Obtain a square box and tape it closed. If you want, cover it in plain brown paper to make it look more uniform or spray paint it white.

Step Two:
Using the circle template below, draw or spray paint dots on each side of the number cube/box.

Step Three:
Allow time for the box to draw and then use as a number cube in your game!

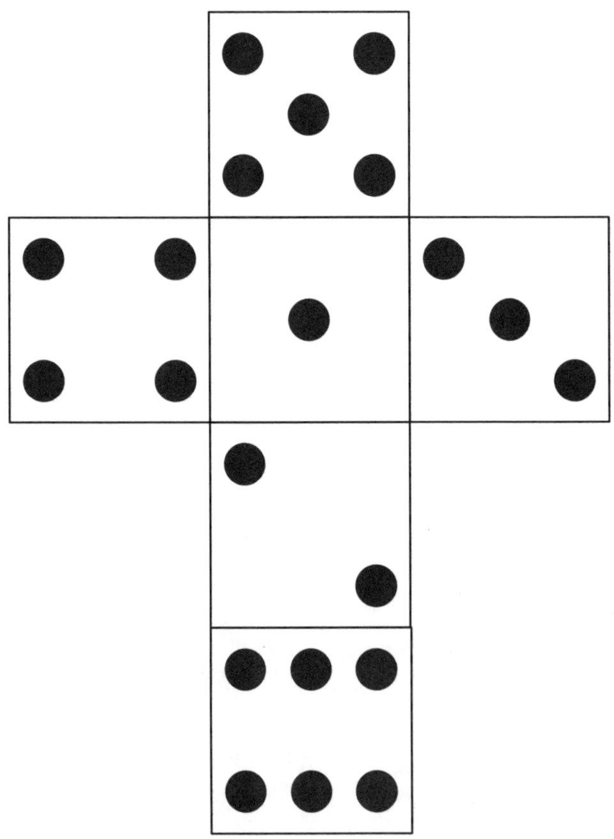

Individual Games

Individual Races

Seek and Find Games

Partner Games

Team Games

Team Races

New Testament

More RoseKidz Books from Lindsey Whitney

Check out these great titles:

Teach the best 50 lessons from the popular Instant Bible Lessons series. *The Top 50 Instant Bible Lessons for Preschoolers* includes quick and easy-to-use resources for Sunday-school teachers with reproducible hand-outs, arts and crafts templates, puzzles, games and step-by-step instructions. Ages two to five years.

ISBN-13: 9781628624977

More great lessons from the popular Instant Bible Lessons series. *The Top 50 Instant Bible Lessons for Elementary* includes the same types of resources for Sunday-school teachers as our preschool book: reproducible hand-outs, arts and crafts templates, puzzles, games and step-by-step instructions. Ages five to ten years.

ISBN-13: 9781628624984

The RoseKidz Top 50 series continues with the *Top 50 Memory Verse Lessons*. Memory verses are vital to hide God's Word in the heart and mind of every child. This book is packed with fun, interactive, creative and engaging ways to get children excited about memorizing Scripture. The 50 verses are in an easy-to-learn format. Ages five to ten.

ISBN-13: 9781628625059

This ready-to-go resource will help you guide preschoolers *A to Z Thru the Bible!* Lindsey Whitney's twenty-six lessons teach children foundational biblical truths while reviewing early education basics. The familiar alphabetical structure makes the key points easy-to-grasp—and remember. Features step-by-step instructions; age-appropriate crafts; fun, interactive activities; and MORE! Ages three to five.

ISBN-13: 9781628627435